MAHADEV GOVIND RANADE

Socio-Economic Ideology

Indian Freedom Fighters Series-41

Mahadev Govind Ranade

Socio-Economic Ideology

S.R. BAKSHI

Anmol Publications
New Delhi (India)

ANMOL PUBLICATIONS
4378/4B, Ansari Road
Daryaganj, New Delhi-110 002

Mahadev Govind Ranade : *Socio-Economic Ideology*

ISBN 81-7041-605-1

PRINTED IN INDIA

Published by J.L. Kumar for Anmol Publications, New Delhi and Printed at Renu Printers, Maujpur, Delhi-53 .

Preface

In the long-drawn political struggle in our sub-continent, the role of Mahadev Govind Ranade is most significant. Born in a middle class family, he rose to the position of the Judge, Bombay High Court and Member, Bombay Legislative Council. His deep contacts with prominent contemporary leaders greatly contributed to the socio-economic causes as well as our freedom movement. He was a fine speaker and a superb writer. Even British officials greatly respected him in social circles.

The chapters deal with his early career, his social ideology, role in the freedom movement and the assessment of his public work which had deep linkage with Indian nationalism.

I have consulted the material from the Nehru Memorial Museum and Library, Sapru House Library and the Indian Council of Historical Research Library, New Delhi. I am grateful to the authorities of these institutions for affording me their academic support during my researches.

S. R. Bakshi

Contents

1

Early Career

Mahadev Govind Ranade was born on 18th January, 1842 at Niphad in Nasik district. His father, Govindrao was head clerk to the Mamlatdar of Niphad. When Mahadev was about three years old, his father was transferred to Kolhapur. At a fairly young age, he was well-conversant with reading, writing and arithmetic in Rajaram High School, which later on developed into Rajaram College. By the end of 1856, he completed his high school education. At the age of 13, Ranade was married to a girl of nine, Sakhubai by name. In 1858 he joined the Elphinstone College, Bombay. In 1862, he passed the B.A. examination with distinction. He also showed similar distinction in his law and advocate's examinations also.

Bal Gangadhar Tilak's estimate may also be pertinently quoted, because, the general belief even to this day is that Tilak came to prominent public notice first as an opponent of Ranade and though essentially his disciple, he often questioned his wisdom and once or twice very severely criticised him. But his over-all view of Ranade was given in the obituary of Ranade he wrote in the *Kesari* in which he compared him to Swami Vidyaranya and called him 'the omniscient Madhava'. In another passage Tilak said:

"The first characteristic of Ranade was that he believed in an all-sided and not lop-sided development of the nation.

He was endowed with a mature and comprehensive intellect which examined all aspects of any question and reached correct conclusions. He was clearly of the opinion that we are backward in every way—religiously, socially, industrially, educationally, politically and unless we improved in all these respects we would not come in line with the civilised nations. Night and day, he was engrossed in active work connected with the improvement of our condition in one or other or several of these fields. It was not only Maharashtra that occupied his mind, though that was his immediate arena of activity, but the whole of India. He was fully conscious that every Indian who had the equipment of western education had this public responsibility and he set an ideal example by his own efforts for 30 years for all to follow.

"It is wholly erroneous to suppose that Ranade could achieve all this with comfort and ease. No. His course of action was fraught with dangers and difficulties and Government knew full well that if anybody was educating the people in Maharashtra to work for public weal and agitate for redress of public grievances it was Ranade. It was not for nothing that he was transferred from Poona to Nasik and from there to Dhulia. Why, it was even strongly held during the governorship of Sir Richard Temple that the Sarvajanik Sabha which he promoted and of which he was the soul, was a seditious body. Ranade pushed through all these troublous times with calm courage and amazing equanimity of mind. Any one of lesser grit and pluck would have been broken and would have succumbed. Quiet courage was his most extraordinary quality and that is why his ceaseless industry was crowned with success in Bombay Presidency in the form of great popular awakening. One has only to think of other parts of the country where a man like Ranade was not born. If there is some pushfulness in the public life of Maharashtra and if its publicists are fearlessly expressing themselves on matters of public interest, there can be no manner of doubt that it is the result of Ranade's ceaseless and painstaking work for over 25 years.

"If Ranade's great intellectual and moral attainments could not be harnessed by the British Government to a greater purpose than work as a judge of the Bombay High Court, that is no fault of his. It is the fault of the system of administration. Had he lived a few years more, there was a fair prospect of his openly pursuing the activities he had initiated in the way Dadabhai and Hume had done but that was not ordained by the Almighty. Otherwise why should we have been compelled to write his obituary instead of organising a golden jubilee celebration?"

Mahadev Govind Ranade was born at Niphad, in the Nasik District, on the 18th of January, 1842. His family belonged to the caste of the Chitpawan Brahmans—a section of the community which has given to India a number of remarkable leaders. The family traditions afford a dim glimpe of a far-back ancestor—the great-grandfather of the great-great-grandfather of Ranade—leaving his native village in the Ratnagiri District, on account of economic pressure and family disputes, and migrating to the Deccan, where he settled in the Sholapur District. Ranade's great-great-grandmother was a remarkable woman. After having given birth to twenty children, all of whom died in infancy or in youth, she finally had a son, named Bhaskar Appa. He, according to the tradition, would neither have been born, nor, after birth, have survived, had it not been for the severe religious austerities to which his mother had vowed herself, and which she strictly carried out for twelve years. One of the feats she is said to have performed was to walk a hundred thousand times round a cow, feeding it with *jawri* and herself living on bread made from grains that had passed undigested through the sacred animal. Besides her genuine piety, she was noted for a finely hospitable disposition.

Bhaskar Appa found employment as a clerk in the offices of the Sangli State, and afterwards obtained a post in the army. Once, when in command of a detachment, he stormed and captured a Moghul fort, but he refused personally to touch any of the property which was available as spoil.

Afterwards he was, for many years, Agent for the Chief of Sangli at the court of the Peshwas at Poona. He was no time-server, and was esteemed for his straightness and his wisdom. He was deeply religious, and towards the end of his life used to pass nearly all his time in meditation upon God. He died at the age of 95, his teeth and limbs being sound to the end, and his energy so little impaired that up till six months before his death he was able without assistance to mount his horse.

Ranade's grandfather, Amrutrao Tatya, was the eldest son of Bhaskar. He was the same type of strong, well-made man, and was an excellent horseman. He was a great lover of Sanskrit and a close student of the Hindu sacred books—interests which led to his writing a Marathi commentary on the *Purusha Sukta*. He entered Government service as clerk in a court of justice, and rose to be a *mamlatdar.*

Amrutrao Tatya had four sons, of whom the second, Govindrao, was Ranade's father. His employment up till the time that Ranade was two and a half years old, was that of Government clerk at Niphad. Thereafter he served in the Kolhapur State, and was promoted to responsible positions. The post of Khasagi Karbhari—a kind of administrating private secretary to the ruling Prince—to which he was appointed in 1862, carried with it a salary of Rs. 250 a month—*i.e.*, about £ 200 a year. When Ranade was born, however, his father's salary would only be about Rs. 35 a month, but even then, we are told, the family was, in accordance with the prevalent standard of life, comfortably off, being neither rich nor poor. Govindrao lived until the year 1877. He was a man of obstinate will, though he had also a kindly side to his disposition. He many a time displayed a prodigal generosity, running himself into debt to assist his brothers and other relatives on occasions when custom required extravagant expenditure, and in order to assist them in education. He was rivetted to Hindu orthodoxy, and genuinely believed and feared the religious sanctions as Hinduism presents them. Ranade's filial piety bound him to his father with a strong tie, but it was a tie of respect and duty rather than of congenial affection. Though his father never treated him harshly, there was an awkward stiffness in their relations. Except at meal times, he always stood in his father's presence. When they were alone together Ranade would speak as little as possible, and would take himself away as soon as possible. It does not appear that either of his parents markedly influenced the development of his mind and character. But in the story of Ranade's life his father looms out of the background like a symbol of hereditary and traditional restraints. The grip of the dead past upon the living and developing present, the shrinking of conservative pietism from the sacrilege of reform, the pain of uncomprehending traditionalism in conflict with *the new*—these seem actually embodied in the gloomy tussles that took place between father and son.

The first recorded words of Ranade were spoken in 1845, on the occasion when a very curious accident had befallen him. His mother, Gopikabai, had set out from Niphad along with her infant daughter, Durga, and her little son. The party went in a bullock-waggon, travelling by night and resting during the heat of the day; and was escorted by one of Gopikabai's relatives, who was mounted on horseback, and by a sepoy. It was about two o'clock in the morning, and under the soporific effects of the darkness, the coldness, and the gentle wind, everyone in the waggon fell asleep, the bullocks meanwhile ambling on by themselves. Soon, however, the road took a steep dip which caused the animals to break into a run. Mahadev had in his sleep rolled to the edge of the waggon, and the sudden jerk that occurred when the bullocks started to run, made him fall out on to the road. His mother being in a deep sleep did not waken, and while the change in the bullocks' pace aroused driver and sepoy, the rattling and rumbling of the waggon prevented them from noticing that any mishap had occurred. So the vehicle went on for about a mile and a half. It was not until the child had been lying on the road, alone in the darkness, for nearly a quarter of an hour that the horseman reached the place where he lay. Hearing the sound of the horse's hoofs, Mahadev called out, "Uncle Vithu, here I am fallen out." The uncle's surprise and alarm can be imagined! He speedily lifted the child, and urging his horse forward soon drew level with the waggon. When he called to Gopikabai, "Are you awake! Are the children in their places all right?" she sleepily murmured that everything was all right. Thereupon Vithu shouted, "You are still asleep, look if the children are beside you." She then began to grope round the waggon with her hands, and soon realised that Mahadev was missing. Vithu however at once removed the dread which fell upon her and which made her cry out with fear; and as he placed the child safely in the waggon again, he said, "What a great mercy God has shown to us this day."

Ranade's childhood from the age of three to the age of thirteen was spent at Kolhapur. When he was six years old he was sent to the Marathi school there, and in 1851 he was sent to the Kolhapur English School. He used afterwards to speak very highly of the English teaching he had received from the headmaster of the English School, Mr. Rrishnarao Chaphaji. It is curious to find that both Ranade's parents and his teachers regarded him as being in no way a specially promising boy. Indeed he seemed to be rather dull and backward. Until quite a big boy he was unable to articulate certain letters of the alphabet. He would persistently substitute the "T" class of letters for the "K" class. His mother used to be quite concerned about him, and would exclaim, "What is to become of Mahadev? Will he ever be clever enough to earn ten rupees for his wife?" As a boy he was rather clumsy and ungainly—and his college nick-name, "the baby elephant," shows that further development did not alter this characteristic. But he inherited the "Ranade" constitution, and was very robust in body.

From his early days he displayed a calmness and steadiness of balance that prevented him from being exhilarated, excited, or upset by happenings which are usually reacted to in a disturbed manner. For example, he would keep to himself news which most children would be bursting to tell. It would not enter into his head to announce to his parents that he had passed in the school examination. The children of the neighbours would come home, telling of their passing, retailing all that the examiner had asked and what they had answered, but Mahadev would be quite silent about it all. When his mother learned from the other children that Mahadev had passed, she would say to him, "Why ever did you not tell us?" And he would calmly reply, "What is there to talk about in that? If we go to school every day and do our work, then we are bound to pass. What more is there in it?"

Another characteristic which reminds us that the child is father of the man, was the boy's absorption in the interests of his work. When he was learning his letters, he would come home after the school was dismissed, and would sit for the rest of the day repeating the letters over slowly to himself and drawing them on the wall with his finger. His work and his recreation tended to be identical. When playing alone in the street, he would sit on the ground drawing arithmetic table in the dust.

From his carly years Ranade had a keen sense of right and wrong. Certain incidents, in which his conduct was guided by a delicate sense of honour, remind us strongly of the lines of Robert Burns[1],—

> "Where'er ye feel your honour grip,
> Let that aye be your border."

Once his mother put into his hands a large piece and a small piece of a cake of which he was very fond, indicating at the same time that one bit was to be given to a poor peasant boy who was standing near. She was surprised to see Mahadev hand the large piece to the other boy, and said, "I meant you to give him the small bit and keep the large one for yourself." But Mahadev answered that that was not what she had said, and that he had done what he understood was her wish.

1. In the poem entitled, "Advice to a Young Friend."

As a boy he was very fond of the game called *songatya*—a game in which dice are flung and pieces moved in accordance with the result of the throws. On one occasion, in his tenth year, lacking any one to play with, he sat down in front of one of the verandah pillars and, imagining it to be his opponent, started a game. Playing with his right hand for the pillar and with his left for himself, he carried the game through to the end. The victory fell to the pillar. When chaffed about allowing a human being to be defeated by a wooden post, he quietly replied that a fact is a fact, that the pillar had obtained a more advantageous throw of the dice, and that there was surely no disgrace in that. The answer, if it does not foreshadow much promise of humour, yet reveals an innate sense of rectitude, a recognition that facts must guide and that matters are not to be arranged simply in accordance with our whims.

Mahadev used to treat with scanty respect the ornaments in which his mother loved to see him decked. With considerable sacrifice, for she was not rich, she would put a necklet, a bracelet, and a ring on him. But Mahadev would so arrange his *dhotar* that it covered the gold necklet. The bracelet he would move up to the top of his arm so that it was hidden by his sleeve. And he would turn the ring round on his finger and close his fist on it, so that it was as little visible as possible. One of his relatives once asked him indignantly why he did not wear the ornaments properly, seeing that his mother was so anxious to have him nicely bedecked. His reply was to compare himself with the poor Brahman students[1] who came to the house every day, and to ask why he should wear ornaments when they did not.

The year 1854, when Mahadev was twelve, was a year of bereavement and of marriage in the Ranade household. In that year his mother died, in giving birth to her eighth

1. In accordance with what is known as the *Mahdukari* system poor scholars went every morning from house to house of the Brahman community, getting a little cooked food from each, and so securing enough to provide them with two meals.

child—none of the eight surviving beyond infancy except Mahadev and Durga. His father married again within about sixteen days. A few days after that event the marriages of Mahadev and of his sister took place. Mohadev's bride was Sakhubai, a daughter of Moropant Dandekar of Wai, and her age at the time of the marriage would be nine years.

By 1856 Ranade had gone as far as the school at Kolhapur could carry him, and so in accordance with his father's desire of giving him a complete English course, and at his own urgent request, he was sent to Bombay, and enrolled in the Elphinstone High School, a Government institution. It was at this stage that Ranade's quality of mind first began to be noticed. His headmaster, on several occasions, indicated that he was a very exceptional lad and prophesied that he would become a famous man. He spent three years at the school, obtaining scholarships of ten, fifteen, and twenty rupees a month, in each successive year.

In 1859 Ranade was one of the twenty-one students who passed the first matriculation examination held by the Bombay University. On the results of that examination he was appointed to a junior scholarship of Rs. 70 a month for three years, and in 1861 obtained a senior scholarship of Rs. 120 a month for three years. In April, 1862, he passed his B.A. examination in the first class. At that time the honours examination and the ordinary pass examination were quite separate. For the honours examination the University prescribed only the subjects, and the student had to prepare himself by reading what books he could obtain that were relevant. Ranade read widely but secured only a second class in the honours examination. The examiner, however, was so much impressed by the intelligence and learning revealed in Ranade's papers that he collected a sum of money among his friends and used it to present him with a gold medal and Rs. 200 worth of books.

From the year 1861 Ranade was on the junior staff of the Elphinstone Institution and had a considerable amount of teaching to do. In 1862 he was appointed English editor of the *Indu Prakash*, an English-Marathi weekly, founded in that same year by G.H. Deshmukh, to advocate political advance, social reform, and material progress. Without neglecting his studies he, for for months, carried on this editorial work, and gave great satisfaction in the doing of it. In 1864, Ranade was granted the M.A. degree, obtaining it automatically in accordance with the five years' regulation. In 1865, he was made a Fellow of the Bombay Unversity and was, indeed, the first indigenous Fellow to belong to that body. He commenced to study Law after taking his B.A. degree, attending law classes four times a week. In 1866, having passed the two examinations, he graduated L.L.B. with first class honours.

Ranade was a student of exceptional quality. One of his professors once said, "Mr. Ranade is the only student in the College who can think." His industry was prodigious, as can be seen from the lists of the books he read, the summaries he made, and the essays he wrote. Like so many other men who have made their mark in life, he was endowed with a very retentive memory. It was said of him that after reading a book he was able with ease to write out the best part of its contents.

Sir D.E. Wacha, a junior contemporary at the Elphinstone Institution, speaking at a meeting of Elphinstonians, drew the following interesting picture of Ranade as he remembered often seeing him in the College library :

"Listless of all that was going on around him, we would find him either intently absorbed in writing his weekly essay or reading aloud his Grote and Gibbon, his Hume and Macaulay, his Locke and Hamilton, and the rest of the standard authors which to us freshmen were such a terrible bugbear to master. The principals and professors, Dr. Harkness and Sir Alexander Grant, Professors Hughlings and Sinclair considered him as one who was destined to make his mark in the public life of this great city and achieve the highest distinction."[1]

1. Reported in *The Times of India*, 2nd February, 1901.

For his teachers Ranade cherished a warm admiration, and especially for Sir Alexander Grant. Sir Alexander, on his side, had a lively appreciation of Ranade's qualities. That however, did not prevent him from making his pupil feel the weight of a stern discipline when he thought he needed it. Like most high-spirited young men, Ranade in his student days was fervently patriotic, but perhaps, not always careful to preserve a due proportion in criticism and attack. It is told of him that on one occasion he drew a very disparaging comparison between British rule and Maratha rule. Sir Alexander sent for him and, after controverting the views expressed by Ranade, said, "Young man, you should not run down a Government which is educating you and doing so much for your people." Besides that, he punished Ranade by suspending his scholarship for six months.

Ranade was by this time thoroughly at home in the English language. Mr. Howard, the then Director of Public Instruction in the Bombay Presidency, once sent a number of his essays to England as specimens of the excellent English written by a native of India. Ranade is also said to have written some very respectable verses while at College. But a much deeper thing than the attainment of facility in the use of a foreign language had been happening to Ranade. His English education had given him the key of entry into a new world of ideas. The Western mind has its roots in the Renaissance, in the Reformation, in the political philosophies, and in modern science. The Hindu mind has its roots in the Vedas, the *Upanishads*, the *Puranas* and the *Bhakti* Cults. The two mentalities differ enormously both in their outlook and in their atmosphere. The falling of the seed of Western education upon a mind nurtured in the Hindu tradition, and at the same time so able and so assimilative as Ranade's was, could not fail to be a momentous event. Ranade's English education was, without a doubt, the most formative influence upon his life and career ; and being the man he was his reaction to that influence had effects which travelled far beyond himself.

In a lecture which he delivered long after his student days (in August, 1878) Ranade uttered words that show how keen was his appreciation of the values which Western education can impart to the Oriental world. He set himself to answer the question, "What advantage is there in knowing the English language ?" And he answers :

"No one can understand its advantage by mere telling, and indeed it is not possible merely to tell it. It is necessary to study the language and the knowledge, for only from the basis of experience can the advantage be really appreciated. The English language is to be regarded not as simply an English affair, but rather an affair of all the advanced nations of the West. If it be asserted that there is no need to go to a foreign language, for surely India has its own language and learning, then the answer is that the Indian learning even in its most flourishing period has to be pronounced immature, whereas to-day European knowledge has advanced to a mature stage. The important thing about any body of knowledge is that it should tell us what we are, what our duty is, what we are to do in this world, what our rights are, and such like matters. This is the knowledge we ought to seek after, no matter whether it originated in our own country or in a foreign country. Now that knowledge has been more or less discovered by the European learning, whereas even in the flourishing times of our Indian learning there is no trace of it...The English rule should be regarded, as a fortunate occurrence for India, and not as a reason for refusing the proferred knowledge. Japan and China and other nations seek with great expenditure and labour to acquire this knowledge... India is in a fortunate position as compared with the Chinese and Japanese, since she is so favourably situated for acquiring it without difficulty. Instead of decrying the impact upon India of Western thought the true lover of India will rejoice in it. He will himself acquire as much of it as he can, will get acquainted with his rights, and by means of the modern knowledge will remove the cloud that has enveloped his country for thousands of years."

The extraordinary amount of reading that Ranade did, had a serious effect upon his already defective eyesight, and for some time it was feared that he would go blind. The trouble began in 1863. In 1864 the doctor gave him strict injunctions that he was not to use his eyes at all. Every morning one or other of his friends used to lead him to the doctor's house, where the green bandages that covered his eyes were removed, the eyes cleaned, fresh ointment applied, and the bandages put on again. This state of affairs lasted for six months, and one can imagine what an exasperating disability it must have been to Ranade with his insatiable appetite for reading. However, the burden of his affliction was lightened by the good-heartedness of fellow-students, some of whom used to take turns in reading to him, and so he was able to keep up his studies. Ranade seems to have had what psychologists call the "aural" type of memory, for it is said that he did not grasp the meaning of sentences without either himself uttering the words aloud or hearing someone else utter them. Probably that fact, combined with his exceptional strength of memory, made it more possible for him to continue his studies during his blind period than would have been the case, had he been a "visual" memoriser. It must, however, have been for him a very trying period and he had trouble with his eyes more or less until the end of his life.

Ranade had in him the making of a great professor, and it was along the teaching line that he started out in life, though he was soon diverted into a legal career. He began teaching when he was appointed a Fellow in the Elphinstone College, in 1861. He taught history, geography, arithmetic, economics, logic, English composition, and English poetry to the lower classes in the Elphinstone Institution. We are told that he made the study of geography attractive by connecting it closely with history. In dealing with a particular country he would tell the story of some of its great men, and would impart the geographical knowledge in connection therewith.

In 1864 he started teaching economics—the subject which shared with history, his chief liking. The high-priest of economic orthodoxy at that time was John Stuart Mill. Ranade, though never an extreme rebel, yet showed sufficient independence of mind to criticise Mill and to protest against the blind application to Indian affairs of the Millian doctrines, which had been evolved amid conditions of economic life differing radically from those of India. We shall see, later on, the form which this protest took in Ranade's more mature thought. The students were accustomed to confine themselves almost exclusively to Mill's book, but Ranade, never content with a one-book knowledge of a subject, made them read Senior, M'Culloch, Ramsay, Malthus, and Bastiat. In his lectures, having given the gist of these writers, he used at the end of the course to read Mill's book with the class.

Being himself the sort of man who would read everything that he could find bearing upon the subject he was studying. Ranade had no patience with the *cramming* methods of the average student. He considered that a teacher's function is to teach his class the subject and not merely to prepare them for passing an examination. He knew it was possible to pass an examination by means of cram-books, and yet at the end of it all to be destitute of any intelligent grasp of the subject. His own method of study had been very different from the pass-tabloid method that was, and is, so common. "Up till the time of the examination," Mr. Phatak tells us, "the books set by the University would scarcely be seen in his hands. His method of study was to read first the biggest books on economics and history and logic, and digest thoroughly the useful part of them, and then at the end to run over the set books." And similarly in his teaching preparation there was nothing of the "ca-canny" policy. He brought to his classes the wealth that he had culled from wide and varied sources. The mental digestion of the majority of his students was, however, too weak for the rich fare he offered; and we are told that he felt the results of his preparation and teaching to be like the effect made by pouring water on a vessel that the is turned upside down. One feels. however, that Ranade must have been a force making for academic righteousness, and that to the few real students the stimulus of a teacher of such calibre must have been powerful.

In 1862, just after he had passed the B.A., Ranade was appointed Examiner in the Marathi Language for the Matriculation Examination. He performed the duties of the post with much conscientiousness. "To carry out the responsibility that lay on me as an examiner," he wrote in his report, "I read six chapters of Dayaneshwar, perused several parts of *Navanit*, and studied poems of Moropant. It was necessary to get a knowledge of the minutest details of the set course of study, so as to be able to set the questions properly. I spent most of my leisure time in February and March in this work."

In 1866, Ranade was appointed Oriental Translator to the Government of Bombay—his work being to report to the Government on whatever new literature was published in Marathi. This appointment caused him to give up teaching for a time and to go and settle in Poona. Shortly after, he was made *Karbhari* or Administrator of the State of Akalkot, and he went from there to be Judge in the State of Kolhapur in September, 1867. He acted as Oriental Translator for nearly two years, retaining the position while employed at Akalkot and Kolhapur. The books and pamphlets were sent to him at these places, and after perusal he sent his report on them to the Director of the Legal Department.

In March 1868, Ranade returned to Bombay, having been appointed Professor at the Elphinstone College in the subjects of English and History. At the time of his coming his pupils, his old fellow-students, and his colleagues on the staff held a great gathering in his honour and presented him with a gold watch. For the next two and a half years, besides doing his College work, he at different times acted temporarily in the offices of Judge of the Small Causes Court, Police Magistrate, High Court Deputy and Assistant Registrar at the High Court. In 1871, he passed the Advocates Examination, and shortly afterwards he was appointed a Judge by the Government of Bombay, and was sent to take up duty at Poona.

Ranade was essentially a son of his age. He built his inner life out of the deeper urges and the fine aspirations of his time. When he went up to college, ideas of social reform were in the air. Western education, the British administration of law and justice, and the efforts of the Christian missionaries had brought into Hindu society a ferment of new thought. As a result the better mind of Hinduism was becoming acutely uncomfortable regarding such things as child-marriage, the wrongs suffered by widows, and the injustice done to the depressed classes; it was beginning to regret the illiteracy among men, and to doubt the wisdom of opposing the education of women; it was beginning to realizc some of the drawbacks of the caste system, and to chafe at the ban on foreign travel. There was in these days, too, a stirring of the waters in the religious sphere. It was seen in the turning to Christianity of such men as Narayan Seshadri and Baba Padmanji, and in reform movements within Hinduism. There was an interesting society in existence for two or three years after Ranade came to Bombay. It had been founded in 1840 by Dadoba Pandurang and was called the Paramhans Mandal.[1] The objects of this soeiety were the abolition of caste, the introduction of the custom of widow-marriage, and the renunciation of idolatry. Every meeting was opened and closed with prayer. There was to be absolute secrecy regarding the objects of the society until its membership reached thousand, when public profession of the creed was to be made.[2] The Theistic Church known as the *Prarthana Samaj*, i.e., the Prayer Society, can be said to have arisen from the ashes of the Paramhans Mandali.

The impetus of Western life and thought was conveyed into the heart of India's social and religious system largely through the writings and the agaitations of Ram Mohan Roy, the great Bengal reformer and founder of the Brahmo Samaj. Ranade regarded Ram Mohan Roy as one who had turned the flow of the national current in the right direction, by his

1. The Divine Society—*Paramhans* being a designation for the Supreme Deity.
2. See Baba Padmanji's *Once Hindu* : *Now Christian*, Chapter xi, for an account of this remarkable Society.

long fight for the abolition of *sati*[1] and other religious atrocities, and by his endeavour to remove the false accretions of ages and to return to the pure monotheism of Vedic times. He also saw in Ram Mohan Roy one who was a true patriot "long before our era of Congress meetings and conferences". Ram Mohan Roy died nine years before Ranade was born. But as a young man in Bombay, Ranade came into contact with many older men whose minds had absorbed, and whose actions embodied, something of that same reforming spirit that had found so distinguished an exponent in Ram Mohan Roy. Ranade was in touch, for example, in the persons of Dadoba Pandurang and Balsastri Jambhekar with men who were full of zeal for the advancement of education both among boy and girls. In Nana Sankarset he had before his eyes a beloved popular leader who had striven to remove misunderstanding regarding the Government action against sati., who had supported the agitation against indecencies at the Holi festival, who had worked hard for the increase of English education among Indians, and who was a model of enlightened citizenship. In Vishnusastri Pandit he had come into close contact with a man who was carrying on in Western India the great work on behalf of Hindu widows which Vidyasagar had started in Bengal. In Dr. Bhau Daji and others he came under the influence of enthusiastic students of history who were ever seeking to point the contrast between India's ancient glory and her present fallen state. Dadabhai Naoroji was in England during Ranade's student days, but doubtless Ranade often heard and read about the things which that great political pioneer was doing and saying. In connection with the religious quest he must on several occasions have listened to the fiery eloquence of Kesab Chandra Sen. Such men as these were the channels through which the spirit of the times poured in on Ranade's soul. But he absorbed that stream in such a way that it became in him a deep and living spring.

1. The practice of widows allowing themselves—often under heavy social pressure—to be burnt alive at the time of their husban's funeral.

Ranade was just the type of young man in whom the higher urges of the time-spirit would find a welcome, and we see him in his student days eagerly responding to its imperious summons. A society called the Dnyanprasarak Sabha, i.e, the Society for the Spreading of Knowledge, was flourishing when he came to college. He became a member and read some papers before it—"The Duties of Educated Young Men," in 1859; "Maratha Kings and Nobles," in 1860; and "The Evil Results of the Growth of Population," in 1864. When editor of the English columns of the *Indu Prakash*, he boldly upheld the cause of the Indian widow. Moreover, he was a member of the Widow-Marriage Association, which had been founded in 1866. He was of great assistance to Vishnusastri Pandit, at the time of his unequal fight with the orthodox Sastris, when trying to prove that widow-marriages are not in conflict with the Hindu scriptures. The Association brought about a great many re-marriages of widows among the Deccani and Gujarati Brahmans. At the time of the first of these re-marriages—in 1869—Vishnusastri Pandit, Ranade, and five other leading members of the Association were publicly excommunicated by the Sankaracharya of Western India.[1] One or two of the excommunicated men gave in and appeased the authorities, but Ranade, refusing to lower the flag of reform, went on fearlessly with the work of encouraging the widow-marriages. It is true that he had not much to suffer on account of his excommunication —a fact which was due partly to his position, and partly to the circumstance that many of his friends were persons of liberal ideas. Nevertheless, his firm stand would be a powerful help to the cause.

Like R.G. Bhandarkar and V.A. Modak, and many other young men of his time, Ranade longed for a form of religion which would satisfy his mind and heart, and which at the same time would not require a complete break with the Hinduism of his fathers. He found this in the Prarthana Samaj, which was inaugurated in March, 1867, amid the wave of religious enthusiasm that marked the second visit to

1. One of several religious dignitaries whose position in regard to their own particular area corresponds to that of a Pope.

Bombay of the Brahmo Samaj[1] missionary, Kesab Chandra Sen. From the beginning, Ranade had close connection with this new theistic society, and indeed, as we shall see, he took a large part in the forming of its creed.

A child of the East, Ranade might be said to have become a foster-child of the West, though he never forgot his real parentage. He comes upon the scene at a time which, spiritually, politically and socially, can be called a twilight hour—but it is a twilight touched with the glimmerings of dawn. Western thought was streaking with its rich-toned colours the sky of the ancient Eastern civilization. Though his Western education Ranade passed without crisis and without conflict into the new outlook, and became a robust and optimistic herald of the new day. Already, while still a student, his eager spirit was reconnoitring those paths of political, social, economic, and religious progress along which he was, all his life, to be so persistent a striver.

From the close of his college period onwards to the very day of his death we are conscious that Ranade has engaged his powers in the service of an ideal which goes far beyond the attainment of personal ambition, and which sheds a brighter lustre than the individual success of a distinguished legal. career. We see him now going forward to the work to which he has been called, a man of rare mental endowment, burning with a strong and steady flame of patriotism. We see him pursuing, with an exceptional catholicity of interest and wholeness of view, four great lines of combined mental research and practical effort, seeking to forward the social, political, economic, and religious advance of his motherland. It is as though, up till 1871, Ranade had been serving his apprenticeship; after that he had emerged the master craftsman, to wield his tools in the shaping of his country's future. As these interests of reform dominate Ranade's life with clear insistence from now onwards, so the remainder of this

1. This "eldr sister" of the Prarthana Samaj was founded in 1828 by Ram Mohan Roy and, though never large in members, it has exercised an important influence in Bengal.

biography will be concerned mainly with the leading thoughts that Ranade reached and maintained in the social, political, economic, and religious fields and with the efforts that he made to bring into effective operation the practical conclusions fo his thinking. The main incidents of his life, its terms of unwonted stress and dramatic tension, were but the inevitable domestic and official frictions that attended upon a man whom such a quality of patriotism inspired, and who was seeking for his country a pathway from the old to the new, from the valued past to the beckoning future. In the varying occasions and forms of that friction and in the ways in which it was faced, we shall see the character of the man revealed.

His wife reminsced thus; I was married in December of 1873. There was not much of a bridal procession. Actually, after the Vedic ceremony was over, we walked home.

My husband had not eaten anything at my mother's house. Even when he returned home, he spoke to no one. He went to his own room and locked himself in. He was in deep agony that day.

It was just about a month since he had lost his first wife, who had been like a comrade to him. That great grief was yet fresh in his mind. To add to that, he had had to yield to his father's stern insistence and marry again entirely against his resolve. Two principles were sacred to him—never to go against the word of his father; and never to disturb the peace and well-being of his family. For this, he gave up a view which he had accepted as correct over a long period of time, the principle of the justice of widow-remarriage. He gave up his valued friendships. He even flung away his self-respect and the esteen arising from it. For the sake of his principle of devotion to the parental word, he faced the ridicule and lasting calumny of society*. It was but natural then, that the night of his sacred wedding should be one of agony for him.

*The refernnce is to the widespread agitation in Maharashtra at Ranade's giving up his publicly avowed principle of widow-remarriage in his own case.

Even today, so many feel that if there is any black spot in his life, it is the traditional character of his second marriage. But I for one feel that if there is any aspect in his life of self-sacrifice and large-heartedness which is nobler than others, it is this one. Whatever anyone might say, I have tremendous respect for the decision he took in this particular regard, and I am sure whoever thinks of his life with true understanding, will feel likewise.

For a fortnight before the wedding, he used to receive a number of letters from his friends in Bombay. "This is the time", they would say, "when you must tell your father that you will not marry a young girl. You must announce to him that you will marry a widow". The first few letters reached him directly. But when Mamanji came to know of them he grew watchful. As soon as the mail arrived, he would first take it himself. He would remove the letters and telegrams from Bombay and send the rest to my husband upstairs. No one in the family dared say a word against Mamanji. So no one mentioned it to my husband.

Mamanji came to Poona after the death of my husband's first wife and immediately started a hectic search for a new bride for him. He already knew that his son was a staunch supporter of widow remarriage and feared that he would now put his principle in practice. He decided not to give him a chance of being influenced by his friends in Bombay and to get him married again at once.

At this time, my father had also gone to Poona to look for a bridegroom for me. He already knew Mamanji. He met him and said, "I am looking for a match for my daughter. But there is a tradition in our family that our girls do not go out of their home to be considered for marriage. You might be aware of this. My request to you, therefore, is that you might send some one to see my daughter in her own home. If she is considered suitable, she will be brought here. It will be highly derogatory to our family if the girl is brought out for marriage and has to return home without being married."

Mamanji asked Vedamoorti Shri Balambhatji Watwe to go with my father. That learned Brahmin had lived with us since he was ten or twelve years old, and was like a member of the family. He lived a clean life and was rigorous in his rituals and discipline. Mamanji had complete confidence in him. He came to our house with my father and "saw" me. He put me all the usual questions. He stayed with us the whole day, perhaps to observe everything else about our family.

At night before he retired to bed, he said to my father, "I approve of the girl. We shall go with her tomorrow. You may send a telegram and ask the family to come over, after the *muhurta* is fixed."

When this was done, my father, Balambhatji and I left for Poona by mail-tonga. In the meanwhile, my husband tried hard to make Mamanji see his point of view. He said, "I do not wish to marry. I am not young any more, I am thirty-two years old. I can certainly lead a life of thought and retirement. Durga is younger than I and has been a widow since she was twenty-one. You do not love her less than you love me, in any way. And yet no one thinks of her. Why am I being urged to marry ? If you think it would be good for her to lead a life of restraint, it should apply equally to me. If you are afraid that I may marry a widow, I give you my word of honour that I will not do so. You need have no anxiety on that score."

He urged Mamanji in many ways. But it was of no avail. Arguments only made Mamanji all the more furious So my husband said, "Even if you are not willing to listen to me, I must obey you. But leave me free for at least six months. I will go to England during that period." Even that Mamanji would not agree to. So my husband sent him a message to this effect : "You are going to force me to marry. But please do this much. Do not select a girl from this place. She should be from another place and she should belong to a family of good repute. It should also be ascertained that the other antecedents and connections of the family are decent. I do not wish to marry a girl from an ordinary family just for the sake of her looks or age. Our relationship is likely to be a little more happy if a good family is given preference over good looks." A couple of days after this, my father and I arrived in Poona.

Mamanji came to the place where we had put up, saw me, approved of me and fixed up the *muhurta* of the next *ekadashi*. He, however, asked my father to see the bridegroom himself and hear him out. "If he agrees to everything, well and good, if not, you may tell him that you have decided to give your daughter in marriage to our family", he said. My father agreed. In the evening he visited the house and went upstairs to see my husband.

My father had an impressive appearance. He looked dignified, respectable and firm, like one from a high and reputed family. My husband rose to receive him when he saw him and enquired about him and his business. My father told him that he was a *jagirdar* of such and such a place and gave very briefly the rest of the information about himself. Then he said, "My daughter is of marriageable age. I have come to propose a match."

My husband said, "Why do you think I will be an appropriate match ? You belong to an ancient *jagirdar* family. I am a reformer in favour of widow re-marriage. I look hale and hearty, but I have weak eyesight and am also hard of hearing. Besides, I am planning to go to England. I shall not undergo any *prayaschitta* after I return. You should consider all this and then decide."

My father replied, "I have known Bhausahib for years. He has told me everything and I have already taken my decision."

After a long silence, my husband said, "If that is so, I would like to propose that only an engagement should take place. The wedding might be postponed for a year."

But my father urged that it would not be consistent with our family traditions. He requested him to consider the embarrassment to his family and so on. In the end my husband decided that they should both see what Bhausahib had to say and abide by it. At this my father left.

My husband persuaded himself that after he had conceded so many things to Bhausahib, he would certainly agree to postpone the marriage by six months. With that hope he went to his father, told him that my father, Annasahib Kurkelar, had seen him and gave him an account of the talk. Mamanji said, "What was the decision, finally ?"

"We have left it to you. We need not agree to everything he proposes. He should consider some of our points also. I have told him that I shall agree to everything, I shall marry, but not today. It should be postponed by a year or six months."

My husband kept saying this, softly but again and again. Mamanji heard it all, but said nothing for a long time. After about two hours, Mamanji spoke. He first asked all the others who were there to go and to leave father and son alone for an hour or so. They all disappeared quickly, but my sister-in-law stayed nearby, unseen.

Mamanji said, "I have heard all you have been saying and have thought over it deeply. But I do not think I can agree to what you say. I have never distrusted you; nor will I do so now. But don't you realise that you are now in a situation full of temptation? Even the most firm and thoughtful decisions may by defeated be a moment of temptation at this stage. I have a feeling that if I leave you free for a year or six months, I shll lose all my peace of mind in this declining age. I shall tell you why. Your friends in Bombay have sent you a number of letters and telegrams during the last fortnight. I have seen them all and kept them with me. Considering them all, I do not think I should agree to your proposal. You are already strongly inclined towards these now ideas, and your friends are encouraging you. You are also young. If you had any children, it might have held you back to some extent. If you were left utterly free, you would naturally be driven towards these new-fangled ideas. This is what I am afraid of. I am now quite old. You are stepping in to the position of the master of the family. The women and children depend upon you. And you are worthy of the burden. I have put everything before you. You can think for yourself. You may do just what you think right. But I shall tell you what I have decided. If you do not marry now, I have vowed not to send the girl back. It will be derogatory to the family of Annasahib and it will be highly insulting to me too. But, if that has to be, you may take it that I shall leave for Karveer for good. Our bonds will be broken for ever. The rest will be in the hands of Providence." Mamanji said all this, heaved a heavy sigh and got up. He washed his hands and feet and went for his *sandhya*. My husband got up and went up stairs. This account of what happened before our marriage was given to me by my sister-in-law.

And so, as decided by Mamanji, we were married on the eleventh day of the bright half of Margasheersha in Saka 1795 (December 1873) at the auspicious hour of dusk, the hour when the cattle return home. My husband went through the Vedic ritual, but did not allow the customary social ceremonies at all. He did not take leave even on the wedding day. Until he returned from the courts before the hour of the wedding, Mamanji was half afraid that one of his Bombay friends might seize the opportunity and take him away for a walk, just to make him miss the *muhurta*. At the same time, he was sure of his son. He knew that once he had given his word, he would never depart from it, however much it might be against his own wishes. Completely justifying that confidence, my husband came straight home from the courts, without going either for a walk or to the library as he was wont to.

After the wedding, my father returned home leaving me in my new home in Poona. I had come with him alone when the match was being considered. When it was decided and the *muhurta* was fixed, a telegram was to go for my mother, brothers, sisters-in-law, sisters and brothers and all the rest of the family. But the *muhurta* fixed up by Mamanji left no time for that. Besides, my husband declared that he would not allow any ceremonies other than the Vedic ritual. So my father thought it wiser not to send for the whole family and disappoint them with the bareness of the ritual.

The evening my father left, my husband called me upon the terrace after he had returned from the courts. He said, "Has your father left ?"

"Yes."

"You are now married to me. Do you know who I am and what my name is ?"

"Yes."

"Then tell me. What is my name ?"

The Beginning of my Education

When he commanded me thus, I repeated his full name as others spoke it. I did not understand anything well enough to be shy. I remember he seemed to be pleased in a way with my answer. Then he asked me about my family and I told him whatever I knew. He asked whether I could read and write. I could do neither. So that very night I was given a slate and a pencil and the first lesson of seven syllables, 'Shriganeshayanamah'. It was my fist chance to handle a slate and a pencil and my first glimps of the alphabet. It took nearly two hours for me to be able to read and write those seven letters. It was decided to devote two hours every night to teach me. I was taught the alphabet and *barakhadis* and after about a fortnight I read the first lesson of the first reader with some help. My husband seemed greatly relieved that evening.

This reminds me of an earlier incident. My own family was an orthodox, aristocratic one of *jagirdars* of the Maratha days. The women dared not enter the front apartment and come into the presence of the father—not even a daughter who had come home for a short while from her husband's house: nor girls above eight years. Singing and playing about was of course unthinkable. So was reading or writing. The police intervened. Immediately the rowdies took to their heels and the procession proceeded in peace. The wounded were sent to the hospital.

My husband returned home and changed his mud-soiled clothes. When someone in the family asked how mud had been thrown even at him when the police were there, he smiled and said, "Why not, when I was with them all ? Why should they think of whether an individual in the opposition is big or small ? It would be wrong of us to think of personal prestige in such a case."

2

Social Ideology

Ranade's contribution for the upliftment of the socially and economically weaker sections of the society is unique in the annals of our history. Through his speeches, and writings as well as personal model life he left a rich legacy for our generation. Indeed his concern for the poor was proverbial.

To-day I find myself far away in the north, surrounded on all sides by the tradition of a civilization older than the oldest known to history, the land of the Aryan race settled in India, tracing its descent from the self-born Svayambhu Manu, where the Solar dynasty flourished for thousands of years, the land of the Ikshvakus, of Dilip and Raghu, of Dasharath and the incarnate hero Rama, with his illustrious brothers and the still more honoured wife Sita, the land where Vashishta and Vishvamitra lived and flourished. the home of all that is beautiful and true, and lovely and godlike in Aryan history. This favoured land of yours gave birth also in later times, to Shakya Muni Buddha, who has been well described as the perfection of humanity in its highest and noblest development, and whose "Wheel of law" still regulates the thoughts and feelings of half the human race in its efforts to attain beatitude. I propose this time to draw your attention to the turn which the Aryan civilization has taken under the influences represented by the conquest of this part of the country by the Mahomedans, nearly a thousand years back. The one factor which separates Northern India from its Southern neighbours, is the predominant influence of this conquest by Mahomedans, which has left its mark permanently upon the country, by the actual conversion to the Mahomedan faith of one-fifth of the population, and by the imperceptible but permanent moulding of the rest of the people in the ways of thought and belief, the like of which is hard to find on the Malabar or Coromandel Coasts. I propose to draw my materials from the Mahomedan philosophers and travellers who visited India, both before and after the Mahomedan conquest and changed the face of the country. Owing to the absence of the historic instinct among our people, we have necessarily to depend upon the testimony of foreign historians. That testimony is, however, unexceptionable, because it was for the most part given before the Mahomedan domination had effected the separation which distinguishes the old India of the past from the modern India in which we are now living. This domination also separates the line which marks off southern India, of which I spoke last year, from the north, in one of the most representative centres of which we are met here to-day.

At the outset, we must have a correct understanding of what northern India was before Mahmud of Gazni made his numerous expeditions for the plunder of its far-famed cities and temples, at the commencement of the tenth century. Fortunately for us, we have a witness to this period of our history in the writing of Alberuni, whose work on India was written shortly after the time that Mahmud crossed the Indus as a conqueror of infidels. That work has been translated by Dr. Sachau, a professor in the Berlin University, and in its Enlish form, is now accessible to us all. Alberuni was a native of Khorasan, his birth place being near Khiva. Mahmud of Gazni conquered Khorasan, and Alberuni had to shift to Gazni which was then the seat of a flourishing empire the rulers of which were great patrons of Mahomedan learning. Alberuni was in special favour with Masaud, the son of Mahmud, and he was thus enabled to travel throughout India, where he spent many years, having mastered the Sanskrit Language. He was a philosopher by profession and temper, and had a special liking for Indian philosophy which he studied with the same care and attention that he bestowed on Plato and Aristotle. His work on India consists of eighty chapters, relating to Religion, Philosophy, Caste, idolatry, Civil Polity, Literature, Science, Mathematics, Medicine, Geography, Astronomy, Cosmogony, Alchemy and Astrology. He took great pains to give a full description of all that was known to the Hindus under these several heads, and being naturally not a bigoted Mahomedan, his book shows that he wrote his whole work with a single desire to promote the cause of true learning. While Alberuni shows a great regard for the Hindu Philosophy, Astronomy, and Medicine, he was not slow in finding out the weak points of the Indian character. In his chapters on caste and idolatry, in the condemnation he pronounces on the want of practical aptitudes of our people, and in their devotion to superstitious observances, Alberuni did not spare his censures. He contrasted the democratic equality of the Mahomedan people with the innumerable divisions of the Indian races. He notices the helpless position of the women of India, and the filthy customs and habits of the people in those days. He gives praise to the few educated Brahmans whom he separates from the superstitious multitude whose fallen condition he deplores. Even among the Brahmans, he notices the verbosity of their writings and the word splitting which passed for wisdom. He notices the greediness and tyranny of the Hindu princes, who would not agree to join their efforts together for any common purpose, and the timidity and the submissiveness of the people who, in his expressive language, were scattered like atoms of dust in all directions before the invading Moslems. The prevailing feeling among the Mahomedans of the time was that the Hindus were infidels, and entitled to no mercy or consideration, and the only choice to be allowed to them was that of death or conversion. Alberuni did not share in these views, but they were the views of his master Mahmud of Gazni and of the hordes who were led by him on these expeditions. Another traveller, Ibn Batuta, a native of Tangiers in North Africa, visited this country about a hundred years after Kutbuddin established the Afghan kingdom at Delhi. Like him, he was taken into favour by the Delhi Emperor, Mahmud Taghlak, under whom he acted for some time as a Judge of Delhi. Ibn Batuta travelled more extensively than Alberuni. He travelled from the extreme west of Africa to the extreme east of China, and went round the coast from Malabar to Coromandel. He was, however, neither a philosopher nor a scholar. His journal of travels is interesting, but he did not observe the manners and customs of the people with the same mastery of details that Alberuni's work shows on every page. The only points which struck Ibn Batuta in the course of his travels through India were the rite of *Sati* of which he was a witness, and the practice of drowning men in the Ganges, both of which stuck him as inhuman to a degree he could not account for. He also notices the self-mortification of the *jogees* and their juggleries. in describing which last he mentions the fact that in the presenee of the emperor, he saw a *jogee* raise his body up in the air and keep it these for some time. Another traveller, Abder Razzak visited India about 1450 A.D. His travels lay chiefly in the Southern Peninsula, Calicut, Vijayanagar and Mangalore. The narratives of two other travellers, one a Russian and the other a Venetian, who both visited India in the fifteenth century, are published by the Hakluyt Society, and afford most interesting reading. The general impression left on the minds of these travellers was a respect for the Brahmans, for their philosophy and attainments in astrology, but for the common people, the vast multitudes of men and women, their sense was one of disgust and disappointment. Abder Razzak expressed this feeling in his own words in a reply to the invitation of the King of Vijayanagar. He said to the king, "If I have once escaped from the desert of thy love, and reached my country, I shall not set out on another voyage even in the company of a king."

The abuse of idolary and caste struck every traveller as the peculiar characteristic of the country, and gave them offence. The practice of self-immolation, or *Sati*, and of human sacrifices to idols by being crushed beneath the temple car are also mentioned. Finally, we have the testimony of the emperor Babar, who in his memoirs thus describes this country :—'Hindustan is a country which has few things to recommend. The people are not handsome. They have no idea of the charms of friendly society or of freely mixing together in familiar intercourse. They have no genius, no comprehension of mind, no politeness of manners, no kindness or fellow-feeling, no ingenuity or mechanical invention in planning and executing their handicraft work, no skill or knowledge in design or architecture. They have no good horses, no good flesh, no good grapes or musk-melons, no good fruits, no cold water or ice, no good food or bread in their bazaars, no baths, no colleges, no candles, not even a candlestick. They have no aqueducts or canals, no gardens, and no palaces; in their buildings they study neither elegance, nor climate, nor appearance, nor regularity. Their peasants and lower classes all go about naked tying on only a *langoti*. The women too have only a *lang*.' The only good points which Babar could find in favour of Hindustan were that it is a large country and has abundance of gold and silver, and that there is also an abundance of workmen of every profession and trade for any work and employment.

Such was the picture presented to the Mahomedans when they entered India through the passes in successive hordes for three or four centuries. A great portion of the disgust and disappointment felt by these Mahomedan invaders may be set down to ignorance and the pride of race. At the same time, it is always of advantage to know exactly how India appeared in its strong and weak points to intelligent foreigners, such as those I have mentioned above. The question for consideration to us at the present moment is, whether in consequence of the predominance of the Mahomedans for five centuries, which intervened from the invasions of Mahmud to the accession of Akbar, the people of India were benefited by the contact thus forcibly brought together between the two races. There are those among us who think that this predominance has led to the decay and corruption of the Indian character, and that the whole story of the Mahomedan ascendancy should for all practical purposes, be regarded as a period of humiliation and sorrow. Such a view, however, appears to be unsupported by any correct appreciation of the forces which work for the elevation or depression of nations. It cannot be easily assumed that in God's providence, such vast multitudes as those who inhabit India were placed centuries together under influences and restraints of alien domination unless such influences and restraints were calculated to do lasting service in the building up of the strength and character of the people in directions in which the Indian races were most deficient. Of one thing we are certain, that after lasting over five hundred years, the Mahomedan empire gave way, and made room for the re-establishment of the old native races in the Punjab, and throughout central Hindustan and Southern India, on foundations of a much more solid character than those which yielded so easily before the assault of the early Mahomedan conquerors. The domination, therefore, had not the effect of so depressing the people that they were unable to raise their heads again in greater solidarity. If the Indian races had not benefited by the contract and example of men with stronger muscles and greater powers, they would never have been able to reassert themselves in the way in which history bears testimony they did.

Quite independently of this evidence of the broad change that took place in the early part of the eighteenth century, when the Mogul empire went to pieces and its place was taken up not by foreign settlers, but by revived native powers, we have more convincing grounds to show that in a hundred ways the India of the eighteenth century, so far as the native races were concerned, was a stronger and better constituted India than met the eyes of the foreign travellers from Asia and Europe who visited it between the period of the first five centuries from 1000 to 1500. In Akbar's time, this process of regenerate India first assumed a decided character which could not well be mistaken. No student of Akbar's reign will fail to notice that for the first time the conception was then realized of a united India in which Hindus and Mahomedans, such of them as had become permanenty established in the country were to take part in the building of an edifice rooted in the hearts of both by common interests and common ambitions. In place of the scorn and contempt, with which the Mahomedan invaders had regarded the religion of the Hindus, their forms of worship, their manners and customs, and with which the Hindus looked down upon them as barbarous Mlechas, whose touch was pollution, a better appreciation of the good points in the character of both came to be recognized as the basis of the union. Akbar was the first to see and realize the true nobility of soul and the devotion and fidelity of the Hindu character, and satified himself that no union was possible as long as the old bigotry and fanaticism was allowed to guide the councils of the empire. He soon gathered about him the best men of his time, men like Faizi. Abul Fazel and their father Mubarak, the historians Mirza Abdul Rahim, Nizamudin Ahmed, Badauni and others. These were set to work upon the translations of the Hindu epics and Shastras, and books of science and philosophy. The pride of the Rajput races was conciliated by taking in marriage the princesses of Jaipur, and Jodhpur, and by conferring equal or superior commands on those princes. These latter had been hitherto treated as enemies. They were now welcomed as the props of the empire, and Maharaja Bhagwandas, his great nephew Mansingha, for some time Governor of Bengal and Kabul, Raja Todarmal and the Brahman companion of the Emperor, Raja Birbal, these were welcomed to court, and trusted in the full consciousness that their interests were the same as those of the Musalman noblemen. The Emperor himself, guided by such counsel of his Hindu and Mahomedan nobles, became the real founder of the union between the two races, and this policy for a hundred years guided and swayed the councils of the empire. A fusion of the two races was sought to be made firmer still by the establishment of a religion of the Din-i-Illahi, in which the best points both of the Mahomedan, Hindu, and other faiths were sought to be incorporated. Invidious taxation and privileges were done away with, and toleration for all faiths became the Universal law of the empire. To conciliate his subjects Akbar abjured the use of flesh except on four special occasions in the year, and he joined in the religious rites observed by his Hindu queens. In regard to the particular customs of the people relating to points where natural humanity was shocked in a way to make union impossible, Akbar strove by wise encouragement and stern control, where necessary, to help the growth of better ideas. *Sati* was virtually abolished by being placed under restraint which nobody could find fault with. Re-marriage was encouraged, and marriage before puberty was prohibited. In these and a hundred other ways the fusion of the races and of their many faiths was sought to be accomplished, with a success which was justified by the results for a hundred years. This process of removing all causes of friction, and establishing accord went on without interruption during the reigns of Akbar, Jahangir and Shahjahan. Shahjahan's eldest son, Dara Sheko, was himself an author of no mean repute. He translated the Upanishads, and wrote a work in which he sought to reconcile the Brahman religion with the Mahomedan faith. He died in 1659. This period of a hundred years may be regarded as the halcyon period of Indian history when the Hindu and Mahamedan races acted in full accord. If in place of Aurangzed, Dara Sheko had succeeded to power as the eldest son of Shahjahan, the influences set on foot by the genius of Akbar might have gathered strength, and possibly averted the collapse of the Mogul power for another century. It was however, not to be so, and with Aurangzeb's ascent to the throne, a change of system commenced which gathered force during the long time that this emperor reigned. Even Aurangzeb had, however, to follow the traditions of his three predecessors. He could not dispense with Jaisingh or Jaswantsingh who were his principal military commanders. In the reign of his son, whole provinces under him were governed by Rajput, Kayastha and other Governors. The revival of fanatic bigotry was kept in check by the presence of these great Rajput Chiefs, one of whom, on the re-imposition of the Zezia, addressed to the emperor a protest couched in unmistakable terms that the God of Islam was also the God of the Hindus, and the subjects of both races merited equal treatment. Aurangzeb unfortunately did not listen to this advice, and the result was that the empire built by Akbar went to pieces even when Aurangzeb was alive. No one was more aware of his failure than

Aurangzeb himself, who in his last moments admitted that his whole life was a mistake. The Marathas in the South, the Sikhs in the North, and the Rajput states helped in the dismemberment of the empire in the reign of his immediate successor, with the result that nearly the whole of India was restored to its native Hindu sovereigns, except Bengal, Oudh, and the Deccan Hyderabad. It will be seen from this that so far from suffering from decay and corruption, the native races gathered strength by reason of the Mahomedan rule when it was directed by the wise counsel of those Mahomedan and Hindu statesmen who sought the weal of the country by a policy of toleration and equality. Since the time of Asoka, the element of strength born of union was wanting in the old Hindu dynasties which succumbed so easily to the Mahomedan invaders.

Besides this source of strength, there can be no doubt that in a hundred other ways the Mahomedan domination helped to refine the tastes and manners of the Hindus. The art of Government was better unerstood by the Mahomedans than by the old Hindu sovereigns. The art of war also was sigularly defective till the Mahomedans came. They brought in the use of gunpowder and artilley. In the words of Babar, they "taught ingenuity and mechanical invention in a number of handicraft arts," the very nomenclature of which, being made up of non-Hindu words, shows their foreign origin. They introduced candles, paper, glass, household furniture, and saddlery. They improved the knowledge of the people in music, instrumental and vocal, medicine and astronomy, and their example was followed by the Hindus in the perversions of both these latter sciences into alchemy and astrology. Geography and history and literature were first made possible departments of knowledge by their example. They built roads, aqueducts, canals, caravansarais, and the post office, and introduced the best specimens of architecture, and improved our gardening, and made us acquainted with the taste of new fruits and flowers. The revenue system as inaugurated by Todarmal in Akbar's time, is the basis of the revenue system up to the present day. They carried on the entire commerce by sea with distant regions, and made India feel that it was a portion of the inhabited world with relations with all, and not cut off from all social intercourse. In all these respects, the civilization of the united Hindu and Moslem powers represented by the Moguls at Delhi, was a distinct advance beyond what was possible before the tenth century of the Christian era.

More lasting benefits have, however, accrued by this contact in the higher tone it has given to the religion and thoughts of the people. In this respect, both the Mahomedans and Hindus benefited by contact with one another. As regards the Mahomedans, their own historians admit that the Sufi heresy gathered strength from contact with the Hindu teachers and made many Mahomedans believe in transmigration and in the final union of the foul with the supreme spirit. The Mohorum festival and saint worship are the best evidence of the way in which the Mahomedans were influenced by Hindu ideas. We are more directly concerned with the way in which this contact has affected the Hindus. The prevailing tone of pantheism had established toleration for polytheism among our most revered ancient teachers, who rested content with separating the few from the many, and establishing no bridge between them. This separation of the old religion has prevented its higher precepts from becoming the common possession of whole races. Under the purely Hindu system the intellect may admit, but the heart declines to allow a common platform to all people in the sight of God. The Vaishnava movement, however, has succeeded in establishing the bridge noted above, and there can be no doubt, that in the hands of the followers to Ramananda, especially the Kabirpanthis, Malikadasis, Badupanthis, the followers of Mirabai, Lord Gauranga on the Bengal side, Baba Nanak in Punjab in the fifteenth and the sixteenth centuries, the followers of Tukaram, Ekanath and Namdev in the Deccan, Babadalis, Pranathis, Sadhs, the Satnamis, the Shiva-Narayans and the followers of Mahant Rama Charan of the last two centuries—this elevation and the purification of the Hindu mind was accomplished to an extent which very few at the present moment realize in all its significance. The Brahma and the Arya Samaja movements of this century are the continuations of this ethical and spiritual growth. Caste, idolatry, polytheism and gross conceptions of purity and pollution were the precise points in which the Mahomedans and the Hindu were most opposed to one another, and all the sects named above had this general characteristic that they were opposed to these defects in the character of our people. Nanak's watchword was that he was 'Neither Hindu nor Mahomedan, but that he was a worshipper of the Nirakar, or the Formless.' His first companion was a Mahomedan, and Mahomedan authors pay him the compliment of saying that his teacher was a Mahomedan. The Hindus naturally do not admit this claim, with reason on their side. There can be no doubt that, while calling himself neither Hindu nor Mahomeden, Guru Nanak wanted to establish a union between the two faiths. Lord Gauranga had also Mahomedan disciples. Mahomedan saints like Shaik Mahmud, Shaik Farid and Mahmud Kazi were respected by both Hindus and Mahomedans. The abuses of polytheism were checked by the devotion to one object of worship, which in the case of many of the Vaishnava sects was the Supreme God, the Paramatma, and the abuses of caste were controlled by conceding to all, Hindus and Mahomedans alike, the right to worship and love the one God who was the God of all.

If the lessons of the past have any value, one thing is quite clear, viz., that in this vast country, no progress is possible unless both Hindus and Mahomedans join hands together, and are determined to follow the lead of the men who flourished in Akbar's time, and were his chief advisers and councillors, and sedulously avoid the mistakes which were committed by his great-grandson Aurangzeb. Joint action from a sense of common interest, and a common desire to bring about the fusion of the thoughts and feelings of men, so as to tolerate small differences and bring about concord—these were the chief aims kept in view by Akbar, and formed the principle of the new divine faith formulated in the Din-i-Ilahi. Every effort on the part of either Hindus or Mahomedans to regard their interests as separate and distinct, and every attempt made by the two communities to create separate schools and interests among themselves, and not to heal up the wounds inflicted by mutual hatred of caste and creed must be deprecated on all hands. It is to be feared that this lesson has not been sufficiently kept in mind by the leaders of both communities in their struggle for existence, and in the acquisition of power and predominance during recent years. There is at times a great danger of the work of Akbar being undone by losing sight of this great lesson which the history of his reign and that of his two successors is so well calculated to teach. The Conference which brings us together is especially intended for the propagation of this 'Din' or 'Dharma,' and it is in connection with that message chiefly that I have ventured to speak to you to-day on this important subject. The ills that we are suffering are, most of them, self-inflicted evils, the cure of which is to a large extent in our own hands. Looking at the series of measures which Akbar adopted in his time to cure these evils, one feels how correct was his vision when he and his adviser put their hands on those very defects in our natural character, which need to be remedied first before we venture on higher enterprises. Pursuit of high ideals, mutual sympathy and co-operation, perfect tolerance, a correct understanding of the diseases from which the body politic is suffering, and an earnest desire to apply suitable remedies—this is the work cut out for the present generation. The awakening has commenced, as is witnessed by the fact that we are met in this place from such distances for joint consultation and action. All that is needed is that we must put our hands to the plough, and face the strife and the struggle. The success already achieved warrants the expectation that if we persevere on right lines, the goal we have in view may be attained. That goal is not any particular advantage to be gained in power and wealth. It is represented by the efforts to attain it, the expansion and the elevation of the heart and the mind, which will make us stronger and braver, purer and truer men. This is at least the lesson I draw from our more recent history of the past thousand years, and if those centuries have rolled away to no purpose over our hands, our cause is no doubt hopeless beyond cure. That is, however, not the faith in me; and I feel sure it is not the faith that moves you in this great struggle against our own weak selves, than which nothing is more fatal to our individual and collective growth. Both Hindus and Mahomedans have their work cut out in this struggle. In the backwardness of female education, in the disposinion to overleap the bounds of their own religion, in matters of temperance, in their internal dissensions between castes and creeds, in the indulgence of impure speech, thought and action on occasions when they are disposed to enjoy themselves, in the abuses of many customs in regard to unequal and polygamous marriages, in the desire to be extravagant in their expenditure on such occasions, in the neglect of regulated charity, in the decay of public spirit, in insisting on the proper management of endowments,—in these and other matters both communities are equal sinners, and there is thus much ground for improvement on common lines. Of course, the Hindus, being by far the majority of the population, have other difficulties of their own to combat with; and they are trying in their gatherings of separate castes and communities, to remedy them each in their own way. But without co-operation and conjoint action of all communities, success is not possible, and it is on that account that the General Conference is held in different places each year to rouse local interest, and help people in their separate efforts by a knowledge of what their friends similarly situated are doing in other parts. This is the reason of our meeting here, and I trust that this message I have attempted to deliver to you on this occasion, will satisfy you that we cannot conceive a nobler work than the one for which we have met here to-day.

Srinivasa Sastri greatly eulogised his public services on 18th January, 1942. Speaking once about Raja Ram Mohan Roy, Ranade expresed the view that in the case of gods and saints or *rishis* we clebrate their birthday, while in the case of

This address was dglivered at the "Indian National Social Conference," Lucknow, in 1899.

men we celebrate the anniversaries of their death. He proceeded to justify this distinction on the ground that men's greatness is not fully proven until the last moment. The time of passing away, therefore, acquires supreme significance and needs commemoration. Till last year the anniversary of Rannade's death was celebrated in Maharashtra. This year, when the day came round, you decided to let it pass in order that two days later you may celebrate the centenary of his birth with solemnity. By this change Ranade takes rank hereafter with Sankara, Ramanuja and teachers of like calibre, whom popular acclaim has enrolled among those to whom *Jayanthis* are appropriate but not *Sraddhas*. This elevation to sanctity of a dead person is attended in the Roman Catholic Church with formalities calculated to examine and publish the grounds on which it is based. The world is thus furnished with the credentials of the new saint. The proposal is registered before a Congregation of Cardinals, and in the manner of judges trying an important suit, they proceed to hear arguments on both sides. The objections to the proposal are first stated by an officer called Advocatus Diaboli or Devil's Advocate, who tries to make out that the person on whose behalf the honours of sainthood are solicited is not worthy of them. The Congregation of Rites next hears the Advocatus Dri or God's Advocate, who answers the objection and maintains that the proposed elevation or canonisation, as it is called, is fully reserved by the character and pious acts of the candidate, if a dead person can be so called. Ranade's life has been scrutinised over and over again these forty years. Its lights and shadows are known to the last point of minuteness. No fresh evidence or consideration need be waited for. The public, though not assembled in solemn congregation or invested with Papal authority, may well proceed to affirm that Ranade will be gathered unto the brotherhood of saints and prophets of Maharashtra, whose names and deeds he has made immortal. Shall we at this gathering imagine ourselves clothed for a brief hour with the dignity of a Court of Cardinals? Application having been made to Our Eminences that henceforth the 18th of January every year be consecrated as a day of Ranade *Jayanthi*, let us give audience now to the opposing pleader. There he stands in his sable gown, with voice and accent befitting its dignity and betraying no premonition of coming defeat.

The man whom Your Eminences are requested to canonise is no ordinary man. I am not concerned to deny him some good qualities and some good deeds. It is enough for my purpose to show that his character is disfigured by some serious defects and that certain of his deeds fall short greatly of the standard that should be reached by a brave and unselfish servant of God. For many years he advocated the remarriage of girl widows in his community, but when his wife died and he had an opportunity of acting up to his precept, he took a maid of tender years and sheltered himself behind the command of his father. Having taken tea at the table of European missionaries along with other Hindu reformers, he bowed his head to orthodoxy and uuderwent *prayascitta* or penance, leaving his companions in the lurch. Professing to hate idolatry, he would visit temples and discourse to casual crowds on the comparatively refined theism of which he was an avowed adherent, thus proving himself a latitudinarian. He had the dirty habit of taking snuff and was, besides, so shabbily dressed that he shocked European observers by the frayed shirt that peeped through his sleeves and the shortness of his trousers. Though endowed with a fine physique, he never kept it up to the mark by regular exercise, but allowed his health to deteriorate; and, as he at the same time worked hard and incessantly, he is believed to have shortened his life. He presenled to friends and visitors a stern and gloomy aspect and, being devoid of light or amusing talk, was by means a pleasant companion. Even at dinner he would start serious topics and ply his guests with hard questions about social and economic conditions in their neighbourhood. While walking, he would fall into moods of meditation and take no note of his companions or surroundings. When he wished to be rid of an unwelcome visitor, he resorted to the harsh expedient of setting him a literary task, such as summarising a dry Government report, and the unfortunate party could not appear again before him. These counts may appear slight in an indictment on this occasion, but they are evidences of an unsociable temper, which must have prevented Ranade from being a centre of cheerfulness and fellowship. In fact his sensibility seems to have been below par. Seldom moved to an outburst of anger even under provocation, or indulging in a fit of righteous or generous indignation, he seemed almost a pachyderm, and those that approached him scarcely felt the warmth of sympathy or intimate fellow-feeling. In his attitude to money he made no attempt to reach the ideal of indifference prescribed by the requirements of scripture,......which means "regarding gold and rubbish alike," but he was known to measure his charities and gifts with excessive nicety of calcutation. Another ethical precept too, he practised with an odd inversion of emphasis......instead of remaining unaffected by praise or blame he would be impatient when praise was sounded in his ear, but greedily listen to blame, saying he must profit by it to the extent that it was just. An admiring friend once used this quaint phraseology in putting a favourable gloss on Ranade's inability to enter readily into the feelings of fellow-creatures: "He loved humanity at large, and men in units did not interest him so largely." How could a man with so many oddities and crudities win the affection of those around him? To be admitted into the blessed fraternity of saints, one must have had more attractive qualities and more lively sympathies than Ranade ever had. If we added together the comfort he gave to widows and orphans, the sympathy and help he extended to suffering neighbours and the tendance he bestowed on the sick and the afflicted, the sum would be small indeed, considering the opportunities and the facilities with which he had been liberally endowed.

I now take the field as God's advocate. I am upheld by the overwhelming strength of my case.

My learned friend has made the most of a bad case. If this is all he can say, my task is easy. Ranade was not a perfect man. What man is perfect? If a man's nature were fully rounded and smooth, other people could scarcely get hold of him at any point, and everytime they try to make contact with him they must turn back baffled, as from the touch of a freezing object. Don't we want our heroes to have a few human weaknesses to ensure our kinship to them? If they always did the right thing at the right time in the right way, we should suspect that they were not real, but creatures without blood belonging to the realm of pure fancy. Ranade, I admit without hesitation, had his foibles. I am surprised my learned friend did not mention to the Court that Ranade lost one of his eyes largely through excessive reading in insufficient light and was in later years afflicted with a slight deafness. He generously forbore all allusion to the nick-name of Baby Elephant, which his unusual size and awkward bearing earned him among his fellow-students. In the early days he did not join freely in sports and games, but was engrossed in his studies, which had an uncommon range and made him an object of awe and wonder. His friends called him the *enfant terrible* of literature, with pardonable misapprehension of the phrase. Once his Principal, Sir Alexandar Grant, caught him reading aloud from Alison's History of Europe, bareheaded and with legs sprawled on the table before him. Ranade should certainly have disposed of his lower limbs in less barbarous fashion and otherwise also remembered that he was not in his own private place. But if Sir Alexander himself took no notice, why need we? Certain of the short-comings ascribed to Ranade are only seemingly such, they are really good points for which he must be given credit. For instance, it takes a really big man to recognise that even a rustic has some knowledge and cxperience which might be of use to the student of village life and village economy, and Ranade was too big a man to miss an opportunity of learning something. Some play was made with his setting tasks to people in otder to drivc them away. Each one of us knows of one or two fussy friends who have nothing to do and just come into our working room for a chat and will take no hint that you would prefer to be alone. Ranade might make enquiries about the average rainfall of Mahabaleshwar, the number of girls' schools in the Thana district, how Sri Rama disposed of the thousand odd *astras* that he acquired in his travels, the arguments against the *laissez faire* theory brought forward by the German economists or the exact doctrinal differences between the various branches of the Brahmo Samaj. If the visitor had nothing to say on these subjects, what was Ranade to do but to take up the latest Government report on the Police Department and ask him to come back two days later with a summary under five heads? Each was sure of a long holiday from the other. It is true Ranade showed no mercy to his body and when people spoke of his habit of industry he would say, "Habit ! it has become a vice with me." We all wish he had known how to relax now and then, but surely unwillingness to lose even an hour of our brief waking life is not a sin deserving to be punished. He was accused of imperfect sympathy with the wants or sufferings of individuals. It may be true of him as of many others that he loved and cared for man rather than men, but we have Gokhale's unimpeachable testimony that he was by nature kind and sympathetic. Here are his words: "One more great quality of his I would like to mention on this occasion, and that was his readiness to help all who sought his help and especially those who were weak and oppressed. He was accessible to all—even the humblest—at all hours of the day. No one ever wrote to him without receiving a reply. He listened patiently to everyone, whether he was able to help him or not. This indeed was to him a part of his practical religion." If his heart were difficult to touch, how could it be said of him 'There is not one man of whom our departed brother was ever heard or known to have said an unkind word."? He readily forgave, harboured no resentment and made no enemies, if he could help it. By his teachings from the pulpit of the Prarthna Samaj and by his incessant social reform activities he incurred the open and unrestrained wrath of the orthodox party, but he was never known to lose his temper and return abuse for abuse. Even during the violent controversy of 1895 over the venue of the Social Reform Conference his forbearance and equanimity were exemplary. When he made his accustomed speech as President, he mentioned no names, recalled no ugly incidents, avoided all personalities and ascribed the unfortunate turn of events to the fact that in Poona, unlike other places, a variety of methods were adopted instead of one sole method. Of these different methods the one that he most approved was that of persuasion, and the one that he most discountenanced was that of rebellion. To many ardent spirits what they called progress was God's own work, and those that obstructed it were like *rakshasas* whom it was a merit to condemn and destroy. They delighted in war against orthodoxy and thought nothing of separating themselves and forming a distinct group of their own. Social affinities and family ties were consumed by the fire of conviction, and many a young man fancied that, by disregarding parental authority when he heard the call, he was testifying to the sovereign power of social reform. Ranade pointed out that the Brahmo Samaj in Bengal and the Arya Samaj in the Punjab, which chose this heroic path, had come to a standstill when the first momentum was exhausted. His own method was to reason, to expostulate and to allure to brighter worlds. The movement would necessarily be slow, but it would be sure and carry forward the whole community. He never forgot, and would never let others forget, that reform was for all and not merely for a few. When compelled by adverse circumstances to halt, he was content to do so, hoping that the next step would be firmer and longer. A few years later this method of persuasion found a powerful and eloquent exponent in Prof. M. Rangacharya of Madras, who described it as "conciliatory co-ordination." This high-sounding name did not please the ear of Mr. K. Natarajan in Bombay. He was a little more combative in those young days than he is now and called it one of the Professor's characteristic orotundities. At bottom Ranade's heart was gentle and peace-loving. His father was apparently a tyrant and made no attempt to understand Ranade's progressive spirit or his zeal for reform. Occasionally he appears to have adopted questionable tactics to keep Ranade from moving forward. Ranade no doubt struggled and struggled hard, but would not break up his home and go his own way. Many of his friends lamented his failure as an apostasy. But enough has been said to convince those who can judge with charity that Ranade's principle of carrying the community along was the mainspring of his action, and not merely the fear of his father's extreme displeasure. Sir Narayan Chandavarkar, who was close to Ranade in the work of reform, said of him. "The idea of displeasing anybody was too much for him, and he wanted all to unite and work together. He erred because his soul wag gentle, his heart charitable." My learned friend on the other side adopted without reserve or qualification the vedict which the prejudice and passion of the time delivered against Ranade. I have not the hardihood to assert that Ranade was wholly right. But it is safe to assume that, where a complicated question of principle was involved, a man of the moral stature of Ranade struck the balance true and fair and did not allow mere expediency or cowardice to determine his conduct.

Ranade was cast in a big mould in body and in mind. He was a giant. His studies had amplitude and depth far beyond the common. History, politics, economics, blue books, Sanskrit literature and Marathi literature,—these and similar subjects made up his gargantuan fare. His knowledge and experience in the official and non-official sphere were at the service of a patriotism, fervent and sleepless, which comprehended all the sections and elements of our population. Like a true *rishi* he had toleration and mercy for all and planned and laboured for all alike. His Marathi sermons are considered by competent judges to constitute a valuable and inspiring course in the doctrine and practice of theism. He rehabilitated the character of Sivaji and the empire that he founded. Of Indian economics he laid the ground-work, showing how the maxims and principles of English writers would not apply to the conditions of our country unless corrected in great part by the writings of German authorities on the subject. He took a leading part in the growth of the Indian Economic Conference, studied the conditions of agriculture and the peasantry in their various phases and became an unequalled authority on questions of land revenue, land tenure and land improvement. On Indian Finance his views commanded equal attention and equal respect with those of Dadabhai Naoroji. His close study of constitutional and administrative problems of India and other countries was laid under contribution by the organisers and leaders of Indian National Congress and is well known that his advice and guidance were at the disposal of the Subjects Committee wherever it met year after year. The Indian Social Conference was founded by him in 1887, and at every subsequent meeting of that body during the next 13 years he presided and delivered addresses replete with wisdom, comprehension and insight. His mind was also devoted to problems of Indian education, and his membership of the University governing bodies was signalised by unremitting efforts on behalf of the Marathi language and literature and the health and longevity of Bombay graduates. In all departments of national endeavour and uplift he was a pioneer, and it would be the bare truth to say of him that he was the most considerable and influential among the builders of Modern India. He himself once enumerated the elements that go to the making of a great man—"earnestness of purpose, sincerity in action, originality, imagination and above all, the power of magnetism—we might call it vital or spiritual magnetism". These he possessed in rich measure. Add to them the achievements catalogued above, and you have a record of greatness so imposing that a teacher or *rishi* of old may be proud to call it his own. The name *rishi* was in his judgment so exalted in import that, when he desired to pay anyone the highest honour for character, he applied the name to him. More than once in his speeches we see Mr. N.M. Parmanand described as "our political *rishi*". Why, Ranade himself was deserving of the title in the eyes of many of his contemporaries. It was surely nothing uncommon in his life as well as afterwards for his admirers to speak of him as the modern *rishi*. A scene vividly comes to my mind when this happened in my hearing. Some time after I joined the Servants of India Society. Principal F.W. Bain lectured in the Small Hall of Poona, and Sir Pherozeshah Mehta took the chair for him. Mr. Bain, the crusted tory that he was, made some remark deprecatory of the general character of our people or of some particular movement of the time. I forget which Sir Pherozeshah at the end of the meeting castigated him in vigorous phrases and with emphatic gestures, which were greeted with rounds of applause. But the applause rang louder than ever when he cited for authority "the late M G. Ranade the modern *rishi*". Thd order of *rishis* exercised a powerful fascination over Ranade's mind. In the hierarchy of homage he would accord them the throne of eminence. In the address called *Vasishtha and Visuamitra*, the last in the great series (which Gokhale had to read for him in Lahore) the concluding passage is a paean to the glory of these semi divine teachers and a devout wish that their line may be continued without end. It is my proud office to-day to plead that Ranade be admitted to this Holy Order and that this celebration be the first of a succession in future which will redound to the benefit of posterity as well as to the fame of the man who came into the world a hundred years ago to-day.

My task is not complete. I have yet to make out that, if our latest *Acharya* had wisdom pure and undefiled, he had also a tongue, eloquent and commanding, with which to proclaim it. There must be a good few here who have sat at his feet more than once and heard his discourses. That good fortune came to me only once. The scene was in Anderson Hall, Madras, and the time was an evening in December, 1898. A great crowd waited expectantly to hear Ranade on "Shuthern India a hundred years ago." We felt surprise without a touch of admiration, as a big figure moved forward with slow deliberate steps. As the lineaments became clear, a faint feeling of dis appointment rose in our breasts, but we kept it under as somewhat premature. But in a few seconds the figure pulled a kerchief, coloured as I remember, and applied it to the nose which was running and made strange noises. The opening words did nothing to reassure us, and as the handkerchief and the nose persisted in their joint activities, our spirit sank withing us. Whipers of dissatisfaction and poutings of lips went round, but scarcely relieved our feelings. Soon, however, things seemed to change. One good remark caught our attention, we strained our ears. Lo. and behold! the handkerchief went back to the pocket, the voice gained distinctness, the sentiments captured our fancy, and as if by magic the face became bright with intelligence. Half a dozen sentences, and our eyes were fixed on the speaker. Thereafter, all through the speech he held us as in a spell. I thought I was listening to a superior being, all aglow with wisdom which seemed a part of him,—so easily, so naturally, so unostentatiously did it keep flowing into me. There was pindrop silence in the hall, I don't think the audience launghed or cheered once. If they did, I didn't hear it.

The published speeches have solidity and mental nutriment which are astonishing. One may go again and again to them with profit. Sir Narayan Chandavarkar's eulogy is not overdone. "Those weighty and eloquent annual addresses, wise with the wisdom of the heart, powerful with all the power of his great intellect, majestic with the majesty of his lofty and commanding personality." The is no art either in the sentences or in their grouping. You don't come across a light, humorous remark; no passing allusion to the trivialities of thought or gossip. The nearest he comes to a joke is when he asks: "Shall we revive the old habits of our people when the most sacred of our caste indulged in all the abominations, as we now understand them, of animal food and drink which exhausted every section of our country's Zoology and Botany?" The nearest he comes to impatience or indignation is in this passage: "If we were stronger and more manly, more prudent, more abstemious and more thoughtful, millions would not live and breed as if they were members of the brute creation, and not men and women made in the image of God for a higher purpose than to live and die like the butterflies." The joke and the indignation are alike grim. As you read through you seem to see Ranade slowly assembling the details from one quarter and from another, inviting your gaze to the accumulation, and slowly and patiently leading you to a realization of your duties and prospects. The style is by no means varied, picturesque or pleasing. But it is weighty without being ponderous; profound without being mystic; edifying without being homiletic. One reader complains that Ranade has no partiality for Anglo-Saxon. Another grumbles that grammar and idiom do not get the respect due to them.

A third in saddened by the frequent inelegances and solecisms. But all are subdued to attention by the dignity of the diction and the high level on which the argument moves without once declining on a false or discordant note. When you are lifted above the small and the grovelling, when you are freshened by the gentle breezes of the upper air, you forget the unsightly objects you have left behind and the inconveniences through which you have ascended. Or may be you feel like a tourist that has been dragged through mean lanes and pebbly tracks, and suddenly finds himself entering a stately edifice with imposing corridors and noble columns and spacious hails, the *ensemble* harmonizing in every part and ravishing his inner soul with a beauty of proportion and symmetry of which he had never dreamed. Criticism is hushed, judgment is awed, and the only feeling left is one of joy and complete satisfaction. To prove that I have not been indulging my imagination, I pray you to listen patiently while I read a certain passage which concludes one of his addresses. It is not the most familiar of the Ranade quotations, but it appears to have flowed without effort from the body of the discourse.

"The chief point, however, that is to be considered in this connection is, who should be these Gurus of the future? It is with this view that I have endeavoured to place before you a brief account of the true Gurus of the past, namely the Rishis who were both Brahmarshis and Rajarshis, only distinguished from one another by their individual inclinations and abilities. We must keep that ideal before us, if we mean to prove ourselves the worthy descendants of our earliest ancestors. Of course the teachings and the methods and the subjects taught in these days must be made to suit our new exigencies and environments, but the spirit animating the teachings must be the same as that which led the first settlers to cross the Vindhya Range, and establish their colonies in the South. By reviving our ancient traditions in this matter we may hope in the near future to instil into the minds of our young generation lessons of devotion to learning, diversities of studies and personal loyalty to the teacher, without which no system of school or college education can ever bear any fruit. This, however, is not all. In addition to these lessons, our new teachers must know how to introduce their pupils to a correct appreciation of the forces which are at work in the wider world outside, and which, in spite of temporary checks or seeming reverses, represent all that is best in human efforts for the elevation and happiness of man. Our tcachers must enable their pupils to realise the dignity of man as man, and to apply the necessary correctives to tendencies towards exclusiveness, which have grown in us with the growth of ages. They must see that our thoughts, our speech, our actions are inspired by a deep love of humanity, and that our conduct and our worship are freed where neeessary from the bondage of custom and made to conform as far as possible to the surer standard of our conscience. We must at the same time be careful that this class of teachers does not form a new order of monks. Much good, I am free to admit, has been done in the past and is being done in these days, in this as well as other countries by those who take the vow of long celibacy and who consecrate their lives to the service of man and the greater glory of our Maker. But it may be doubted how far such men are able to realize life in all its fulness and in all its varied relations, and I think our best examples in this respect are furnished by Agastya with his wife Lopamudra, Atri with his wife Anasuya, and Vasishtha with his wife Arundhati among the ancient Rishis, and in our own times by men like Dr. Bhandarkar on our side, Diwan Bahadur Raghunatha Row in Madras, the late Keshab Chander Sen and Babu Pratap Chand Mozumdar and Pandit Shivanath Shastri in Bengal, and Lala Hans Raj and Lala Munshi Ram in vour own province. A race that can ensure a continuance of such teachers can, in my opinion, never fail, and with the teachings of such men to guide and instruct and inspire us I, for one, am confident that the time will be hastened when we may be vouchsafed a sight of the Promised Land."

Ever since I gave Ranade a definite place among my heroes, my heart's adoration has gone to him in fuller mesaure every day. Which one among his qualities grips me most? His elevation and datachment. Wordsworth's immortal line occurs to me whenever I think of him. "His soul was like a star and dwelt apart." True he mingled in men's affairs and strove with all his matcless strenght to improve them. His life was one long and unbroken sacrifice. In pre-eminent sense he was—

> Type of the wise who soar but never roam,
> True to the kindred points of heaven and home.

Nevertheless, after his duties to the world were fully done, there remained a part of him above attachment and clear of taint. There his *bhakti* reigned alone and he kept converse with his God in his triple nature as *sat*, *chit*, and *ananda*. Where the air is serene and rare, gross beings cannot follow him. The simple but noble words of Goldsmith are the aptest I know.

> As some tall cliff that lifts its awful form,
> Swells from the vale and midway leaves the storm,
> Though round its breast the rolling clouds are spread,
> Eternal sunshine settles on its head.

CONCERN FOR THE POOR
(1878—1893)

RANADE WAS deeply religious. It was his conviction that love of God and love of man are but expressions of one and the same thing, namely, the religious element in man's nature. Ranade's study of economics was not so much an intellectual search for economic truths as a compassionate striving to eliminate human suffering. Around him, there was plenty of suffering, and his heart bled at its sight. One of his first acts on reaching Poona in 1878 was to organise an economic survey of the neighbouring districts. He addressed himself to the problems of the poor; he examined them in the light of economic theory of which he had made a deep study.

It was thus that he vigourously argued that if Indians in general were to be rid of poverty, *India must industrialise*.

Cottage industries must be replaced by manufactures. Capital required for them on a large scale must be found; people should stint, save, and invest. On the agricultural side, the State must reduce the burden of land revenue.

A perusal of his writings on economic problems of his day impresses the reader with the enormous study and industry behind them. This writing was not part of his official duties; much of it was anonymous. The great labour involved in preparing these lengthy articles and addresses could only be promoted by his resolve to rescue the nation from the bog of poverty. "We need only to walk through our streets" he says at one place, "and study the most superficial aspects of our economic situation, and the fact forces itself upon us that we are a peopic of little resources. Many millions among us scarcely earn a couple of annas a day, many millions more are always underfed and live on the borderland of famine and slow death into which the failure of a single monsoon precipitates them." He wrote on every aspect of Indian economy on which he could suggest improvement, and wrote with obvious earnestness. Agriculture, industries, organisation of credit, public finance, tariff, legal position of cultivators, emigration, census statistics—such was the wide range of the topics he dealt with. His usual method in treating a subject was that he first surveyed in great detail all relevant facts and opinions of all cencerned persons, and then recommended certain measures, which seemed to follow logically from the survey. For instance, writing on reorganisation of rural credit in India, he briefly described the salient features of credit organisation in Austria, Hungary, France, Italy, Belgium and Switzerland, and then showed what could be learnt by India from the experience gained in these countries. Writing on Indian foreign emigration, he first described the extent of Indian emigration in Mauritius, Natal, Jamaica and sixteen other foreign countries in the world, giving an account of the conditions in these settlements; then he made an analysis of the facts so collected, showing for example the general tendency of increase in emigrant population specially of women emigrants and so on; and at the end, he made suggestions as to how associations like the Industrial Conference could make themselves practically useful.

His articles in the *Sarvajanik Sabha Journal* and his addresses before the Industrial Conference speak of his interest and contributions to the industrial field. In brief, his proposals for eradicating poverty from the country were these: Every effort must be made to develop in India manufacturing industries. This would indirectly help the agriculturists also. But to help him more directly in raising his standard of living, land revenue should be reduced and be *permanently fixed* at the reduced level. Next in importance was the setting up *of organisation of credit at* low interest for the cultivator. Another remedial measure was *legal protection to the cultivator against* the greed and wiles of the *money-lender*. In the words of Ranade, "Judicial reform, increased banking and loan facilities, and the guarantee of a permanent settlement, these are the three-fold elements in that organic constitution of our agricultural economy which. . . will alone rescue the country from its present sad plight." "There can be no doubt", he said, "that the permanent salvation of the country depends upon the growth of Indian manufactures and commerce, and that all other remedies can only be temporary palliatives". Again, "When factories and mills on a small or large scale were set up all over the land, the present paralysis would give way to a play of energies which would. . . give a new birth to the activities of the nation".

Ranade welcomed the legislation, called the Deccan Agriculturisis Relief Act, with the three-fold object of protecting the ryot from the frauds of the money-lender, simplifying the procedure of law, and granting relief to the farmer from the weight of indebtedness. He worked for the success of the Act while he was the Special Judge to try cases under it. He defended its continuation when the matter came up for discussion later. But he expressed his opinion time and again that the Act would afford the much-needed relief only on condition that it was accompanied by a more liberal land revenue policy.

The Deccan Agriculturists Relief Act, which placed a ban on charging exorbitant rate of interest; was a negative measure; Ranade's suggestion for creating an additional supply of credit to the agriculturists was a positive measure. The Government should give financial help, and even guarantee, to special banks meant for the benefit of agriculturists. These agricultural banks should lend money to small Sawkars at low rates of interest; and the Sawkars in their turn should lend this money to the agriculturists at controlled rates. Besides, the guaranteed Agricultural Banks themselves should lend money to the agriculturists directly. For this scheme, the Government would require funds; these could be borrowed from the public. "If Indian capitalists prove unable to advance all the capital (needed for farmers), there is abundance of capital in England." He advocated, side by side with these banks, also the setting up of cooperative banks.

The most importan measure of relief to the agriculturists in Ranade's opinion, was the reduction of land revenue and keeping it fixed permanently at that level, making allowance only for changes in prices. In this, his view came in conflict with that of the British officials in India. "We have for the last fifteen years," wrote Ranade in 1881, "exposed the failure of the present system, and advocate a *permanent settlement of land* as the only alternative open to the Government by the side of which reform all other agencies sink into insignificance". The Government in its land revenue policy acted on the theory that the State was the owner of all land. On this theory the State was entitled to any amount it could extract from the cultivator. Land revenue was rent taken by the State as the owner and not a tax imposed by the State on an owner. Recognised canons of taxation did not apply here. The State was not only a landlord but the only landlord owning all land in its territory. It was in a position to impose revenue at an excessive rate, and Ranade claimed that it had done so already. ' The only guarantee against excessive enhancement, which is found effective where land is held in private right,it competition of the landlords among themselves. There is no place for this guarantee under the Indian system, because the land is the monopoly of the State, single and individual. The absence of such a check has resulted in wholesale enhancements all over the country to an extent of which the Government itself is now ashamed." The Government should abandon the theory of State ownership of all land ; it should give up the enhanced rates which have proved detrimental, and guarantee the cultivator that there would be no enhancement in future. It need not hesitate because of fear of loss of revenue : for, "by guaranteeing a permanent settlement fixed in kind, and commutable into money at long intervals according to permanent changes in prices, the Government will not have to forgo the smallest fraction of their just claim". Permanent settlement would so develop resources of the country in general that the Government would be able to realise larger amounts from other taxes. There would be another advantage; "The ryots and the middle classes will look upon their land as theirown property. . .With-out such a guarantee of full property (proprietorship), all ende-avours to ameliorate the condition of the ryots must fail to produce any but temporary benefit." "All improvements in husbandry suggested by science and experience presuppose a great expenditure of capital invested in the land. The magic of property alone can induce people to incur such expenditure. Neither private Sawkars nor joint-stock land banks will venture capital to sink wells or to use manures or throw dams across streams unless the ryots to whom these advances are to be made possess full proprietory rights over the land." "The State monopoly of land and its right to increase the assess-ment at its own discretion are the two most pr.minent obstacles in the way of growth of our national prosperity". In clear terms, Ranade's proposal was this : "A permanent ryotwari settlement, fixed in grain which the land produces, and commuted into money values every twenty ar thirty years, can alone furnish a solution of the agricultural problem."

As early as 1872, Ranade had observed and brought to the notice of the public a dismal feature of India's foreign trade, namely, that her exports largely consisted of raw materials and her imports of manufactured goods. It was a dismal feature because it proved India's extreme backwardness in industry, which in its turn explained why India remained outrageously poor. Industrial development of India was a matter of urgency. Ranade, therefore, on the one hand undertook the task of creating public enthusiasm for industrialisation and, on the other, argued with the Government for active support for the cause. The Indian National Congress was a political organisation; he desired that the members in its annuul gathering should also meet to discuss social reform and industrial progress. He succeeded soon in starting an Indian Social Conference metting in the same pandal after the Congress, but was not successful with regard to an Indian Industrial Conference. However, he was able to organise in 1890 the Industrial Association of Western India. In 1890, Ranade wrote : "Our contact with the world outside and the freedom of exchange with has resulted in consequence hava produced one more undesirable result. They have aggravated the situation (nation's poverty) by making us more than ever dependent upon a single and precarious resource (namely agriculture). The industry and commerce of the conutry, such as it was, is passing out of our hands and. . . the country is fed, clothed, warmed, washed, lighted, helped, and comforted generally by a thousand arts and industries in the manipulation of which its sons have every day a decreasing share." The co-ordination of economic activities in a community implies a due proportion among men engaged in agriculture, industry, and commerce; when these three are thus co-ordinated, the nation thrives. In recent years, this proportion was disturbed; while industries decayed, too many were led to depend on agriculture. Industrialisation alone could restore the healthy proportion; and industrialisation in the current times could only mean development of large-scale manufacture and not small-scale hand-made goods industry.

Objections were raised by the cautious and the diffident. will enough capital be available? How is industrialisation possible when coal and iron, the basic factors, are scarce? What can we do when the Government is so apathetic? Ranade answered all these objections one by one. In an address before an industrial conference, he exhorted with transparent earnestness his audience to discard doubts and work hard. "We have to work with a will to pull long and pull all and to pull till we succeed."

It seems strange today that Ranade had to cry hoarse to urge people to invest in idustries and to argue with the Government to help industries in every way. But in Ranade's time, the situation was altogether different from what it is today, both in respect of the people's as well as the Government's attitude to industries. In his days, Indians showing courage to invest in industrial concerns were rare. To start a factory was helping the industrialisation of the country and thus it was a form of public service. Ranade organised the Industrial Conference just to spread the gospel of financing and starting industrial concerns. Its object was to consider ways and means of promoting industries, whereby national poverty could be removed. On the one hand, he had to persuade with all his might people to save and invest in industries; on the other, he had to persuade with all his learning and debating skill the British Government in India to render active help to the process of industrialisation. The Government was unwilling. Its masters in England were under the sway of the economic philosophy of *laissez-faire*, opposed to any State activity or interest beyond the minimum. A keen student of history, politics and economics that he was, he laid his finger on one successful experiment with State intervention in industries, namely, the Culture System in Netherlands Indies (now called Indonesia). Quoting it as a precedent, he argued that the State in India could do a lot for its economic development without involving much extra expenditure. "The Culture System may be described as a system of encouraging the planting of remunerative crops, and manufacturing them for the European market, by private agency and at private risk, with Government advances, and under Government supervision, and with Government as the sole customer". Roughly following this model, Ranade heid that the Government of India should first select a few industries which might be of importance to national prosperity and in respect of which India possesses special advantages such as iron, coal, sugar, oils from seeds, woollen goods and leather goods. The most urgent need of these industries was capital; "The industry of the country is parched up for want of capital." "The want being national, the nation has a right to expect its rulers to supply the want." Local or Municipl Boards, or specially created Corporate Boards of Trade and Commerce should undertake the development of industries in their areas. The Government has in its possession people's savings invested in Government stock or in Post Office savings accounts; out of these funds, which are lying idle with it, the Government should lend money to these bodies at low interest. They in their turn, should make advances at a slightly higher rate to private 'persons with skill and energy to turn them into account'. Of course, the Government through its officers should supervise the disbursement of this money. The Government should also patronise the products of the concern it has thus helped. Besides, the Government in certain cases should guarantee minimum profits in the initial period; in some cases the Government might even help a company to float its own debentures or lend money itself. The Government should provide technical advice in respect of the choice of the location and so on. By helpinu industries in this way, the Government would create confidence, and people would be more inclined to invest in them.

In one of his addresses before the Industrial Conference, he suggested that we should "take in as much of raw produce from abroad as we need and work it up here, and send in place of our exports of raw produce the same quantities in less bulky but more valuable forms, after they have undergone the operation of art manipulation and afforded occupation to our industrial classes. To illustrate, in place of oil seeds, send oil; in place of raw cotton, send cotton goods, in place of hides and skins, send prepared and tanned leather."

His articles and addresses on economic questions concluded with practical suggestions. He refrained from suggesting protection to help industries, though he firmly believed in it, because there was not the slightest chance of the suggestion being accepted. "We cannot expect the Government here," he bitterly remarked, "to do what France or Germany does for their shipping trade and their sugar industry, and ask Government bounties and subsidies to be paid out of general taxes. These are heresies according to English Political Economy, such as is taught to us, and whether they be really so or not, it is useless to divert our energies in fruitless discussion and seek to achieve victory over free trade." Elsewhere he said; "Notwithstanding these disadvantages and the free trade policy of the Government, we may win."

On Indian fincnce, he cordially endorsed the views of the well-known economist of the British Liberal Party Prof. Fawcett. Among the conclusions of the latter were the following: India is extremely poor. Its revenue resources are inelastic, while an ever-growing expenditure has to be met out of them. The factors which increase the expenditure include, among others, excessive military expenditure, burden of public debt due to the Afghan War and the railways. It is not possible to suggest any sensible method for additional taxation. It therefore follows that (a) severe retrenchment and (b) substitution of the cheaper services of Indians for the expensive services of European civil servants are the only remedies open to the Government. Fawcett condemned the surrender of the cotton import duties by the Government of India at a time when it was faced with financial difficulties first, because the duties were probably not protective as was claimed and, secondly, because the surrender was motivated by the ruling party's desire to please cotton industrialists in England.

Ranade tried hard to knock these ideas into the heads of the officials in India, but in their proud obstinacy they spurned them. Besides, most of them placed British interests above the Indian, and hence could not help disagreeing. They swore by the science of economics, and Ranade's proposals were treated as amateurish. The current economic doctrine, the doctrine of the classical school of Adam Smith,

Ricardo and Mill, led to the theory of *laissez-faire*, of rigid non-interference by the State in economic affairs. On the contrary, Ranade's main suggestions (except regarding the land revenue policy) involved vigorous State activity. Ranade therefore decided to attack the economic policy of the bureaucracy, and carried the battle on to the field of economic science itself. Ranade embarked on a review of the whole economic theory, right from its beginning to its latest development. And he observed that the latest trends in the Western economic thought supported the remedies suggested by him and not those of his opponents.

In 1892, Ranade chose Indian Political Economy as the subject of his address in the Deccan College, Poona. In it, he assailed the classical economic theory on which the Government of India and its officials took their stand. They held that the truths of classical economics, like those of physical sciences, were universally true, and hence should guide the policies of the State in India as well as England. Ranade pointed out that these truths or laws were founded on a number of assumptions, such as that each person pursues self-interest, that each has perfect knowledge of his interest and the capacity of acting according to this knowledge, and that there is perfect mobility of labour and capital. Ranade dealt in two ways with these assumptions. First, quoting the authority of what was then the latest school of thinkers known as the historical school, Ranade argued that it was wrong to study economics on the basis of universal assumptions but from observed facts studied in their historical setting. This approach alone could give us knowledge of actual economic conditions. Secondly, Ranade argued that the assumptions of classical economics had hardly any validity for such a society as was found in India. Here, an average man was the very antipodes of the economical man of the classical theorists: The family was more powerful than the individual in the determination of status: self interest was not only or the primary motive in guiding activity, and custom and state regulation were far more powerful than competition. For this reason also the dogmas mentioned above lost all their force in a country like India. The dogmas of the classical school of economics, therefore, could not be made to veto the remedies which Ranade, and following him, other Indian publicists were proposing for the eradication of poverty in India.

In the last quarter of the nineteenth century, there was a crop of similar political and economic ideas flourishing in all parts of the country. Placed in the same situation and faced with similar problems, there was a tendency among Indians who took interest in public affairs to think alike. A few of them thought and wrote on economic problems; Dadabhai Naoroji who had taken residence in England, Dinshaw Wacha and K. T. Telang in Bombay, Ranade and G. V. Joshi in Poona and Satara, R. C. Dutt in Bengal and G. Subramania Iyer in Madras wera foremost and the most brilliant among the thinkers. But, except Ranade and perhaps G. V. Josi, each of them dealt with a special group of Indian problems. Dadabhai concentrated on India's poverty and the 'drain' of wealth to England, Telang on the necessity for protection to industries, Dutt on the urgency of lowering land revenue and making settlement permanent. They were all developing, in mutual co-operation, a common point of view, At one place R. C. Dutt paid fine compliments to the Sarvajanik Sabha and its journal; while Ranade, reviewing a book by Dababhai Naoroji, complimented the author saying, "Prof. Dababhai has done right yeoman's service in meeting the enemy on his own lists, and removing the veil from these mysteries of Indian administration." Differences between these Indian writers were of a minor nature, and by mutual interchange of ideas they developed a common viewpoint. In this development Ranade's contribution was the greatest, because he excelled them in the study of this department of knowledge. Sir J. C. Coyajee, the well-known economist of a later generation, said of Ranade: "He was the first economist in India. He was the first in the sense of approaching almost all the most important economic problems of our country and in giving a comprehensive view of these in the light of a proper background of economic theory. While his contemporaries and co-workers like Dababhai Naoroji and Telang were content to criticise individual points in the policy of the Government, Ranade was aiming at a comprehensive view of his subject. Again, while several of his co-workers were animated by the spirit of the advocate and were fearful of making concessions to the opposite side, Ranade was characterised by a spirit at once judicious and judicial and he never attempted to gloss over the weak points of his nation and country." It was Ranade who provided a theoretical basis to the economic thought of his Indian contemporaries: it was he who demonstrated that system of economic theory superior to the classical school and latest in development, namely, the historical school, was behind what Indian economic writers were propounding. He was the first to show that List and not Ricardo shed light on Indian problems and suggested solutions. Ranade well deserved the title of the 'Father of Indian Economics'. which the later economists conferred on him.

(*Commemoration Address on*
The Telang School of Thought)

You are aware of the nature of the business which has brought us together in this place on the present occasion. It is a function of a friendly and social commemoration, and must be undertaken by every one of us in the spirit which suits the occasion. A meeting like this ought to have been held earlier, and it was arranged accordingly; but owing to unforeseen engagements of the most pressing character, the managers of the Club had to put it off to a more convenient day. Death, as you all know, has been of late so very busy among us that, notwithstanding the absorbing distractions of our everyday life of toil and enforced rest, our minds are in a more serious mood attracted naturally towards those who have been gathered to our forefathers—some of them prematurely, long before their mission in this life had been accomplished. Our minds are, as each fresh loss comes upon us, with its sudden surprise, distracted with grief for a moment; but such is the providential uift of our elastic temperament that we soon recover our usual equanimity, and seem apparently to forget the past. It is not, however, always the case. There are times and there are seasons when even in these absorbing distractions, our thoughts are turned from the present day engagements to converse in spirit and solitude with those with whom we worked in various fields in the past, and whose company we now miss in the great responsibilities that come upon us as each day rolls on and makes room for its successor. It is not, therefore, without reason that our wise ancestors ordained it as a part of our religious duty that once at least in the course of the year there should be a fortnight set apart for these commemorations, so that each one in his own small sphere, and all of us in our collective sphere, may take stock of the fact that our present existence here is an existence limited by conditions over which we have no control, and that unless we teach ourselves to regard it only as the place for fitting and preparing ourselves for a better existence, we fail to understand the mission of the life with which we are so much absorbed. Last month was the month in which these commemorations were held throughout the country, in domestic circles and more at large in high places, where the claims of the dead commanded a larger circle of mourners. These commemorations remind us of our duties to those who have left this troubled life of ours, and it is to some extent with a similar object in view that the members of this Club have felt it to be their duty, which they had long put off for various reasons, to meet together in this place, and to commemorate in a proper spirit the loss which the Club has sustained in the death of its late President. Mr. Justice K.T. Telang. Five years and more have now elapsed since that eventful departure from our midst took place of one whom we all knew so well, and loved so dearly. It was thought by the members of this Club that this long period of time should be allowed to elapse, for in the excess of our present grief we might be tempted to put too high a value upon the loss that we had suffered, and that it was far better to wait and see if, like many of our other sorrows, these five years of separation might not reconcile us to the loss that we had suffered and make us forget it, as we do forget many other affections that trouble our existence here. Five years have passed, and yet every one of us, I believe every one who is in this hall, and many hundreds who may not be here to-day will admit with me that these five years have not reconciled us to the loss and made us forget the estimation in which we held the late President of this Club during his short but brilliant career. It was on this account that the members of this Club thought that the time had now come when we could discharge this duty without being exposed to the charge that we made too much of our loss.

Of course, on such occasions, when we meet here for such a solemn purpose as this, memories rise before the mind's eyes of many familiar faces, and the shades of the dead flit before our vision with a reality which is almost as vivid as life itself. Not to recall to your memory the great men of the past generation, about whom many of you have no personal knowledge, but whose works we read and admire—not to go so far back as that period, and confining ourselves only to the past five or six years, the memory of which is so fresh with us, our hearts and our recollections are drawn to many familiar faces whom we miss now as the miser misses his wealth, or the mother her lost child. We miss,for instance, the sturdy features of Mr. K.L. Nulkar, than whom a more sustained worker in all the higher activities of our life, a more earnest sympathiser in all that was good, did not breathe in this part of India. Another loss we feel is that of my friend Mr. S.P. Pandit, whose cast of features indicated an unbending will, coupled with a tenacity of purpose and undaunted courage peculiarly his own. His was a life, though short, of great and continuous struggles and noble achievements on behalf of posterity. We further miss the familiar face of Dr. Atmaram Pandurang who, during three-score years and ten took the lead in our Society, in all good works of benevolence and charity. I prize him more not on account of his ministering to our bodily maladies, but on account of his ministering to our spiritual longings. His loss is still so fresh, and the debt we owe him has been so badly discharged by us that I do not feel myself at present disposed to say more about him. We miss again the face of Mr. W.A. Modak, the great educationist, and a man whose life was an example to us in all things good, a man who applied himself devoutly to every secular duty. We miss him as his shade passes before our vision with a poignancy of grief that I at least cannot describe in words. We miss our Political Rishi, Mr. N.M. Paramanand, confined to his bed for ten years and more of one continuous suffering and yet a friend from whom we never heard a word of complaint or of sorrow. In matters of religious, social or political elevation a purer life and a purer soul never lived with us and never worked with us till the last breath left him. Another gap is that left by my friend Mr. Javerilal U. Yajnik. A soul formed in a higher mould, a soul above vanity, and in its capacities equal to all that we expect in our great men, joined with humility and resignation that was unequalled by any who lived before him or who might come after him. We miss Mr. V.N. Bhagwat, a silent worker in the higher fields. I know his charity was a silent charity. It was a charity which he loved to hide from all his most intimate friends, a man whose independence of character was never sullied by any blemish of irreverence or fault-finding.

We miss all these and many more. It would be too long a list for me on an occasion like this to recall to your minds all the shadows flitting before our eyes, some more clearly perceptible than others, and we miss above all, our friend, for the commemoration of whose death we have met more especially on this occasion here. Our friend Mr. Telang was not a man whose reputation was confined to this city or this Presidency. He was India's representative, the type, I may say, of New India. Had it not been that the cruel hand of death took him away from us all too soon, there was every promise that year after year the rose that had blossomed with such beauty and with such fragrance in our midst, would have filled the whole country with its sweet scent. His simplicity of life was exemplary, his sympathies were always foremost in the support of everything that was good and true. Noble in mind himself, contact and converse with him made every one, even a stranger who visited him for the first time, discover in the man the nobility of character which only those that have this magnetic power developed in them by the gift of nature can realize. His countenance is before you all; no photograph can ever portray his features, that calm life which I believe we all realize, though it is not possible to describe it. The intellectual cast of that countenance was of a character which I had the privilege to mark in its very first stages. Some five and thirty years ago it was that I noticed in the young man who then attended the college, a power and force concealed which would carry him up to the very highest stages of our social and political life. There were lines in that countenance which marked him out as an intellectual giant before whom all our modest performances would look as if we were only trying to follow him, but could never get up to him. Those who heard him speak—there must be thousands here—will remember his silver voice, his persuasive and earnest eloquence; it was all one sweet flow of reason. Those who heard him speak still remember him not as an orator who could thunder, but as one who gave light, heat, motion, and hope to the masses about him in a way to make them feel that they had profited by listening to him, even for a short space of time. Such was the man as he was seen and as he was heard, but when we went beyond the spheres of sight and hearing, and when we met the man in converse, when we saw him at work in his own house, or when we saw him as he was engaged in his multifarious duties, our estimation of him which might have been formed by hearing him or seeing him, developed into a love which we liked to cherish as a privilege. Our intimacy with him grew day by day and inch by inch into a privilege of citizenship which under no circumstances we would be induced to forego. Never out of temper himself, he always put other people into their best temper, always thinking that there was something in everybody else which deserved his admiration. As a scholar, as a speaker, as a politician, as a judge, as a member of our political and official bodies, his services are on record. Though his friends have not done their duty by him in letting his life remain unwritten, and in allowing the reminiscences of his life to be still gathered from the remarks made here and there, that work has been undertaken by an English friend far away separated from India, and by a Parsee gentleman who, however, has not been able to understand him and his life properly. I can imagine one reason why it has been found impossible by some intimate friends of his to do full justice to the man. Their excess of love for him made it impossible for them to put their thoughts in writing in such a way as to do adequate justice to the great excellences of his character.

To those who may think that the claims of future existence have no regard for us, and that all that we need care about is our present existence, and that after death their is an end of all things to us, an end that can never be recalled to them, there is no hope and no joy in store. But most of us cherish the faith in a future existence for the soul where opportunities, denied here, are given to us in abundance; where our powers are still further developed, and where our foibles, if any, are corrected, our temper is strengthened, and our virtues are enlarged. This is the belief of Mr. Telang's friends; and it is this belief of theirs that gives them consolation, and partly reconciles them to the loss they have suffered in the departure of so many of our great and good men. What converse shall we hold with these spirits, who are hovering over our heads in and about this place? What shall we converse with them? Certainly not of our petty disappointments and sorrows; not of the many toils and trials that we have to suffer. What shall we converse about with souls like these? Everyone has to fix in his own mind what we shall converse about. They all have a family likeness which distinguishes them from many of our other friends who have gone either before them or after them, to the existence from which there is said to be no return.

And while you are contemplating in your own minds what converse you should hold with these spirits, I shall suggest to you the particular features of this likeness. What are these features of family likeness which distinguish those whose memory I have brought to your recollection? Some of you may think that there is no family likeness; that there are no common features in the great and good work done by these men, which would justify my calling them a school; and still I want to show to you, if I am permitted to do so, that they do form a school. In the absence of a better name I may call that school, as representing all its best characteristics—I may call it the Telang School of Thought and Action. Shall we make ourselves worthy to be the followers of this school in our present existence, either as teachers or disciples? For teacher and disciple are alike in the same condition in respect of this high spiritual converse. Teaching is learning in such matters; teaching is discipline; learning is discipline again. What then are these common features which bring all these great and good men together in our estimation? What makes all these great men and good people rise together before our minds as if they were members of one family; as if they were members of one society; as if they were members of an association with common purposes and objects? Such of you as knew these persons intimately need hardly be reminded of the particular and salient features of this school. I do not deny that there are other schools with distinguishing features; I should be the last person to deny that, Though my love for this school grows higher every day, still I should be the last person to deny that there are other schools, and possibly the members of those schools might have equal right to assert their own superiority. But on this occassion we have been invited at the members of a Club of which Mr. Telang, though not the founder, was a most distinguished leader. We meet here to store up in our minds in this commemoration all the lessons with which his life, his teachings, his actions, and his sufferings are so fraught; we shall carry those lessons by way of discipline and by way of encouragement to us all.

The first common feature is that they were all *hopeful men.* You may perhaps not understand me when I say that this privilege of hopefulness is one which many disentitle themselves from claiming a share in; some of you may not be able to see what grounds for hopefulness can exist in our present abasement when the whole world is pointing the finger of scorn at us. And yet it is a fact that they were all hopeful. If any one wishes to become a member of this

Telang school of thought and hold converse with these great teachers of this school, he must first learn the lesson that *hopefulness is the badge of the school.*

We should be unworthy of ourselves if we are not hopeful with our traditions which transcend the tradition of every other nation of the world. You may take the map of Asia Europe, Africa, or America, and you will find that there is no other country in the world which presents such a continuity of existence over such a long period of time. Races and creeds have risen, thrived, and decayed in other lands, but India is favoured that notwithstanding its abasement in many other particulars, the people of this country have been preserved from dangers, as they were a people with a special mission entrusted to them. We, of the present, or those of our ancestors of the immediate past, may not be worthy to bear the standard of that mission, but still there is the fact that we represent a continuity of creed, of traditions, of literature, of philosophy of modes of life and forms of thought which are peculiar to this land, and which have been carried to other countries by our illustrious ancestors in the past from this land. What is there in this circumstance, you may ask, that we should feel hopeful on this account. It cannot surely be for nothing that this particular favour has been shown to us under providential guidance. If the miraculous preservation of a few thousand Jews had a purpose, this more miraculous preservation of one-fifth of the human race is not due to mere chance. We are under the severe discipline of a high Purpose. This is one ground of the hopefulness which has been the characteristic feature of the school. They were hopeful men, they felt proud of the past, and they were hopeful of the future. They were hopeful that if they lived under this discipline, they might in time be fitted to take their proper place in history.

What is the nature of this discipline which unites our dislocated races together and makes us one in aspiration and thought? All the creeds and civilizations are gathered in this land; all the spiritual forms and beliefs are here; all social and political experiments are being tried on a large scale; and this is the only land where you will find all these creeds represented by hundreds and thousands, and millions, living peaceably together and partaking of the charities, learning, and excellence of each in a spirit of toleration for all which you will nowhere find on the broad face of this earth. This is a discipline which has not been vouchsafed to any other country in the world. The Jews were punished in Egypt; they were taken captive to Persia and were brought back and restored to their promised land, and finally again scattered to the four corners of the world. We also have been punished for our wrong doings, and still the providential discipline keeps its hold upon us, but we have not been scattered to the winds. We are slowly being prepared by discipline and trained to be what we were certainly intended to be—fulfillers of the mission which has still not been fully accomplished. Our great ancestors accomplished it in part, their successors failed to accomplish it and suffered the reverses that we are now labouring under, and we feel hopeful that this work has come to our hands, and we are being trained to undertake it in a proper spirit. If we can take away with us this source of strength from this commemoration, then we shall have taken the first steps in the lessons which are taught in this school.

You will recognize that shis *sturdy hopefulness* is the golden mean between stolid indifference to change and the sanguineness of temper which desires to accomplish the work of centuries in as many decades and the work of decades in as many years and the work of years in as many days. The stolid indifference to change represents the decresitude of old age and the sanguineness of temper represents the difference between the child and the man. Many of us are still in that state of mind when every little success elates us and every little depression dejects us. Give them a little start in life, and they feel as if they have mastered the whole situation; a little piece of good fortune happens to them and they feel that they are the luckiest men in the world. People who have got this spirit of sanguineness developed in them are, I say, clearly to be distinguished from those who, while they feel hopeful of the final result, are still weighed down with the thought that they have to undergo a long discipline, and have no heart for boisterous displays or dreams of mock revivals of past glory. The results are to be achieved in ourselves and not by change of extraneous circumstances. And these results are to be achieved and change has to be brought about in a way which it would be difficult to anticipate at present but such change must come if we aspire to fulfil that mission which has been left half accomplished. We know that we should not be oversanguine in such matters.

Our difficulties are really not outside us but inside us; the difficulties are in us, in our inertia, in our weakness, in our physical inability to sustain hard work, in our inaptitude to work long for great results by great toil. These are our difficulties; old habits are to be changed; we have by long centuries of debasement learnt to be like little children who are disappointed on being deprived of a toy or like old men we are irritable and querulous. We should learn to be men, stalwart puritan met, battling for the right, not indifferent nor sanguine, trustful but not elated, serious but not dejected. That is the change in character which has to be accomplished.

One word of caution is necessary here. It is not the immediate past of which we are to feel proud, but of the past of our great ancestors in whose time our philosophies were developed, our literature and sciences grew up and our people went to foreign lands, far off to Java, to the East, and far away beyond Mongolia to the North. About these times we ought to have intense reverence. The more immediate past has brought us to our present position and stranded us into the difficulties in which we find ourselves. We are creatures of that more immediate past, we are suffering the penalty of our weakness, hesitation and self-seeking and mutual jealousies. That immediate past has landed us into our debasement. There have been periods even in that immediate past about which we may be all as legitimately proud as of the days of our great ancestors. There have been lights blazing on the mountain tops which shone with a brilliancy as great as of the Rishis in the olden days. These lights have, however, been extinguished. They were so few and far between, and the work to be accomplished was so great that lights failed and we are to some extent involved in our own darkness; and that veil has to be lifted, and nobody can lift it unless we welcome the light ourselves. Vast agencies are set in motion, by the guiding hand whose kindness it is our privilege to recognise at every step, but it is a work which takes years and years, and centuries after centuries before it can be fully accomplished.

Now these are some of the distinguishing features of this school. What else is there to be said about the common family features of this group of great and good men that we have called to converse with us? There is this further common feature—that they all agreed in holding that the work to be accomplished is not one-sided work. *The liberation that has to be sought is not in one department of life, or one sort of activity, or in one sphere of thought, but it is an all-round work in which you cannot dissociate one activity from another.* Take the improvement of our physique alone. To do that you may take many decades, you may take centuries, as the result of false ideals of life, evil habits, and bad institutions can only be counteracted by persistent efforts to combat the mischief.

But besides physical development the other duties that have to be performed are of even still more peremptory characters. And what are they? They are the improvement of the social surroundings about us. The very air in which we live, move and breathe has to be purified. These environments have to be in a sense reordered in a way that would help not merely our physical growth, but also out intellectual and moral growth. That was the idea in the mind of our friend, the Political Rishi. Those who knew him, lying as he had been in bed in sorrow and suffering for ten or twelve years, knew that if there was anything which preyed on the mind of that man it was not the pain that he suffered—though that pain was excruciating, but it was this thought, that some of us were attaching too much of importance to one form of evil and paid little attention to the other forms. There was the work of religious regeneration to be attended to. Not that we need go to a foreign country and borrow our faith from foreign masters. Spiritual life was developed into the highest perfection, not merely in the writings, but in the actual existence of great men who flourished in the past. We have to revive that life in us; we have not to set up a particular doctrine which separated one friend from another, and one church from another. Too much importance is attached to that. We have preserved the outward forms and symbols while the spirit has evaporated—the spirit which teaches us to do justice between man and man, and between man and woman too, and high and low alike.

While we developed new forms of thought in philosophy we circumvented ourselves with new temptations, and we are now in a fix, being able neither to move out, nor move with the mass, and yet the social emancipation, or if you want to call it by any other name, religious or social revival if you please—is a task that has to be accomplished.

Next there is the economical and industrial movement. Our industries are in the same condition in which they were when man first entered on the agricultural stage. Millions of people are working and toiling all the year round in a most desultory fashion, managing to eke out their living in some form or other. Labour is unskilful, capital is scarce and without organization, our material resources are either not utilized or undeveloped. It is difficult to accomplish a revolution like that unaided. But Providence has placed us in a most favourable state to secure the development of this side of human character in its best form. We have been put to school under the best living captains of industry and organisation.

We have, lastly, to learn to take interest in the political well being of our people, and though it is thought to be a very easy lesson to learn, it is one which is most difficult to accomplish, unless ordinated with it, we secure the regular development of other useful activity in us.

You may frame a system, you may fashion a machine, you may build a house, but you cannot manufacture men in the way in which you can manufacture dead machines. You must have men to deal with this system, to live in this house, and to work this machine. There are other schools in this country proclaiming a dozen other missions. But the great characteristic feature of what I have called the Telang school is that you cannot develop the chest without developing your other organs; you cannot starve yourselves and yet desire that your muscles shall grow and your nerves have the same elasticity as before. There is an interdependence between the parts, so that it is not possible to do justice to one without doing justice to the other also. This, I believe to be a very difficult lesson to learn and yet every one of those men that I have named, every one of them lived and died in a steadfast faith in this great doctrine. I may bring to your recollection the work done by our friend, whose death we have met here specially to commemorate. He was, as you know, a writer, a social and economical reformer, and he was the most active worker in the political field. He was a man who was a great scholar; not a scholar in the old sense of the word. He was a scholar whom the Pandits of the West and the Pandits of the East had learnt to revere, and learnt to understand. He combined all these activities in himself and he was trying to give a helping hand to all in other fields when he could not himself work. In such matters as these, people think that they cannot help one another. I should be the last person to entertain an idea like that. The strongest among us has sometimes his moments of weakness. A man who does not get the support of his friends at such times feels that he is left alone and sinks occasionally and sins badly. We are for a moment led to believe that we cannot make use of greater opportunities without running greater risks. This is one of the mistakes which the weakness of human nature always entails upon the strongest of our men. It should be our duty to try and remedy this weakness and to see that such a mistake may not occur. When you find that you have made a mistake you must not try to hide it or defend it, but you should seek help, and try to see that it does not occur again. That is the lesson that we have to learn from true hopefulness; that hopefulness is based on the belief that there is a mission assigned to us; that mission is not assigned by any one among us, but assigned by One who alone has the power to assign the mission. And that belief is based on a sure foundation, not on the foundation of our common sense, or our powers and capacity. But it is a religious belief that there is this short of guidance given to us, only on one condition, that we fully realize that we have to work our own liberation and our own betterment, and that betterment not in one field or in one direction. Our muscles and sinews have to be hardened; our hearts have to be humanized to the sense of justice in all directions; and our intellect to be freed from prejudice and prepossessions; freed from the beliefs of superstitions which have been long dominating over us. This is a work of a very difficult character, and yet each one of us, unless he puts his hand to the wheel, can never help himself to obtain success in his own emancipation. I said that there are other features relating to this particular question which I cannot describe at present. I have thought about them, but I do not at present feel that I can do justice to them. I am quite sure that many of you here had the privilege of longer intimacy with the friend I have now brought to your recollection, whose memory we have now come here to commemorate. Teachings of the Telang School are seen in the life and writings of the men whose family likeness I have brought to your recollection on this occasion. We have a duty to discharge; we all owe a debt of duty, not of course in feeding them with things which they do not want, but to feel for a moment that you are not of this world, that you are in some better existence than in this world, and that your soul converses with their souls in the other existence in order to throw off its bondage. This is an object to the accomplishment of which occasions like this should be utilized I hope you will be able to do that work. I trust that this Club in which Mr. Telang took so much interest, and a Club in which, I fear, there is something wanting to make it clubbable, will prosper, and that occasions which bring us together will multiply and make us feel the want of Club life, till we raise this Club to the position occupied by the Clubs of the other communities in this city. A Club without common feelings may be said to be a rope of sand. Every one of you has got a function to perform in this connection. The common feature of Club life is co-operation and association. I believe I am not far wrong when I say that the few principles which I have tried to place before you now find response in your hearts, and there are many more to which your attention may hereafter be directed. In the meanwhile there is no reason why we may not join in common fellowship which is likely to be productive of such good results.

REVIVAL OR REFORM

The Reports of this year's work which have been received from nearly sixty Associations, large and small, and which have been summarized up to date, complain that their work for the year has not been as successful as in the previous two years. And yet to those who can read between the lines, there are manifest signs which show that the work has been as earnestly pursued as ever. To instance a few cases:—Under the head of Female Education, the Bethune College of Calcutta the Girls' High Schools at Poona and Ahmedabad, the Kanya Maha Vidyalaya at Jallunder, the Sabha's Girls' School at Lahore, the Maharani's Girls' School at Mysore, the Mahakali Pathashala organized by Mataji Tapasvini Bai, a Mahratta lady, in Calcutta, and the Sylhet and Mymensingh Unions, all show a record of progress, each in its own line of development. There is not a single Reform Association of any position in the country which has not lent its best efforts to raise the standard and popularize the system of Female Education. Many Associations, Sabas, and Samajas maintain independent girls' schools of their own, and others have their home classes more or lees actively employed in carrying on the work of the

Note : This address was delivered at the Hindus Union Club, Bombay, in 1895.

schools to educate the more advanced students. Others again have their lectures for ladies, and Ladies' Associations such as at Ahmedabad, Bombay, and Madras, started and maintained by the ladies themselves. Though the common of female education is still very backward and though the experiments that are now carried on are on different lines, the signs are clearly visible that throughout India the national awakening to the necessity of developing the moral and intellectual capacities and aptitutus of our sisters has found universal recognition.

As regards another sign of this liberal movement which see us to do equal justice to the rights of female as of the nill sex, it is satisfactory to note that though the number of widow marriages this year has been smaller that the of the previours years, still all the provinces have then part in the movement. The reports show that in all twenty-five widow marriages were celebrated throughout India during the past year :—in the Punjab ten, Bombay six, the Central Provinces four, Madras, North-West Provinces and Bengal, one each. The widow marriages in the Central Provinces have been all brought about directly or indirectly by the persistent efforts of Rao Bahadur Kolhatkar, the President of this gathering. For the marriages in Punjab the credit is due to Dewan Sant Ram and his friends of the Widow Marriage Association there, and in regard to Bombay the same honour is due to Mr. Bhagwandas, the son of the late Mr. Madhvadas Ragunathdas, in whose house two re-marriages were celebrated. The credit of the widow marriages celebrated in Madras is due to Rai Bahadur Vireshlirgam Pantulu. There was thus not a single province in which friends of the casus did not manifest their active interest in it, which remark does not equally hold good for the prevoius years. The paucity in the total number was partly due to the calamities of the year, and partly to the prohibition of all marriages due to the year being a Sinhastha year. Another good sign of the times which may be noted is the fact that some of the castes, in which no re-marriages had been celebrated before, joined in the movement for the first time this year. It was also reported in the papers that the Maharajah of Nabha, in the Punjab, had exercised his influence in favour of bettering the condition of Hindu widows, and inducing influential Hindu gentlemen to support the widow marriage movement. In the Chandraseniya-Kayastha Prabhu caste of Bombay, a similar pronouncement was made by the leaders of the community in favour of remarriage, and it was resolved to bring up the subject before the next Kayastha Prabhu Conference to be held Baroda. Another satisfactory indication of the time is furnished by the fact reported from Guzerat, that the Audicha Brahmin community at Damun has made a similar pronouncement in favour of widow marriage in their caste. The Widows' Homes at Baranagore and at Pooda have also been successfully maintained notwithstanding pecuniary difficulties, and the numbers of widows attending the homes has slightly increased, thanks to the efforts of Mr. Shashipad Bannerjee and Professor Karve of Poona.

As regards Foreign Travel, the year has had a good record to show. Several gentlemen of the Saraswata Brahman community have returned from England, and though the *Guru*, High Priest, of the caste has refused admission to them, the reform party at Mangalore and in North Canara have succeeded in openly showing their sympathies with these men. Raja Nowloji Rao Gujar, a scion of the princely house of Nagpore, returned from England, and was well received, and Messrs, Booti and Alonikar of Nagpur, Mr. Krishna Rao Bholanath of Ahmedabad, Professor Gokhale of Poona, and Mr. Ketkar of Gwalior, have similarly, though not formally, been admitted by some of their caste people, and the opposition has not ventured to place any difficulties in their way. Two Bhatia gentlemen, for the first time in that community, left for England with the full support of their caste. In the Punjab, several young men in the Biradadri castes, who had been to England, were admitted back without any opposition. Two young men from the Aurorbans caste went to England last year. The liberal section of the Cashmere Pandit's Sabha is strongly in favour of foreign travel. These instances show that slowly but surely, in all parts of the country, the prejudice against foreign travel is on the wane, and that before long the orthodox community or communities will learn to tolerate these departures from custom as an inevitable change.

In regard to the question of Inter-Marriage, the Bengal papers announced an inter-marriage in high life between two sub-division of the Kayastha community, which hitherto kept aloof. In the Punjab, there was a betrothal between two sub-castes of the Serin community. This was the first instance of an inter-marriage between these two sub-divisions. Many of the widow marriages have also been instances of inter-marriages, and for the first time last year two instances of inter-marriage between Madrasi and Bengali gentlemen and ladies were reported. The North-West Provinces reports show instances of similar fusion between sub-divisions of the Kayastha caste there, and in Guzerat there is a similar tendency manifest in some of the castes to amalgamate together.

As regards the postponement Infant marriages, the reports from all provinces show a decided tendency to increase the limits of marriageable ages of girls and boys. In the Punjab, the Aurorbans Sabha has passed a resolution that no girl belonging to the caste should be given in marriage unless she completed her twelfth year. In the Madras Presidency, the opinion is gaining ground that the time has now come for applying to Government for legislation on the subject to fix at least the marriageable age for boys, if not for girls, and to lay down a maximum limit of age for old persons who marry young girls, on the plan adopted by the Mysore Government. The Madras Provincial Social Conference and the Godavery District Conference expressly passed resolutions on this subject. The Hindu Social Reform Association at Madras has also appointed a committee to draw up a memorial with the same object. The Hon. Mr. Jambulingan Mudaliyar is reported to be contemplating the introduction of a Bill in the local Council there on this subject. There have also been individual instances in some parts of the country where grown-up girls have been married without experiencing any very bitter opposition from the caste.

Nearly all the Associations have been pledged to support the Purity movement, including the anti-*Nautch* and Temperance agitation, and the work done during the year shows considerable progress under both these heads.

To turn next to another question in which the Conference has been interesting itself for the past few years—the Admission of Converts from other faiths,—some progress has been made during the year. The Shuddhi Sabha admitted nearly 200 Mahomedan converts this year. Hitherto, the movement for the readmission of converts to other faiths back into the Hindu society was chiefly confined to the Punjab. This year, however, there have been also instances of such conversions in Bengal, the North-West provinces, and far away in Burma, one of them being a convert Christian and the others Mahomedans. The Shuddhi Sabha of Lahore and the Arya Samaja there have deservedly taken the lead in this movement, and it will be a source of great strength to them that the movement has been taken up in the other Provinces also. The Central Provinces report for the year show that Mr. Shanker Shastri of Jubbulpore has published a pamphlet on the subject, an it is a strange coincidence that Professor Rajaram Shastri Bhagwat of Bombay read this year a paper before the branch of the Royal Asiatic Society there, showing how in old times the non-Aryan races were brought within the fold of the Aryan system.

As regards the reduction of extravagant expenses in marriage, a very important movement was started in Calcutta under the auspices of leading Kayastha gentlemen, including such men as Sir Romesh Chundra Mitra and the Hon'ble Mr. Madhava Chandra Ghose, who met at Babu Ramnath Ghose's house, and passed several resolutions which are likely to be attended with good results. Nearly every one of the reports of the North-West Provinces contains details of the manner in which the Kayasthas, the Bhargavas, the Chaturvedis, the Vaishyas, the Jains, and the other castes have tried to lay down sliding scales of marriage expenditure, curtailing extravagance under many heads, abolishing *Nautch* parties, fireworks, and other useless items. In the

Punjab, the Aurorbans have very considerably reduced the extravagance in marriage expenses. On the Bombay side, the Bhatia *Mandal* and the Dasa Oswal Jains have successfully worked in the same direction. Even in far off Baroda, the Dasa Porwad Bania caste people have been moving in the matter. Following the example of the Rajputra Hitakarini Sabha, many non-Rajput castes in Rajputana and Malwa have laid down rules which are enforced by the same sanctions as those of the principal Sabha.

As regards Conference work generally, it may be noted that caste Conferences are the order of the day in all parts of India. I have, on previous occasions, mentioned the gatherings annually held this week in several large towns in the North-West Provinces of the Kayastha and the Vaishya community. This year was distinguished by the holding of the first Provincial Social Conference in Madras, in which Presidency also we had two district Conferences, one on the East Coast in the Godavery District, and the other on the West Coast at Mangalore. New associations are being formed under very favourable auspices in many parts of the country, notably in the districts of Bombay and Madras Presidencies, to support the work of the Conference and to give effect to its resolutions.

Encouraged by the success which has attended the efforts of the Mysore Government, and the Malabar Marriage Law passed in the Madras Council, two Bills of great social importance have been introduced, one, in the Imperial Council, to bring under better control religious Charities and Endowments, and another, in the Madras Council to remove all doubts and to codify the law in regard to what constitutes self-acquired property under the Hindu joint family system. Both these Bills have suggested subjects for discussion at the ensuing Conference this year, and it is not, therefore, necessary for me to enlarge upon their importance. There is a third measure before the Viceroy's Council which, though it relates to a particular section of the Mahomedan community, has a wider bearing which interests us all. The Memon section of this community in Bombay were originally Hindu converts, and though they embraced Mahomedanism, they retained their old Hindu customs in regard to inheritance and succession, and these customs were recognized by our Law Courts. A majority of that community, however, now desire that, in place of the Hindu customs, the Mahomedan Law should govern their succession to the property of deceased persons. The Government of India, accordingly, intend to pass a sort of a permissive measure, by which a member of this community may retain or abandon the old rules by a formal declaration of his choice, which choice, once made, will be final. The subject bristles with dfficulties, but the permissive legislation, if it proves a seccess in actual operation, will furnish a precedent which may prove of considerable help to those who wish to have more liberal laws of inheritance and succession without a change of religion.

Such is the brief record of the principal social events of the year. Many ardent spirits amongst us will, no doubt, be very much dissatisfied with the poverty of this record. At the same time we must bear in mind that hundreds and thousands, may, millions, of our countrymen regard this poor record as very revolutionary, and condemn this as one of the unseen causes which have brought about the physical and moral catastrophes upon the land by way of punishment for the sins of the Reformers. These are the two extreme sides of the question, and it is not for me to say to an audience like this, on which side the balance of truth may be found. The Arya Patrika of the Punjab which is a recognized organ of the Arya Samajas there, has, in its words of advice to the Conference, expressed its view that we are radically in the wrong in seeking to reform the usages of our society without a change of roligion, and it seriously suggests that we should in the first instance become members of the Arya Samaja, and this conversion will bring with it all the desired reforms. Many enthusiastic friends of the Brahmo Samaja entertain similar views and give us similar advice. All I can say to these welcome advisers is that they do not fully realize the situation and its difficulties. People have changed their religion and yet retained their social usages unchanged. The native Christians, for example, especially the Roman Catholic section among them, and many sections of Mahomedans, are instances in point. Besides, it has been well observed that even for a change of religion, it is too often necessary that the social surroundings must be liberalised in such a way as to help people to realize their own responsibilities, and to strengthen in their efforts. Lastly, these wellmeaning advisers seem to forget that the work of reform cannot be put off indefinitely till the far more arduous and difficult work of religious conversion is accomplished. It may take centuries before the Arya or the Brahmo Samajas establish their claims to general recognition. In the meanwhile what is to become of the social organization Slowly but surely, the progress of liberal ideas must be allowed to work its way in reforming our social customs, and the process cannot be stopped even though we may wish it. In the case of our society, especially, the usages which at present prevail among us were admittedly not those which obtained in the most glorious periods of our history. On most of the points which are included in our programme, our own records of the past show that there has been a decided change for the worse, and it is surely within the range of practical possibilities for us to work for a better state of things, without stirring up the rancorous hostilities which religious differences have a tendency to create and foster. There is no earthly reason whatsoever why we should not co-operate with these religious organizations, or why they should not rather co-operate with us in this work in which our interests are common, because the majority of our countrymen hold different views about religion from those which commend themselves to these Samajas. I am speaking these words a full sense of my responsibility, for I am, in my own humble way, a member of one, if not both the Samajas, and I am a sincere scarcher after religious truth, in full sympathy with the Arya and Brahmo Samaja movements, and I hope, therefore, that these advisers of ours will take my reply in the same spirit, and will not misunderstand me. Schismatic methods of propagation cannot be applied with effect to vast communities which are not within their narrow pale.

On the other side, some of our orthodox friends find fault with us, not because of the particular reforms we have in view, but on account of the methods we follow. While the new religious sects condemn us for being too orthodox, the extreme orthodox section denounce us for being too revolutionary in our methods. According to these last, our efforts should be directed to revive, and not to reform. I have many friends in this camp of extreme orthodoxy, and their watchword is that Revival, and not Reform, should be our motto. They advocate a return to the old ways, and appeal to the old authorities, and the old sanctions. Here also, as in the instance stated above, people speak without realizing the full significance of their own words. When we are asked to revive our old institutions and customs, people seem to me to be very much at sea as to what it is they seek to revive. What particular period of our history is to be taken as the old, whether the period of the Vedas, of the Smritis, of the Puranas, or of the Mahomedans or the modern Hindu times? Our usages have been changed from time to time by a slow process of growth, and in some cases, of decay and corruption, and you cannot stop at any particular period without breaking the continuity of the whole. When my revivalist friend presses his argument upon me he has to seek recourse to some subterfuge which really furnishes no reply to his own question. What shall we revive? Shall we revive the old habits of our people when the most sacred of our castes indulged in all the abominations, as we now understand them, of animal food and intoxicating drink, which exhausted every section of our country's Zoology and Botany? The men and the gods of those old days ate and drank forbidden things to excess, in a way no revivalist will now venture to recommend. Shall we revive the twelve forms of sons, or eight forms of marriage, which included capture, and recognized mixed and illegitimate intercourse? Shall we revive the Niyoga system of propagating sons on our brother's wives when widowed? Shall we revive the old liberties taken by the Rishis and by the wives of the Rishis with the marital tie? Shall we revive the hecatombs of animals sacrificed from year's end to year's end, in which even human beings were not spared, as propitiatory offerings to God? Shall we revive the Shakti worship of the left hand, with its indecencies and practical debaucheries? Shall we revive the *Sati* and infanticide customs, or the flinging of living men into the rivers of over rocks, or hook-swinging, or the crushing beneath the Jagannath car? Shall we revive the internecine wars of the Brahmins and Kshatriyas or the cruel persecution and degradation of the Aboriginal population? Shall we revive the custom of many husbands to one wife or of many wives to one husband? Shall we require our Brahmins to cease to be landlords and gentlemen, and turn into beggars and dependants upon the King as in olden times? These instances will suffice to show that the plan of reviving the ancient usages and customs will not work our salvation, and is not practicable. It these usages were good and beneficial, why were they altered by our wise ancestors? If they were bad and injurious, how can any claim be put forward for their restoration after so many ages? Besides, it seems so be forgotten that in a living organism, as society is, no revival is possible. The dead and the buried are burnt once for all, and the dead past cannot, therefore, be revived except by a re-formation of the old materials into new organized beings.

If revival is impossible, this reformation is the only alternative open to sensible people, and now it may be asked what is the principle on which this reformation must be based. People have very hazy ideas on this subject. It seems to many that it is the outward form which has to be changed, and if this change can be made, they think that all the difficulties in our way will vanish. If we change our outward menners and customs, and change our food and dress, sit in a particular way, or walk in a particular fashion, our work, according to them, is accomplished. I cannot but think that much of the prejudice against the reformers is due to this misunderstanding. It is not the outward form but the inward form, the thought and the idea which determines the outward form that has to be changed, if real reformation is desired. Now what have been the inward forms or ideas which have been hastening our decline during the past three thousand years? These ideas may be briefly set forth as isolation, submission to outward force or power more than to the voice of the inward conscience, perception of factitious difference between men and men, due to heredity and birth, a passive acquiescence in evil or wrong doing, and a general indifference to secular well-being, almost bordering upon fatalism. These have been the root ideas of our social system. They have, as their natural result, led to the existing family arrangements, where the woman is entirely subordinated to the man, and the lower castes to the higher castes, to the length of depriving men of their natural respect for humanity. All the evils we seek to combat flow from the prevalence of these ideas. They are mere corollaries to these axiomatic assumptions. They prevent our people from realising that they really are in all conscience neither better nor worse than their fellows, and that the average man, whatever garb he may put on, is the worse for his assuming dignities and powers which do not, in fact, belong to him. As long as these ideas remain operative on our mind we may change our outward forms and institutions, and be none the better for the change. These ideas have produced their results, and we must judge of their good or had qualities, as St. Paul says, by their fruits. Now, that these results have been disastrous nobody disputes or doubts, and the lesson to be drawn for our guidance in the future from this fact is that the current of these ideas must be changed, and in the place of the old worship, we must accustom ourselves and others to worship and reverence new ideals. In place of isolation we must have fraternity, or rather elastic expansiveness. At present, it is everybody's ambition to pride himself upon being a member of the smallest community that can be conceived, and the smaller the number of those with whom you can dine or marry or associate, the higher your purity and perfection. The purest person is he who cooks his own food, and does not allow the shadow of his nearest friend to fall upon his cooked food. Every caste and every sect has thus a tendency to split itself into smaller castes and smaller sects in practical life. Even in philosophy, it is a received maxim that knowledge and salvation are only possible for the esoteric few, with whom only is true wisdom and power, and for the rest of mankind, they must be left to grovel in superstition and vice, with only a colouring of so-called religion to make them respectable.

Now all this must be changed. The new mould of thought must be cast, as stated above, in fraternity, or all-attracting expansiveness, and cohesion in society. Increase your circle of friends and associates slowly and cautiously if you will, but the tendency must be to turn our face towards a general recognition of the essential equality between man and man. That will beget sympathy and power. It will strengthen your own minds by the sense that you have numbers with you, and not against you, or, as you foolishly imagine, below you. The next idea which lise at the root of our helplessness is that we were always intended to remain children, to be subject to outside control, and never to rise to the dignity of self-control by making our conscience and our reason the sole guides to our conduct. All our past history has been a terrible witness to the havoc committed by this misconception. We are children, no doubt, but the children of God, and not of man, and the voice of God in us is the only voice to which we are bound to listen. Of course, all of us cannot listen to that voice when we desire it, because from long neglect we have benumbed the faculty of conscience in us. With too many of us, a thing is true or false, righteous or sinful, simply because somebody else has said that it is so. Duties and obligations are duties and obligations, not because we feel them to be so but because somebody, reputed to be wise, has laid it down to be so. Of course, in small matters of manners and courtesies, this outward dictation is not without its use. But when we abandon ourselves entirely to this helplessness, and depend on others' wills it is no wonder that we become as helpless as childern. Now, the new idea which should take its place is not the idea of rebellious independence and overthrow of all authority, but that of freedom responsible to God alone. Great and wise men in the past or in the present, have a claim on our regards. But they must not come between us and our God—the Divine principle seated within everyone of us, high or low. It is this sense of self-respect, or rather of respect to the God in us, which has to be cultivated and it is a tender plant which takes years and years to cultivate. But we have the capacity, and we one it as a duty to ourselves to undertake the task. Reverence all human authority, pay you respects to all prophets and revelations, but subordinate that reverence to the Divine command in us. Similarly, men differ from men in natural capacities and aptitudes, and heredity and birth are factors of some importance in our development, but it is at the same time true that they are not the all-important factors that we have learnt to regard them from sheer idleness, as determining our fates by a sort of moral necessity. Heredity and birth explain many things, but neither they, nor the law of Karma, explain all things, and what is worse, they do not explain the mystery that makes man and woman what they really are, the reflections of the image of God. Our passions and our feelings, our pride and our ambition, lend strength to these factitious agencies, and with their help, the doctrine of Karma completes our conquest, and enforces our surrender. Heredity and birth can be controlled and set back by a properly trained will, when this will is subservient to a Higher Will. This misconception is very hard to remove, perhaps the hardest of the old ideas, but removed it must be, if not in one life or generation, in many lives and many generations, if we are to rise to our full stature.

The fourth old form or idea, to which I will allude here, is our acquiescence in wrong or evil-doing as an inevitable condition of human life, about which we need not be year particular, as after all human life is a vanity and a dream, and we are not much concerned with it. It is in fact atheism in its worst form. No man or woman really ceases to be animal who does not perceive and realize that wrong and evil-doing, impurity and vice, crime and misery, and sin of all kinds is really our animal existence prolonged. It is the beast in us which blinds us to impurity and vice and makes them even attractive. There must be Nautches in our temples say our priests, because even the gods cannot do without their impure fairies. This is only a typical instance of our acquiescence in impurity. There must be drunkenness in the world, there must be poverty, and wretchedness, and tyranny, there must be fraud and force, there must be thieves and robbers, and the law to punish them. No doubt these have been facts, and there is no use denying their existence. But in the name of all that is sacred and true, do not acquiesce in them, do not hug these evils to your bosom, and cherish them. Their contact is poison, and the worst poison, because it does not kill, but corrupt men. A healthy sense of the true dignity of our nature and of man's high destiny is the best corrective and antidote to this poison.

I think I have said more than enough to suggest to your reflecting minds what it is that we have to reform. All admit that we have been deformed. We have lost our stature, we are bent in a hundred places, our eyes lust after forbidden things, our ears desire to hear scandals about our neighbours, our tongue wants to taste for bidden fruit our hands itch for another man's property, our bowels are deranged with indigestible food. We cannot walk on our feet, but require stilts or crutches. This is our present social polity, and now we want this deformity to be removed, and the only way to remove it is to place ourselves under the discipline of better ideas and forms such as those I have briefly touched above. Now this is the work of the reformer. Reforms in the matter of infant marriage and enforced widowhood, in the matter of temperance and purity, intermarriages between castes, the elevation of the low castes, and readmission of converts, and regulations of our endowments and charity, are reforms, only so far and no further, as they check the influence of the old ideas and promote the growth of the new tendencies. The reformer has to infuse in himself the light and warmth of nature, and he can only do it by purifying and improving himself and his surroundings. He must have his family, village, tribe, and nation, recast in other and new moulds, and that is the reason why social reform becomes an obligatory duty, and not a mere pastime which might be given up at pleasure. Revival is, as I have said, impossible—as impossible as mass conversion into other faiths. But even if these were possible, they would only be useful to us if they reformed us and our surroundings, if they made us stronger, braver, truer men, with all our faculties of endurance and work developed, with all our sympathies fully awakened and refined, and with our heads and hearts acting in unison with a purified and holy will,—if they made us feel the dignity of our being and the high destiny of our existence, made us love all, work with all, and feel for all. This is the reformer's work, and this, in my opinion, is the reason why the Conference meets from year to year, and sounds the harmonies in every ear which can listen to them with advantage.

PHILOSOPHY OF INDIAN THEISM*

Nearly three thousand years ago, in one of the primeval forests of Northern India, Bhrigu, the son of Varuna, approached his father, and entreated him to teach him what Bramha was—that Bramha from which all beings sprung into existence, that which keeps them alive when born, and that to which they tend, and in which they are finally absorbed. His father, Varuna, told him at first that Bramha was Food, as Food generated life and sustained it after birth, and finally, on decay, resolved itself into the food of other generations of life, and being. Bhrigu long pondered over the matter, but was not satisfied with the finality or sufficiency of the explanation. He again approached his father with the same question, and he was successively told that Bramha was the Breath of life that Bramha was the Mind, that Brahma was self-conscious Reason. None of these answers stood the test of Bhrigu's further thought, and finally, he was told that Bramha was the Joy and the Blessedness which pervaded the universe; and this reply satisfied the deepest cravings of the young student. These three stages of thought, the first stage representing 'Sat,' 'absolute existence,' as the cause of all inanimate or animate

*Delivered at the Free General Assembly, Wilson College, Bombay.

matter, second 'Chit,' identifying it with 'mind and self-conscious reason,' and the third 'Ananda,' as the source of all joy and blessedness', these three stages represent the three different phases of thought which have dominated over men's minds throughout history. The spirit of joy and blessedness here described is further spoken of as pervading the universe. '*If there were no spirit of joy in this universe, who could live and breathe in this world of life* ?—(Yajnavalkya Upanishad). He makes us feel joy and gives us peace of mind when it becomes sinless and fearless. This represents the practical side of the subject I propose to-day to take up for your consideration.

There are those among us who are disposed to think that we have had enough of these old-world topics about birth and death, soul and immortality, sin and punishment, and all that can be known about them has been discoverd long since, and all beyond the first few steps is mere blind guess. They would dissuade men from the pursuit of this wild goose chase, and characterize the students of this dismal science as preternaturally old men. They will have us turn to more useful pursuits, which will secure for us the comforts of this world, as the world understands comforts. Now, if there has been any teature of our national history which has been its glory and its reward for much suffering, it is the firm belief that 'not what a man hath, but what a man is, or can become,' constitutes his real wealth. This is the protest which Indian thought has raised from all time, and which, it will continue to raise to the end of time. The contrary view derives also no support from the highest Christian or European ideals before us. The whole mission of Christianity and civilization is meaningless for those who read in it nothing but the progress of physical comforts, and the means of realizing them. On this point, as in others, the highest teaching of the two religions is identically the same. When the great Apostle of the Gentiles reached Athens, he addressed the Athenians by appealing to the Unknown God to whom they had erected an altar, and he described the Bramha in words, which are only a paraphrase of the passage quoted at the beginning from the Upanishad:—

In Him we live and more, and have our being : that is; Outside Him there is neither life nor motion nor being possible.

The hand of God in History is but dimly seen by those who cannot recognize in the contact of European with Eastern thought a higher possibility for the future of both races. Already the morning dawn is upon us, and we can see glimpses of the bright future reflected in our ability to see and appreciate each other's strength and excellence. Not to refer to the Theosophical movement, have we not seen before our eyes the fact that for the first time after many centuries of stagnation, Indian preachers are reciprocating in other lands the sympathy which sends to our shores the many thousand missionaries, who have laboured among us for generations to spread the truth as they understand it. The labours of English and German Professors are taking a new turn, and the foundations of the Gifford and Hibbert series of lectures, and thc holding of the Parliament of Religions, these are not events which we can afford to ignore or which it will profit us to pass by unheeded. The Lectures of Dr. Fraser on the Philosophy of Theism, of which I propose to give you a brief summary to-night, from an Indian student's point of view, are an important contribution towards this same end, and I am firmly persuaded that I cannot hope to find a more appropriate place for dwelling on this subject than the premises of a College which represents the highest philanthropy of the West actively at work in the East.

What, then, is the problem which the Philosophy of Theism proposes to solve ? This is how Dr. Fraser puts it :— What is the deepest and truest interpretation that can be put by man upon the immeasurable actuality with which he is brought in contact and collision ever since he becomes percipient and self-conscious ? In what sort of environment, and for what purpose do I exist ? What is this Universe, for ever changing the appearances it presents to me ? What is the origin and outcome of this endless flux ? Is the principle which finally determines all events reasonable and trustworthy or chaotic and misleading, or must man for ever remain ignorant about this and unable to adapt himself to it ? What light can enlighten me upon may present duties or my final destiny as part of this investerious whole ?

The eminently human character of these questions will be at once perceived by those who are not blinded to their importance. If there was no human element in them, or as our forefathers said, if there was no 'Rasa,' 'light and sweetness' in them, it is hardly intelligible why the highest thought of man in all ages and countries has been busy over this mystery! It is our highest privilege that we feel the full force of this mystery and are drawn towards it. This is the highest fruition of humanity and its final goal. The awe it inspires is the seed of all religion. The devotion of the mind to this study of the Infinite is the working force of philosophy. The successive steps of progress towards this knowledge constitutes the hierarchy of science. The existence of evil and sin here below, and the contemplation of Death, and what becomes of us after death, intensify the human character of such studies and make us pause, with Shakespeare, to consider if Death is a sleep, or a dream, or else only a shuflling off of the mortal coil. Both individual and social well-being depend upon the answer we give to this question of questions. It dominates morals, it shapes our legislation and the practical art of government. In the words of the Upanishad, "*If there be no spirit of joy over-ruling the universe, how cau we live and breathe in this world of life*?"—(Yajavalkya).

Having proposed the problem and shown its human character, we have next to see what final interpretations have been attempted of this problem of existence, the articulations, so to speak, of the human mind with reference to it. The two postulates underlying all thought are, the 'I' and the 'Non-I', the subject and the object. This is the quality of finite existence, each a mystery by itself. This is, however, not an ultimate analysis; for the question arises when the Infinite and the Eternal dawns upon us, whether besides the Ego and the non-Ego there is a third postulate of supreme existence which synthesises both, by being in and outside both, the one in which and by which we live and move and have our being. In the philosophy of the Ramanuja sect of Vedantism, we have these three postulates, 'Chit,' human soul, 'Achit,' matter, and 'Brahma,' Supreme spirit; the '*Chit*' and '*Achit*' having no separate existence, from Brahma, in the 'Avyakta,' unmanifested form, and appearing separate only when 'Vyakta,' manifested or individualized. This same view is in all other Indian systems of philosophy variously emphasised, some maintaining the existence of three separate principles, others two, and some affirming only the real existence of one principle. In the European systems of philosophy also, the difference between system and system resolves itself into the exaggeration of one or other of these first postulates to the point of negativing the absolute separate existence of the other two. One thing, however, is common to all : the human mind is not at rest with the dual solution of the Finite, which alone its senses grasp. It yearns to find the Finite linked together in some bond with the Infinite: it may be by faith or reason, hope or fear, by aspiration or by love. Man finds that his own existence for a moment of time is not intelligible unless there is a background for it to rest upon. He feels that the flux of things is not intelligible unless it also finds its rest in something which knows no flux. Whether the Infinite Being is potential matter, energy, mind or spirit, these are the points on which philosophy has proposed various interpretations and solutions. The mystery surrounding this third postulate of existence is not more enigmatical than what is involved in a right understanding of what constitutes the Ego and the Non-Ego. We cannot comprehend the one more clearly than the other. Each of us can realize the fact that he exists, and that something outside him also exists. His own existence and the existence of the Non-Ego become more intelligible to him when he also lears to realize the existence of the Infinite.

All the errors of superstition, scepticism and mysticism spring up from our inability to keep our hold on the three distinct postulates of existence. We should not either explain away or exaggerate any of them. When we localize God in place or time and connect Him with uncommon particular events or places, superstition creeps in and overturns the balance of our mind. When we exaggerate our own powers we end in mysticism. When we unduly allow nature and her forms to dazzle us, and belittle our capacities, we become sceptical. It will be useful to see what element of partial truth and falsehood there is, in each of the systems which exaggerate and emphasize the one or the other postulate of existence to the prejudice of the others linked with it inseparably. And first of materialism, which sits at the feet of the material forces and magnifies nature and its powers. In European thought this school has occupied a more prominent position during the last few centuries than it ever occupied in this country. But even in our land two out of the six Darsanas are partially or wholly materialistic, that of the Sankhya system of Kapila and the atomic system of Kanada. As a corrective of extreme idealism, this philosophy has done good service. Its other service to humanity is that it has laid the axe at the root of that conception of the Universe, which made the earth the centre of the universe and man the centre of the world. The sun and the moon, it was thought, shine for us, the planets revolve and the stars twinkle for our benefit. The anthropomorphic conception of God ruling men and things as a great patriarch of old with the full display of exaggerated human passions and force, and also human weaknesses at times, this conception has been dissipated by the discoveries of modern science which have reduced the earth to its true insignificance and man to his true position on earth, so far as he is a physical being. The discoveries of Astronomy and Geology have especially led to this result, and they have enabled men to understand the full mystery of the Infinite in space and time. Scientific evolution has also enlarged men's conceptions of the methods of operations pursued in the genesis of life and being. The equivalence and conversion of different kinds of force have paved the way to much clearness of thought on these and kindred subjects. The brilliancy of these results led men to the other extreme and to dream of abolishing mind and spirit altogether from the universe. This mechanical and chemical interpretation of Nature, however, solves nothing. It takes us a step or two back and then it leaves the mind more bewildered in the labyrinth of chaos. The manner of working is explained to some extent, by the interpretation of second causes, but the efficient and ultimate cause remains as shrouded as ever, and as impervious to human vision as when Moses saw the glory on the top of Sinai and received the Commandments. Materialism explains co-sequence and not causation, and it explains co-sequence and by making it out to be a casual assemblage of atoms chancing to evolve order out of chaos. This solution appears to give no satisfaction to the enquirer. Shankaracharya has in his Bhashya very cleverly turned the tables on the atomic theorist.

The first quality of matter is inertia, so our senses tell us. This inertia is overcome by force outside it, and what is this force or energy is still as much a mystery as the mystery of mind and spirit. Why should the molecules be attracted and repelled in a particular way though all time and space? And then, if mind and spirit are left out of view, how comes it that this casual combination of molecules results in the ascending scale—first, of life, next of conscious life, further on of thought, self-consciousness and responsible will, which does not come within the domain of chances, but is guided by purpose which is the negation of chance? This philosophy thus fails to interpret Nature where it most needs rational interpretation. The anthropomorphic conception of a patriarchal God is more intelligible than this materialistic conception of Nature without a Providence overruling it to accomplish purposed ends. Society, law, morals, poetry and art, not more than theology, thus become anachronisms or solecisms, if man and Nature are interpreted as chance combinations of molecules brought out without purpose and both liable to be dis-severed by chance at any time. Man feels instinctively that this surely is not a rational interpretation of the order he sees in the Universe.

He then falls back on himself, and begins to think that there is no truth in this universal flux of things about him and that the only reality is himself. Things exist for him only because he perceives them. Outside his perception of form and colour, primary and secondary qualities, things have no existence in themselves, and from this the inference is drawn that the only real existence is the individual soul. Homo Mensura becomes the rule of thought. It is a useful guide within certain limits, but when pushed too far it becomes self-destructive. Self-consciousness may be a good reason for man's certain belief that he exists, but it is hardly sufficient to make him equally assured that the external world of matter and force obeys any laws or enjoys permanence outside his changing consciousness about it. Science thus becomes impossible, when scientific truths have no basis except in the fiction of his brain, and even sentient beings like himself have no existence independently of his belief about them. This comes out logically as the result of any philosophy which makes the individual soul the final and only measure of being. There is a similar collapse of our moral nature also, when no relationship subsists between one soul and another. Man feels instinctively that, though he may not be able to say how the world of matter exists, it existed before he came into life, and will exist after, he and his race cease to live. It is only demented humanity which can find rest in merely human interpretation of the Universe, and it is to the glory of mankind that there has been no systematic school which has given it currency either in this country or in Europe, though individual thinkers have used it as a powerful weapon to expose the vagaries of rival systems.

The human mind being thus foiled in its worship of Nature, and the deification of Man as an all-sufficient explanation of being, seeks refuge in an exaggeration of the third alternative, which makes out that the Supreme Spirit alone exists, and both Nature and Man are but its reflected manifestations, not separable from it in essence, but only seen to be separate by reason of our ignorance. This is the system which had its representatives in late. Greek and Stoic and modern European, especially German, thought, and which, with shades of differences, has found its chief home in India.

It has several advantages over the other systems. It is an adequate explanation of the infinity of matter we see around us. It is also an adequate interpretation of the infinity of force we see around us. It dispenses with the necessity of explaining the origin of things and the problem of creation or evolution. It has an element of truth about it, in that the Supreme Being is immanent in all beings animate or inanimate. This is a much higher and truer conception of Supreme Existence than any which has found expression in many religious creeds of the world, which seek to separate God from Nature and Man by making Him out to be a being among being, only more powerful and wise.

There is, however, a notable distinction in this respect between the pantheistic teachings of European thinkers and their prototypes in this country. One of the most current mistakes is to regard the 'Advaita,' Monistic system of thought as formulated in the great Bhashya of Shankaracharya on the Vedanta Sutra, as the only characteristically Indian explanation of pantheism in this country. As a matter of fact both before Shankaracharya's time and after his death, the modified Advaite system of Ramanuja has played a great part in Indian philosophy, and to it may be traced the rise and progress of the Vaishnava Sects throughout India, which sects have attained to a higher and truer conception of Theism than any of the other prevailing systems. In Shankarcharya's own system the existence of objective Nature was not categorically denied. The position taken up was that neither existence nor non-existence could be affirmed in regard to it in the same sence in which the human soul and the Supreme Spirit are known to exist. Besides Shankaracharya freely admitted that Brahma, the Supreme existence, as soon as it conceived the idea of creation, became by reason of that thought 'Ishvara,' Creator, and all that was created has phenomenal existence. For all practical purposes this philosophy is strictly theistic in its beliefs. The European thinkers, on the other hand, exaggerated the doctrine so as to negative all other existence.

The European pantheists, while asserting that God was the only substance, the only reality, under the changing apparances of all finite things and persons, fall into the error of consubstantiating this reality with all material things and all individual minds, making it co-extensive with them, so that whatever is predicable of them is equally predicable of the reality. The absolute reality is thus at once Infinite and finite, the substance and the mode, undifferentiated and determined in necessary forms. This error has been avoided in the Indian forms of pantheism as formulated by the great Acharyas. This complete effacement of individual things and persons, and the apprehension of separate appearances as being only an illusion of the imagination ends by reducing the absolute reality itself to a being of two dimensions only, extension and thought, the Sat and Chit of our philosophy. There is no room for the higher spiritual manifestation of Anancia, without which God is an empty substance, without any spiritual relations towards His creatures, these last being only illusory manifestations, of His substance. Pantheism thus ends in becoming, like Materialism, or Egoism, an interpretation of what we see around us, which fails to satisfy our intellectual, moral and spiritual perceptions. We are conscious of our difference, we are conscious of our freedom as well as dependence. We are conscious of our sense of right and wrong, and our responsibility for self-determined action. When the Infinite is thus allowed to swallow up all finite existence in time, space, and causation, the result is that there is no succession in time and space, and there is nothing like cause and effect. Nothing happens but only exists eternally and necessarily. Nothing is originated or changed. There is no perfeticn or imperfection, nothing good or evil in men and things. In short, the undifferentiated and impersonal unity which extreme pantheism teaches, is an interpretation of the universe to which the conditions of our self-conscious being can never permanently be reconciled, and this unity must always remain a more or less curious speculation with little permanent hold on the head or heart of men, except in moments of poetic or mystic ecstasy, in which both in Europe and India pantheism finally sublimates.

Having thus examined all the possibilities of reducing the three postulates of existence to a single postulate, man's mind, in despair, has taken shelter in doubt or scepticism, not of the aggressive or militant kind, but in a more resigned form of it, in which it seeks to rest satisfied with the position that nothing certain can be grasped in connection with these great problems. This is the latest development of modern European speculation, and is known as agnosticism, and we have now to see how far the human mind can resign itself to a conclusion which may be likened to a paralysis of thought as it withdraws itself, tortoise-like, from all contact with such speculations. They all demand logical proof and are not satisfied with practical or moral certitude. It is just possible that practical or moral conviction is all that is needed and therefore attainable by the human mind in its search after the Absolute, and in that case the demand for logical proof may itself be an unconsonable demand. If practical certitude is attainable, it does not follow from our inability to furnish a logical demonstration by way of proof, that nothing can be positively and certainly known about these matters. The failure of the human mind to attain to a living knowledge of the Absolute has partly arisen from this confusion of certitude with demonstration. This disability is not confined to philosophy or religion only. There are large departments of knowledge where demonstrative proof is not possible and be content ourselves with the next best alternative and substitute faith for knowledge and act on that faith and suffer for it. Our Earth, or even the Solai system, is not the Universe, nor is our time Eternity-Finite existence in time and space becomes intelligible only when they discover their background of the Infinite. Second causes linked together necessarily suggest a first cause which holds the links together. In our own personal consciousuness, the fleeting perception and even thought of each moment cannot furnish the origin of true knowledge. That basis is widened by the more permanent results of self-consciousness, which memory holds together over a great length of time in what we recognize is 'I' with its past experiences. Further, connecting our individual thought with those of others, we come to rest our knowledge upon the collective thought of humanity. It would be intellectual suicide or madness if we followed any other principle. We can never demonstrate logically our reasons for the faith that we feel in continuity of nature and the uniform operation of its laws. All science ultimately resolves itself into a product of our faith in the trustworthiness of the ever-changing universe. This sense of trustworthiness is the slow growth of ages, but it none the less the basis of scientific truths as we apprehened them. If this basis of faith is not repudiated by science, it has equally legitimate claims upon our acceptance in the philosophy of the Absolute.

This conformity of the material universe with our faith in its trustworthiness establishes the link which joins man with the universe in which he lives and moves had has his being. We do not feel as if we were like fish taken out of water or like the soaring eagle made to walk over earth. This harmony between our thoughts and the operations of Nature is the highest natural revelation. This harmony springs not from man's consciousness only, nor is it born of inert matter. It not only links us with Nature, but it links us and Nature alike with the Infinite existence whose purposes of wisdom and benevolence, beauty and power, are thereby disclosed to our eyes of faith and knowledge. Science thus holds the torch of faith to the mystery of religion. If this torch were extinguished or set aside not only will Theism suffer, but with it science itself will cease to be scientific, for it also rests ultimately on faith in the harmony of the Universe, and the permanence of its laws and methods of work.

The threefold postulates of existence are thus seen to be distinct and yet harmonized together. All attempts to assimilate and reduce them into one absolute existence fail, because they are bound to fail. At the same time, they are not distinct in the sense of being disjointed parts of a mechanical whole. They are one and yet they are many. Nature and man, each have definite relations of subordination to the great Infinite which rules over them and harmonizes them, and the discovery of these subordinate relations is the special domain of the philosophy of Theism. Even agnostic philosophers have admitted the existence of power and wisdom, benevolence, as manifested in the operations of Nature. In the infancy of science, this power and purpose was concieved as not the work of any single unseen agency and will, but as the play of good and bad deities—Devatas, angels, spirits, and ghosts, the gods and goddesses of mythology of tribal and local origin, which had larger powers and more subtle influences over Nature than man. This stage of thought naturally led to polytheism and to idolatry. It obtain still in this and other countries among people who cannot understand the universal harmony of Nature's laws as science discloses it. Later on, science taught men to classify these agencies into good and bad angels, Devas and Daityas, Ahriman and Ahuramazad. A hierarchy of gods, bigger and smaller, under the banners of the principles of good and evil, was thus evolved, and it is best seen in the early faith of the Hindus and Parsis and has left its stamp on the Mahomedan and Christian systems of faith. Finally, with the triumphs of scientific investigation, the idea dawned upon men's minds of the world of Nature and Man being pervaded by one power, wisdom and purpose, which superseded the old gods and goddesses and the division of good and evil principles. This was the work of Theism. This God was not, as in the older forms of Theism, apprehended as a being among other beings, a fashioner or mechanician setting the watch in motion from outside, but a God immanent in everything and over-ruling the Universe, a God who was not exhausted by the limits of His work, but was, in the words of the Purushasukta, 'Bigger than the Infinite Universe, and encircling as He did, the created world of matter and man, exceeded it on all sides.' It was the peculiar glory of the Upanishads to have discoursed of such a God. 'The winds blow from fear of Him, and the Sun rises and sets as He hirects. Fire and Indra and even Death run on His errand'. In one of the Upanishads there is a beautiful account of the way in which the mythological gods of Fire, Indra, etc., tried their strength in contest with this Supreme Brahma, and were foiled in the attempt and submitted to do His bidding. He saw, or rather thought, and the world and the inhabitants thereof were created. This is also the teaching of the Old Testament. Order means reason, conscious mind, or personal will. God's immanence in Nature is seen in the order and the purpose which animates Nature.

This account of the origin of things does not make the work of creation an event in time or history. It is as much a development of infinite thought, as though it had no beginning in time. Both Geology and Asteonomy, however, show to demonstration that Cosmos, as we now see it ordered and regulated, had a beginning, and a development or evolution from imperfect to perfect, and from simple to complex orders of beings. In this latter view, the important point for us to note is not the question of time but of causation. If causation is seen to be at work in infinite time and space, it is a sufficient explanation for the purposes of practical certitude.

There can be no natural agents in the proper sense of the word. Matter is in its essence inert and the so-called agents are only signs by which the divine reality regulates the purposes of law and order, beauty and benevolence, power and wisdom. This divine activity is what is signified by the phrase, 'God immanent in Nature.' These activities are interpretable by man and become trust-worthy, because they are His activities and not mere casual combinations and permutations of lawless and purposeless chance. Material agents are like the telegraph wire through which messages are sent across time and space, and deciphered by man, whether they are messages of science or of religion. An interpretable universe brings man face to face with God as the ever acting immanent cause of all natural changes, and the spirit which animates and regulates the world.

Just as Nature is supernatural in this view, Man has also a super-human element in him. The distinguishing features in man are his self-conscious reason and his volition which is free to act or not to act within certain well, defined limits. Free volition can hardly be said to be present in brute creation. They are solely guided by their instincts and impulses, and are not in the strict sense of the word responsible for their actions (Man alone possesses a sort of delegated freedom to choose between right and wrong, between good and evil. He alone has the power of self-determination and of being a causal agent. There distinguishing features constitute his highest glory and his greatest responsibility. They furnish the bases of all law and government, morals and manners, social and family arrangements, literary and scientific culture, and finally of religion and worship. He is not a mere creature of necessity, not a mere diagonal result of opposite forces acting upon him, as is the rest of the world including even the brute creation. Man thus occupies a higher plane of being and the question arises how this higher existence is subordinated to the over-ruling Providence which regulates the universe including man a physical being. In man's case his spiritual relations with thus universal Soul are made manifest by the sense of conscience in him, which makes him feel that he is responsible for the proper exercise of his delegated freedom. He feels that the spirit immanent in the universe about him manifests His presence in him through this faculty of conscience which accuses him when he goes wrong, and helps and guides him when he is on the right path. The bitter remose he feels when he demeans himself, and the sense of satisfaction which rewards him when he does his duty, are the connecting links between his soul and the spirit he realises as the Soul of his soul. It is this communion which opens to him the gates of another and higher world where love and justice reign supreme. Intelligent, self-originated volition under obligation of duty and sense of personal responsibility, this is in the case of man the divine; that is the super-human and super-natural element in him. This ethical and personal conception of man's relation with the universal Soul is a higher revelation than what nature discloses, and this is the realm where faith and knowledge becomes faith which elevates man from mortal into immortal existence. Though we cannot know all that we might wish to know about these mysteries, these revelations of Man and Nature teach us that the deepest and truest thought man can have about the outside world is that it is the immediate manifestation of the divine or Infinite person in moral relations to imperfect persons who are undergoing intellectual and spiritual elevation in divine surroundings. At the same time God is not to be conceived of as merely man made infinite, in his qualities and without his imperfection. This was the error of Buddhism which elevated the wise man above the old mythological Gods and even displaced the spirit from the universe. This is the form of idolatry against which all religions have raised their protests, and in none more emphatically than in the Aryan system of Faith. The Upanishads have said that 'He who thinketh that he knoweth God doth not know Him, while he who thinks that he doth not know Him knoweth Him. From Him the speech of man recoileth in despair how to describe Him. The mind of man cannot grasp it. Only through faith, hope and love can He be approached'.

This is the teaching of Theism. It has to be supplemented by further revelations of God in history which form the basis of all historical religions and religious movements. Historical revelations of Theism must differ from one another according to the circumstances of the age and country in which they occurred. Their historical surroundings are, however, destinc d in course of time, to fade in importance as their work of national education is accomplished, and they converge together to supplement each other's work in the final goal which they are all intended to reach. Alone in all the countries of the world, India has had the privilege of witnessing this convergence of historical faiths actively at work without losing its own individual characteristics. With her, revelation has not ceased at any point of time. The stream has flowed and still continues to flow in the lives and teaching of every saint and prophet of this or of other lands. From the worship of the elements personified, Indian Theism, or as I have elsewhere called it, the Bhagavata Dharma, developed into the worship of the power which rules over the elements. This power then became clothed with ethical and moral grandeur, banishing the old gods and elements into a lower order of beings and Devatas, Deities. The capacities of the human soul next attracted attention, and in the Upanishads the divine nature of the soul was first formulated and carried up even to the point of identity. Then came the Buddhists who strengthened the moral side of our nature, and substituted for the old animal sacrifices the sacrifice of the animal in man, as the highest form of worship and the only road to salvation. Next followed the aggressive domination of the Mahomedan faith which had its own purpose in enforcing the claims, of strict Monotheism not only in intellectual apprehension but in practical conduct; and now Christian influences are at work. The power of organisation, active hatred of sin, and indignation against wrong-doing in place of resigned indifference, a correct sense of the dignity of man and woman, active philanthropy and a feeling of fraternity, freedom of thought and action, these are Christian virtues which have to be incorporated into the national Character, and this work is actively going on in all parts of the country. The Bhagavata Dharma has many points of contact and kinship with the Christian system of faith. The Supreme Spirit is apprehended in both as being the Ocean of life in which we live and move and have our being. The three persons of the Trinity have their more logical counterpart, in the One without a second, who is absolute existence, 'Sat'; the Logos, or the Word eternal is the 'Chit', and the third person, the Holy Comforter is 'Ananda', joy and peace, who inspires joy and peace in all. The Hindu ideal of the soul becoming one on emancipation with the universal spirit is materialized in the Christian mystery of transubstantiation. Both systems recognize incarnation, the difference being of one or many. In both sacrifice has played an important part. With these elements of kinship there are essential differences which cannot be overlooked. The characteristics of Indifan Theism, which have enabled it to maintain its identity, will cling to it through all times. They are first its non-historical character. It is associated with no particular saint or prophet, though it has room for reverence to all saints and prophest. It is not bound down to any particular revelation but is open to the best influences of all revelations. With it, revelation is a perpetual stream which never ceases to flow. Above all, Indian. Theism is built on the rock of the direct communion of the individual soul with the Soul of the Universe to which it is linked by the tie of faith, hope and love. India Theism does not limit its education of man to a single trial in this world. The modified law of 'Karma' which distinguishes it from fatalism, which connects the past with the present and future, is no where better realized than in this country, though it is much exaggerated in some of its over-logical conclusions. The national mind has been cast in a spiritual and religious mould, which does not allow it to sink into the worship of this world and its riches and power as the highest object of desire, but always looks upon the hereafter as its chief resting place. The Universe is not merely His handiwork, but He is the Soul, Who fills the universe and moves it. Lastly, Indian Theism teaches toleration to all, self-sacrifice, and the duty of Love, not only of man to man but to all animated beings. It was not, therefore, without reason that the Rev. Dr. Miller, in an eloquent address he gave at Madras, asked the Christians to bear in mind that God was at work in India long before any missionary, Catholic or Protestant, set his foot there, and that the Hindu system, amidst all its corruptions, contains elements of Divine Truth. The *Christian World* commenting upon this has observed that India will not give up all its moulds of thought at the bidding of British or Christian organisations, but it will draw into itself the divine life which these organisations enshrine.

Gentlemen, I hope you will excuse this last digression from the professed purpose of the present address. I have tried to present before you on parallel lines the substance of Professor Dr. Fraser's lectures which represent the latest phase of European thought, and illustrated it by references to our own ancient works. The parallelism is very suggestive, and I hope it will prove an incentive to some of you to follow up these studies. If that result is achieved, I shall consider myself amply rewarded.

HINDU PROTESTANISM*

Once more we meet on this platform to take steck of our gains and losses of year that is about to close. Many familiar faces that cheered us in our work and helped us with their sweet encouragement, have left us, and their vacant places have not yet been filled up in our hearts and memories. The sad reflection comes upon our minds as we recollect these losses, whether after all, this Theistic movement is, or is not destined, to out-live those who first founded it in our midst twenty-eight years ago, and if we were left upon our resources this feeling of dismay might overpower us with its heavy weight. The fact, however, is that the movement has struck its roots deep in the past, and its growth in the future may, therefore, safely be expected to embrace a longer period than is represented by the lives of the present generations of our leaders. During the last few years I have been trying to set forth from this platform, and in other place also, the past history of the origin and progress of what has been well described by our saints and prophets for two thousand years and more, as the Bhagavata Dharma, of which the present Samaja movement is only a faint reflection and a humble off-shoot. One of the essential features of the Bhagavata Dharma is its Protestant character. As among the Jews, prophet after prophet has risen among us, and in their lives and precepts have protested against and denounced certain habits of thought and principles of action which have an inveterate tendency to encrust the true spirit of our faith and to give a human coating which obscures from view the essentially divine element. Bhagavata Dharma may, therefore,be safely described as Protestant Hinduism, and I would be speak your favourable attention to-day to the chief feature of this long-continued protest, which has done such great service in the past and which is likely to do still greater service in the future. Our students are tolerably familiar with the fact that the searching of the spirit, and the cleansing of the heart which culminated in the growth of Protestantism in Western Europe were con-

*Anniversary Address at the Prarthana Mandira, Bombay, *1895*.

temporaneously working as powerful agent in this our own country, and with a similar beneficial result. The Christian leaders of modern thought protested against the supremacy of the Latin language as a vehicle of expression and thought in the schools and churches. They protested against the excess of the ascetic ideas of the monks of different orders and the necessity of priestly intervention in all rites and ceremonies. They protested against indulgences, and they protested against pilgrimages, fasts, confession and casuistry. They protested against the image-worship and relic-worship and pompous ceremonies, which did not tend to elevate the heart and the mind of man. They succeeded in their own time wonderfully not only by the direct of their action in their own communities but still more by their reflex effect on the Roman Catholic Church, which not only purified itself in the struggle and kept up its authority over a large part of Europe, but with renewed vigour, has again been able to raise its heant as the oldest and noblest representative of constituted authority in its struggle with emancipating reason. The need for protest was not over with the century which produced Luther and Calvin, Knox and Latimer. The established faith has always and everywhere a tendency to grow too rigid and authoritative, too mechanical and formal to retain the celestial fire pure and burning. The Puritans and the Covenanters of the seventeenth and the Wesleyans and Methodists of the last century are all valuable only as protests against the weakness and corruption of the es ablished order of things. I need not pursue this topic further here, as my main concern is to trace the growth of the Protestant movement in our own country. With a view to prevent misapprehensions I may at once state, for the information of my audience, that I have based my own history of this movement on the biographies of sainsts and prophets, not written by any one of us, but by writers such as Nabhaji, Uddhav-Chidghan, Priyadasa, and rendered familiar to us by Mahipati's great work written more than a century ago. Mahipati's collection makes us acquainted with the history of one hundred saints and prophets, out of which about fifty are from Maharashtra, and the rest from other parts of India. The saints and prophets, it may be noted, include about ten women, and as many Mahomedans, and the rest, about eighty, comprise about an equal number of Brahmins and non-Brahmins, and among these last are representative men of all castes and creeds : butchers, spinners and weavers, goldsmiths, barbers and mahars kings and farmers, bankers and soldiers. This is the most noteworthy feature of the lauders of the Protestant movement in India. No country in the world can present such a galaxy of pure and pious men born in humble circumstances, who struggled and strove for the cause, and won it not by their own strength, but by their humility. The genuinely natural character of the movement is attested by the fact that it spread to all classes and touched all hearts, both of men and women, and of Hindus and Mahomedans alike. There is always good reason for despondency and despair, so long as any movement is not so general in its character. This has been the weakness of the Samaja movement, both of our own and of the Arya and Brahma Samaja, that they have failed as yet to stir the heart of the nation, and their influence is only operative over a few souls brought up in a particular atmosphere. It is on this account that the study of this old history becomes to us a matter of paramount importance. These one hundred men immortalized by Nabhaji and Uddhav Priyads and Mahipati, cover a period of five or six hundred years, and even yet the stream has not been dried up altogether.

We have next to see what were the principal features of the potest that these men raised each in his own place and time, each in his own manner and method. Their struggles led to neither wars nor bloodshed nor persecutions, inquisitions, or banishments. They worked silently as God's spirit works in us, silently but surely. These men protested against the supremacy of the old Sanskrit language as a vehicle of learning, and they enriched, each in his own time, the stock of their vernacular treasures. The battle of the Vernacular against the Classics is not of our own time only. It is an old struggle. Pandits pounce upon Ekanath and Tukaram for daring to popularize the old so as to make it accessible to the meanest of the mean. The story of the drowning of

Ekanath's and of Tukaram's works at the bidding of the Pandits is well known. The same struggle was main tained by Ramdas against Weman and by Rasal against Namadev. The saints conquered in the end, and so far the growth of the vernacular in each province of India has been the measure of the geowth of the protestant element in that province. The protest was raised by these men against the tendency to exaggerate the importance of rites and ceremonies as helps to the growth of the religious spirit. Rites and ceremonies are after all symbols, and if their symbolical character is not vividly presented to the mind, they obscure the religious vision and usurp the place of the purity of heart and of true devotion for which they were intended to be auxiliaries only, and not masters. Nearly everyone of the saints worked for righteousness in this direction, and it would take too long if I were io enumerate the triumphs they achieved. Jesus protest against the Pharisees and Sadducees was reproduced in the lives of every one of these men in their struggles with orthodoxy and Brahminism. Their success in this department has not been equal to that which they achieved in breaking down the monopoly of Sanskrit learning, but anybody who can read our Smritis and religious ordinances and compare their strictness with our present customs and practices, can alone measure the greatness of the work already achieved. The third protest raised by these saints was against the hold of the Yoga system of austerities and the supposed powers it conferred on the Yogi of performing wonders. In this direction the success is almost complete. Our countrymen have learned to discern the vanity to their foolish attempts to strive after occult power, which even, when possessed in full, means no real gain. The contrast exhibited in the lives of Dnyanadev and Changadev, and of Dnyanadev himself and Namadev, typifies this feature of the protestant movement with reamarkable accuracy, and leaves nothing to be desired. The fourth feature of the movement was directed against the relaxation of the strictness of caste rules and distinctions. The inclusion of mahars and barbers, cobblers and hutchers, the inclusion of women and Mahomedans among the saints, represented an enlargement of view to which you will scarcely find a parallel elsewhere. The lives of Ekanath and Kabir, Ramdas and Tukaram, typified the highest efforts of true religion in this direction. The success here is not so permanent and assured as in other respects, but still much ground has been gained. The next protest was raised against cruelty and impurity, against animal and human sacrifices, against the worship at cruel deities and the performance of Shakta rites. The success hereis complete. The next ground of protest was equally strong against Polytheism though not against idolatry, except in the advanced sects of Nanak and Kabir. The saints were practically worshippere of one God, and their efforts not to admit a multiplicity of rival gods was heroic. The protest was equally loud in favour of proclaiming that God was a loving God, and that his spiritual Providence cared for the meanest of His creatures wtih more than a mother's and father's love. This sense of a loving God who spoke to and walked with, and comforted the worshippers, that sense is our richest treasure, though the stories told of this inter-communion with men have been often of a very grotesque character. These then are the points in which Indian Protestantism has done us service, and if we are true to our great ancestors, this is the work and these are the lines on which we should carry on the struggle. Coming in contact with Mahomedans, the Hindu Protestant Saints made converts of thoughtful Mahomedans by making concessions which implied an unity of Providence, whether it was called Rama or Rahim. We have come in contact with Christianity and we have our own concessions to make. But, whatever we give in or take from our surroundings, one thing we must never forget—that it is not a movement started by a few English educated natives, and that its founder was this or that man in Bengal or the Punjab. The movement is older than Modern India, and it is not confined to the English educated classes in the towns. Its roots lie deep in our history and we must study it there all along the line if we want to understand how we really stand, and whither we have to go. Authority in matters of faith is as essential as authority in matters of secular happiness. Authority is not a creation of the imagination. We cannot create the same which teaches us to bow to noble and good men of the past, and we cannot dispense with their help. We must seek them as our guides. Our domestic guides are in such matters to be preferred to foreign guides, because these last have not been the flesh of our flesh, and the bone of our bone. If we would bear that in mind and work the movement on the lines of the Bhagavata Dharma in the times to come, success is sure, because it is His work, and He will carry it through by the hands of poor med, if only we swear fealty to Him and hold by Him through good and bad report.

THE SAINTS AND PROPHETS OF MAHARASHTRA

We propose in this chapter to trace in rough outline the history of this religious upheaval in Western India. Our main sources of information will be the voluminous biographies of the saints and prophets of Maharashtra, written by one of our own poets, Mahipati, towards the close of the last century, long before British influence was felt in these parts as a factor of any importance. Like the political struggle for independence, the religious upheaval was also not the work of a single man, or even of a single century. Its early commencement can be traced even anterior to the Mahomedan conquest of the Deccan. Under the rule of the Yadav Kings of Devagiri, Dnyandev, the first saint and prophet of Maharashtra, wrote his famous commentary on the *Bhagavad Gita* in the spoken language of the country. Mukundraj, who lived under the Ballal Kings, also wrote his famous work, the first of the kind in Marathi, in the twelfth century. The Mahomedan invasions for a time seem to have paralysed all activity, but gradually the national spirit regained its healthy elasticity and just about the time of the rise of the Maratha power we had a galaxy of saints and prophets, whose names have become household words with the people of the country. The stream continued to flow in full tide for two centuries, and then it appears to have dried up, and with its ebb, the political domination also became a thing of the past. Roughly speaking we may state that the history of this religious revival covers a period of nearly five hundred years, and during this period some fifty saints and prophets flourished in this land, who left their mark upon the country and its people so indelibly as to justify Mahipati in including them in his biographical sketches. A few of these saints were women, a few were Mahomedan converts to Hinduism, nearly half of them were Brahmins, while there were representatives in the other half from among all the other castes; Marathas, *Kunbis*, tailors, gardeners, potters, goldsmiths, repentant prostitutes, and slave girls, even the outcaste *Mahars*. Much of the interest of this religious upheaval is centred in the facts we have noticed above, as they indicate plainly that the influence of higher spirituality was not confined to this or that class, but permeated deep through all strata of society, male and female, high and low, literate and illiterate, Hindu and Mahomedan alike. These are features which the religious history of few other countries can match or reproduce, unless where the elevating influence is the result of a widespread popular awakening. In Northern and Eastern India a similar movement manifested itself much about the same time. Nanak stirred up the Punjab to rise and made a supreme effort to reconcile Hinduism with Mahomedanism. Chaitanya in the far Fast sought to bring men back from the worship of *Shakti* and *Kali* to the faith of the *Bhagavat*; while Ramanand and Kabir, Tulsidas and Surdas, Jayadev and Rohidas, contributed each in his own way to the work of spiritual enlightenment. Their influence has no doubt been great and abiding, but it cannot be compared with the work done by the saints and prophets of Maharashtra. The names of Changdev and Dnyandev, Nivritti and Sopan, Muktabai and Jani, Akabai and Venubai Namdev and Ekanath, Ramdas and Tukaram. Shaik Mahomed and Shanti Bahamani, Damaji and Udhav, Bhanudas and Rurmdas, Bodhle Bava and Santoba Powar, Keshav Swami and Jayaram Swami, Narasimha Saraswati and Ranganath Swami, Chokhamela and the two potters, Narahari Sonar and Savatia Mali, Bahiram Bhat and Ganesh Nath, Janardanpat and Malopant, and many others that might be cited, furnish an array which testifies to the superior efficacy of this movement in Maharashtra. The Brahmins in these parts furnished a much larger proportion of saints and prophets than was the case in any of the other parts in India where the *Kashatriya* and *Vaisya* castes furnished a much larger contingent than the Brahmins.

As is the case with all biographies of saints, the popular imagination attributes to these persons wonderful and miraculous powers, notably those of raising the dead to life, healing the sick and feeding the hungry. The stories which are told of the way in which they were helped by supernatural agency in their mission of love may or may not be accepted in these days of vigilant criticism. As Mr. Lecky has remarked, it is the atmosphere of childlike credulity which pre-disposes men to require and accept these wonders and miracles as events of ordinary occurrence. The saints and prophets themselves did not claim miraculous powers. They were meek and suffering men who placed their trust in Providence, and their trust was justified beyond their expectations, often times to their own surprise. The moral interest of these biographies centres however, not in their miraculous feats, but in their struggles, and in the testimony their lives afforded in vindication of the eternal verities of the moral law and man's higher spiritual life. It is with this aspect of their life that we are more immediately concerned in the sequel, and we hope to show that in this respect the work they accomplished was priceless and blessed beyond all comparison.

There is a curious parallel between the history of the Reformation movement in Western Europe and the struggle represented by the lives and teachings and writings of these saints and prophets who flourished about the same time in Maharashtra. The European reformers of the sixteenth century protested strongly against the authority claimed by the priests and the clergy with the Roman Bishop at their head. The clergy and the Pope represented a tradition of authority which had come down from the remote past, and had done signal service in its own time in humanising and civilising the hordes of the barbarian conquerors who devastated the Roman provinces. In course of time, the priests, instead of being the servants, claimed to be masters and rulers, with temporal and spiritual powers, and intermediaries between God and man. The exercise of this intercession was hedged round by numberless rites and ceremonies, and in course of time many abuses crept in and alienated general sympathy. These abuses assumed their worst forms about the time that Luther rebelled against the authority which issued indulgences and levied Peter's Pence, not as charity, but as a tax to subserve the temporal power of intriguing Popes and their vicious Cardinals. The Reformation in Western India had its counterpart in this respect. Ancient authority and tradition had been petrified here, not in an ambitious Bishop and his clergy, but in the monopoly of the Brahman caste, and it was against the exclusive spirit of this caste domination that the saints and prophets struggled most manfully to protest. They asserted the dignity of the human soul as residing in it quite independently of the accidents of its birth and social rank. The circumstances of their own birth and education naturally predisposed some of these preachers to take up such a position. As observed above, nearly half of them were of castes other than Brahmins, and some of them of very low castes indeed. Many of the Brahmin reformers also had some stain in their inherited purity which led or forced them to rebel against all artificial restraints. Dnyandev and his brothers and sister Muktabai were born to their father after he had retired from the world and became a Sanyasi. His spiritual guide, Ramanand, came to know that this Sanyasi had not obtained his wife's willing consent to a change of Ashram and he ordered him to go back to his native place and live with his wife. The children so born to the *Sanyasi* became marked objects of caste aversion, and the Brahmins refused to perform the Initiation ceremony when the brothers reached the proper age. The children remained in this unrecognised condition all their life, and were revered notwithstanding this defect in their caste respectability. Another saint, Malopant, was married to a low-caste girl, whose caste was not discovered till after the marriage, and the husband did not abandon her, but only held no intercourse with her, and when on her death, he performed her death-rites as usual, a miracle was displayed which satisfied his worst enemies, that Malopant and his *Mahar* wife were both holy by nature. Jayaram Swami's master, Krishnadas, was similarly married to a barber girl, and the inferiority of her caste was discovered after marriage. The holy life of the man had, however, such an effect that at last, after much persecution, even the high priest Shankaracharya of the day raised no objection. Ekanath, it is well-known, made no secret of the little importance he attached to caste distinctions. He fed a hungry *Mahar* at his house, and, when out-casted, allowed himself to be taken to the river for purposes of purification, when a miracle took place by which the merit of feeding a hungry *Mahar* was proved to be far greater than that of feeding many hundred Brahmins, for the former merit cured a teper of his foul disease, when the latter failed to make any impression on him. A very common miracle is reported to have been performed by many of the saints, notably by Dnyandev, Ekanath, and Naganath, when, on the refusal of the Brahmins to officiate on *Shraddha* ceremonies in their places for breach of caste regulations, the deceased fathers of the obstinate Brahmins were made to descend to earth, and shamed their incredulous sons into the belief that their caste exclusiveness was wholly out of place. In Namdev's biography, his God of Pandharpur, who had allowed Namdev to invite Brahmins to a feast and himself partook of that feast with the saint, was himself excommunicated, and then the story relates how Dnyandev, who was present in spirit, remonstrated with the Brahmin persecutor.

He said:—There was none high or low with God. All were alike to him. Never entertain the thought that I am high born, and my neighbour is low of birth. The Ganges is not polluted, nor is the wind tainted, nor the earth rendered untouchable, because the low born and high born bathe in the one, or breathe the other, or move on the lack of the third.

The most touching incident, however, is that which occured in the persecution of the out-caste *Mahar* Chokhamela for his having dared to enter the temple of Pandharpur. When remonstrated with for his temerity, Chokhamela replied that his God took him inside by force, and he did not go of his own accord. He remonstrated with the Brahmin worshippers of the temple in this strain—What availeth birth in high caste, what availeth rites or learning, if there is no devotion, or faith? Though a man be of low caste yet if he is faithful in heart, and loves God, and regards all creatures as though they were . . . himself, and makes no distinction between his own and other peoples' children, and speaks the truth, his caste is pure, and God is pleased with him. Never ask a man's caste when he has in his heart faith in God, and love of men. God wants in his children love and devotion, and he does not care for his caste. The Brahmins, as might be expected, were not converted by this preaching of high wisdom, and they complained to the Musalman officer of the place, and he like another Pilate of the Bible story, ordered Chokhamela to be punished by being tied to and driven by a team of bullocks, and tortured to death in this cruel fashion. God, however, miraculously delivered his worshipper, and baffled the oppressors, for the bullocks would not move from their place. The story of Bahiram Bhat is also interesting in this connection. Being a *Shastri,* he did not find rest in Brahminism, and therefore became a Mahomedan under the impression that its monotheism would satisfy the cravings of his heart, but failing to find the satisfaction he desired, he returned back to Brahminism. Both Brahmins and Mahomedans found fault with him for these changes of faith, but he disclaimed being either Hindu or Mahomedan. Bahiram Bhat challenged the Brahmins to make him a true Brahmin as long as his circumcision mark was not removed, and he challenged the Mahomedans to fill up the holes in his ears, which showed that he was still a Hindu. The Mahomedan converts to Hinduism, represented by Shaik Mahomed's followers even to this day observe the *Ramzan* fasts and the *Ekadasi* fast, and make pilgrimages to Mecca as also to Pandharpur. There are many other saints of great renown who, like Kabir, Nanak and Manik Prabhu, are claimed both by Hindus and Mahomedans as belonging to their respective communities, and worshipped and reverenced as such by both. These examples will suffice to show how the lives of these men have tended to elevate the national conception of man's spiritual nature, and shake the hold of caste intolerance.

The result of all this elevated teaching is seen in the fact that caste exclusiveness now finds no place in the religious sphere of life, and it is relegated solely to the social concerns of men, and even there its restrictiveness is much relaxed. The relaxation is most accentuated at the time of the annual Pandharpur pilgrim gatherings, and the mixed greetings with which the Lord's Feast is celebrated on the last day. Just as in Europe, men ceased to believe that the priest was a necessary medium between God and man for purposes of salvation, in this part of India, the domination of the Brahmin caste as the gods of creation, whom the other castes should serve and worship, lost much of its potency, and men and women, high and low, came to feel that they were free to attain salvation by faith and love in spite of their low origin.

There was a counterpart of the European protest in the way in which our saints and prophets raised their voice against self-mortification and fasts, and meaningless penances and endless pilgrimages. The same spirit prompted them to condemn austerities practised by those who followed the *Yoga* system with a view of acquiring the power of woking wonders which, it was supposed, the *Yogis* enjoyed in consequence. This contest between *Yoga* and *Bhakti* is well illustrated by the encounter of the proud Changadev with Dnyandev, when the former, in reliance on his *Yoga* powers rode on tigers, and used serpent whips and was put to shame by Dnyandev riding on a wall. There was a similar encounter between Dnyandev and Namdev, when the former, by the exercise of *Yoga* powers, became small in size, and drank the waters of a deep well, while Namdev, by his devotion, brought the waters to overflow the well for all time, so that all who passed by, and felt thirsty, might drink to their hearts, content. These stories most beautifully typify this feature of the teaching of the saints and prophets of Maharashtra.

The story of Kanoba Pathak, who was unbraided by a

Brahman of Benares for his incordinate love of children, and astonished his critic by throwing away his child into a well with seeming indifference, illustrates the vanity of the vows of celibacy, which cannot by themselves produce equableness of mind, and indifference to pains and pleasures. Ekanath all his life lived with his wife and children, and so did Tukaram and Namdev, though they were not blessed with sympathetic female relations. Bodhale Bawa, Chokhamela, Damajipant, Bhanudas, the two potter saints, and many others lived in the midst of their families. Dnyandev's father who had become *Sanyasi* without obtaining the free consent of his wife, was directed by Ramanand to return to his home, and live with his wife. All these incidents prove that a very high conception of the sanctity of family-life was realised by these saints and prophets, and they did their best to correct the national weakness which shrinks from trouble and anxiety by retiring from the world's conflit. The lives of the female saints have a special interest in this connection. The biographies relate that, owing to their devotion and implicit faith, God helped them out of their difficulties by assisting them in their daily household work, and, by assuming strange disguises, permitted them the freedom they wanted in order to serve Him without being missed by their jealous relations. There is a danger in all such stories of making providential intervention too cheap, but this fault is more than balanced by the high moral which underlies these accounts. The sanctity of married and family life was nobly vindicated by these saints and prophets, and this was a signal moral triumph over the past traditions of asceticism.

All students of modern European history are aware that the Reformers achieved their most permanent success in the liberation of the national intellect from the thraldom of scholastic learning, and the oppressive preponderance of the classical Latin in which all the best books were till then written. The Bible was, by the help of these Reformers, for the first time made accessible to all, high and low, and the monopoly of learning, till then enjoyed by the priests, was shaken to its foundations. Here, in India, the process of liberation was carried out on the same lines. The professors of the old Sanskrit learning found for the first time, to their great surprise, that the saints and prophets addressed the people, both in speech and writing, in their own vernacular, and boldly opened the hitherto hidden treasures to all and sundry, men and women, Brahmans and Shudras, alike. The final victory was not achieved without much struggle and considerable suffering. Dnyandev was the first adventurer to stray into these forbidden regions, and his example was followed by Ekanath and Ramdas, Namdev and Tukaram, Vaman Pandit and Mukteshwar, Shridhar and Malopant. These last four gifted men are more celebrated as authors and poets than as religious teachers, but they derived their inspiration from the same sources. It is true the *Vedas* and the *Shastras* were not translated as the Bible was, but there was a sufficient reason for this difference. These early Marathi writers knew that modern India, after the Buddhistic revolution was less influenced by the *Vedas* and *Shastras* than by the *Ramayana* and *Mahabharat*, the *Bhagavata Purana* and the *Gita*, and these latter works were translated and made accessible to all. The pioneers in this field, Ekanath and Tukaram, were each made to bear the brunt of Brahmin opposition. Their works were not burned as in Europe, but they were ordered to be thrown into water. The river gods, however, so the story runs, would not let them be destroyed, and the works remained dry and would not sink, and thus became more famous than ever. Vaman Pandit, the great Sanskrit scholar, who would not deign to speak or write in the popular language, as being unfit to be used by a Pandit, was, when brought in contact with Ramdas, made to see the error of his ways; and a Brahmin translator of the Ramayana, named Salya Rasal, who was over-proud of his superior learning, was similarly put to shame by a message from his goddess that he should get the work corrected by submitting it to the revision of the tailor Namdev. Dnyandev also was made the instrument of performing a miracle, by which a buffalo was said to have recited the *Vedas* by heart. This story is obviously an allegorical parody of the mental condition of those who prided themselves upto their ability to recite the *Vedas* without understanding their contents.

The struggle between the claims of the Classical Sanskrit and the Vernaculars, of which we hear so much in these days, is thus an old conflict, the issues in which were decided in favour of the Vernacular or living languages long ago, and whatever scholars and antiquarians may urge to the contrary, there can only be one answer to the question,—the answer which was given by the saints and prophets when they laid Sanskrit aside as useless for their work, and spent all their energies in the cultivation and growth of their mother tongue. It may safely be said that the growth of the modern vernaculars in India is solely the result of the labours of these saints, and that the Provinces which showed most decided tendencies in the way of reform, also showed the most healthy development of their Vernacular literature.

The Protestant reformers in Europe achieved another change of great importance in the way in which they raised their voice against the excesses to which imageworship and saint-worship were carried in the Roman Catholic Church. On our side, also, this protest was raised, but it did not assume the iconoclastic form which the Protestant reformers, especially the stricter sect among them, adopted. Polytheistic worship was condemned both in theory and in practice by the saints and prophets of Maharashtra. Each of them had his own favourite form of the divine incarnation, and this worship of one favourite form left no room for allegiance to other gods. Ramdas, for instance, worshipped God under the name of Rama; Ekanath and Jayaram Swami worshipped Him under the name of Krishna, Tukaram, Chokhamela and Namdev under the name of Vithoba; Narahari Sonar and Naganath under the name of Shiva : Janardhan Swami and Narasimha Saraswati under the name of Dattatraya : Morya Gosavi and Ganeshanath under the name of Ganpati, and so on for the rest. Strange stories are told in these biographics of the way in which the saints, when they visited other shrines, refused to see the image in the form in which they did not worship God, and, as a consequence, the image manifested itself to them in the form familiar to them. The supremacy of one God, One without a second, was the first article of the creed with every one of these saints, which they would not allow anybody to question or challenge. At the same time, as observed above, the iconoclastic sprit was never characteristic of this country, and all the various forms in which God was worshipped were believed to merge finally into one Supreme Providence of *Bramha*. This tendency to the national mind was a very old tendency. Even in Vedic times, Indra and Varuna, Marut and Rudra, while they were separately invoked at the sacrifices offered for their acceptance, were all regarded as interchangeable forms of the One and supreme Lord of Creation. This same tendency explains the comprative indifference with which the saints and praphets treated the question of mage-worship. It is a complete misunderstanding of their thoughts and ideas on this subject when it is represented that these gifted people were idolaters in the objectionable sense of the word. They did not worship stocks and stones. In Vedic times there was admittedly no idol or image worship. It came into vogue with the acceptance of the incarnatian theory, and was stimulated by the worship of the Jains and Buddhists of their saints. Finally, it got mixed up with the fetish worship of the aboriginal tribes, who were received into the Aryan foldand their gods were turned into incarnations of the Aryan deities. The saints and prophets, however, rose high above these grovelling conceptions prevalent amongst the people. Idol worship was denounced when the image did not represent the Supreme God. Both Tukaram and Ramdas have spared no words in denouncing these aboriginal and village'gods, and their frightful rites and sacrifices. In the life of Bhanudas it is stated that he told the King of Vijayanagar that the Goddess he worshipped served his God at Pandharpur in a menial capacity as a sweeper, and the king found it to be the truth when he visited Pandharpur. In the lives of two other saints it is stated that the Goddess Kali, to whom human and animal sacrifices were offered, was so frightened by the protest of the saints in the name of Hari against such cruelty, that the sacrifices were given up by the command of the Goddess not only for time, but for all time. These illustrations will serve to show in what light image-worship, as an aid to devotion, was utilised by these saints, and unless this distinction is borne in mind, it will be impossible to understand the true position occupied by these teachers in this important matter.

These is one point, however, in which the reforming saints and prophets in this country differed essentially from those who were working in the same cause elsewhere, the contemporary protestant reformers in Europe. From the Vedic times downwards, the *Aryan* gods have been gods of Love and Brightness, of sweetness and of light. There were, of course, terrible gods also, such as Varuna and Rudra, who inspired awe and filled the mind with terror. But the national tendency was to dwell with affection on and contemplate chiefly the bright side of divine Providence, and was unlike the Semitic idea which dwelt upon the terrific manifestion of a distant God, whose glory could not be seen save through a cloud, a severe Chastiser of Human frailties, and a Judge who punished more frequently than He rewarded, and even when He rewarded, kept the worshipper always in awe and trembling. This conception lies at the root of all Semitic religions, and it is to the credit of Christianity that it attempted and partly succeded in bridging the gulf by securing the intervention of God incarnate in the flesh, as Jesus Christ, who suffered for mankind and atoned for their sins. This intervention was never found necessary in the *Aryan* religions of Greece or Rome, or of India. God, with us, has always been regarded more as a father and a mother, a brother and a friend, than a judge and a chastiser and a ruler. Not that He does not judge, or rule; but He judges, reles, and chastises with the love of a father or a mother, ever ready to receive the repentant prodigal son back into his arms. The orthodox Brahminical conception does not bring out this feature of kindly Providence so prominently as it is found to be realised in the teachings and life experiences of our saints and prophets. They are emphatic in their assertions that they were able to see their God, and hear His words, and walked and talked with Him, and held intercourse with Him. In their higher moments they, no doubt, describe Him as One who did not speak, but their most normal condition of mind was one of satisfaction when they realised His presence as we realise the presence of sensible things. The *Yogis* and the *Vedantis* only talk in their waking dreams of being one with God, but Namdev and Tukaram, Ekanath and Dnyandev, were not content with this distant and difficult union, which did not last during all the moments of their conscious life, and compared their own happiness in such daily intercourse with God as being above all the attainments of *Yoga* and *Vedanta*. We may believe the miracles ascribed to these saints or disbelieve them, but we cannot disbelieve their emphatic statements on this point. All the love that in Christian lands circles round the life and death of Christ Jesus has been, in India, freely poured upon the intense realization of the every-day presence of the Supreme God in the heart in a way more convincing than eyes, ears or the sense of touch can realise. This constitutes the glory of the saints, and it is a possession which is treasured up by our people, high and low, men and women, as a solace in life beyond all value.

As a consequence of this conception of God's relations with man, the supreme efficacy of devotional Love, *Bhakti*, over all other methods of attaining to His knowledge became the cardinal creed of these *Vaishnara* sects. There is not a life in all these sketches drawn by Mahipati in which *Bhakti* and Faith, *Bhawa*, are not emphasised as being far superior in virtue to all other forms of worship, such as the performance of rites and ceremonies of external worship, pilgrimages and ablutions, self-mortifications and fasts, learning and contemplation. These have relation only to the body or the mind while the Spirit is what God desires to see engaged in His service. The rites and ceremonies may be performed as indifferent matters, just as food may be taken and thirst quenched, and the rest of sleep enjoyed, as they come naturally without effort or unnecessary anxiety about them. The best ablution is when the senses are drowned in the ocean of God's presence about us, and the same presence is made to fill us inside and out. The best sacrifice and the highest *Dana* or gift is when we surrender ourselves to His sweet will and for His service, and claim nothing as our own. The best mortification is that which makes the spirit humble before Him, the best contemplation is when His glory is sung with all our powers. Neither knowledge nor *Yoga* powers. health nor wealth, nor children nor possessions, not even *Mukti*, freedom from birth and death, is desirable in itself. What is desirable is to be always full of love for Him and His works including all creation, men and animals. Namdev cried while removing the bark of a tree, because he thought ne saw blood coming out from the stroke of his axe, and he struck himself with the axe to see how he felt, and realised what the tree might feel. Shaik Mahomed, being sent by his father to practise the butcher's trade, first cut his own finger with his knife to see how the animal would feel, and the pain he felt drove him to forswear his trade, and retire from the world in which such pain had to be inflicted for earning one's livelihood. Tukaram felt that there must be something wrong about him, when, on seeing him, the sparrows left the field he was sent to watch, though he did not intead to disturb them. This intense spirituality and absolute surrender of Self may sound somewhat unreal to men not brought up in the atmosphere these saints breathed. But, there can be no doubt about the fact, and there can also be no doubt that the national ideal of spiritual excellence has been shaped by these models. It may be that a stronger backbone and more resisting power are needed in the times in which we live, but in an account of the saints and prophets as they flourished more than two hundred years ago, we cannot afford to interpolate our own wants and wishes.

It may be interesting to note how these saint, thought and spoke, and how, when they came in contact with a militant religion like Mahomedanism, they faced their troubles and conquered them. The lives of Namdev, Ramdas, Ekanath and others are full of such incidents. The most noteworthy fact in their connection is that several Mahomedans became converts to the Hindu faith, and obtained such a public recognition that their help was invoked by the Hindu authors who wrote in those times, along with the Hindu saints. Shaik Mahomed and Kabir may be cited as examples of thin catholic spirit of recognition. On the other hand, Tukaram and

Ekanath were so infioenced by their contact with Mahomedanism that they composed verses in Urdu of so catholic a character as to be unobjectionable to the strictest Mahomedan Ramdas did the same when one of his disciples, Udhav, god into . . . at Bedar. The story of Damajipant, a servant of the Bedar Kings, is well known to all. In a time of famine he distributed the Government stores of grain among the poor and on being taken to task he was relieved by an unexpected remittance of the full value of the grain to the King's treasury. The saints came out well in their struggles with their foreign rulers and they prevailed not by fighting nor by resistance, but by resignation to the Will of God. There was a tendency perceptible towards a reconciliation of the two races in mutual recogninion of the essential unity of Allah with Rama, and by the time Shivaji appeared on the scene, this reconciliation seems to have becn almost complete, though occasional outbursts of Mahomedan fanaticism were not altogether unknown even then.

We have thus noticed all the principal features of the religious movement, which, commencing with Dnyandev who lived in the fifteenth century, can be traced to the end of the last century as a steady growth in spiritual virtues. It gave us a literature of considerable value in the Vernacular language of the country. It modified the strictness of the old spirit of caste exclusiveness. It raised the *Shudra* classes to a position of spiritual power and social importance almost equal to that of the Brahmins. It gave sanctity to the family relations and raised the status of woman. It made the nation more humane and at the same time, more prone to hold together by mutual toleration. It suggested and partly carried out a plan of reconciliation with the Mahomedans. It subordinated the importance of rites and ceremonies, and of pilgrimage and fasts, and of learning and contemplation, to the higher excellence of worship by means of Love and Faith. It checked the excesses of polytheism. It tended in all these ways to raise the nation generally to a higher level of capacity both of thought and action, and prepared it in a way in which no other nation in India was prepared to take the lead in re-establishing a united native power in the place of foreign domination. These appear to us to be the principal features of the religion of Maharashtra, which Saint Ramdas had in view when he advised Shivaji's son to follow in his father's footsteps, and propagate this Faith, at once tolerant and catholic, deeply spiritual and yet not iconoclastic.

VASHISTHA AND VISHVAMITRA*

About this time last year I had occasion, at the inauguration of the Conference held at Lucknow, to dilate on a text of Nanaka, in which he proclaimed himself to be 'Neither a Hindu nor a Mahomedan.' To-day, I find you have come together in the extreme North-West corner of India, in the land of the Five Rivers, the original home of the Aryan settlers who composed the Vedic hymns and performed the great sacrifices. You have met to-day in the land of the Rishis, where Vashistha and Vishvamitra lived and flourished at a time when the caste institution had not taken its root in our Indian soil, when men and women enjoyed freedom and equality, asceticism had not overshadowed the land, and life and its sweets were enjoyed in a spirit of joyous satisfaction. The Punjab, during its eventful history, has well deserved the compliment that it is the land of the Rishis. The question, then, naturally arises, who were these Rishis ? What was the condition of society when they lived ? What thoughts stirred them; and what actions ennobled their lives and their struggles? For most of us, long habit has rendered it impossible to imagine a state of society where men were not split up into petty divisions of caste, with its artificial barriers, limiting men's activities and narrowing their sympathies. It is a revelation to many of us to be taken back to two or three thousand years ago; to a state of society when class divisions, such as Brahmins and Kshatriyas, Vaisyas and sudras, were unknown, or not well established, and the only distinction

Note: This Essay has been extracted from Ranade's History of the Rise of Mahratta Power.

* Inaugural Address, Lahore Conference, 1900.

recognized in practice was between the Aryans and non-Aryans. To illustrate the gulf which separates our own times from the days when the Rishis flourished, we need only mention the fact that Lopamudra, the daughter of the king of Vidarbha was given in marriage to Agastya. Another Raja, by name Lomapada gave his daughter Shanta in marriage to one Rishya-Shringa. The King Trinabindu also thus gave his daughter Gou to Pulasti, and Bhagiratha gave his daughter Hamsi to Koutsa Rishi. The King Sharyati's daughter Sukanya was given in marriage to Chyavana Rishi. Instances where the Brahmins gave their daughters in marriage to kings were also not uncommon. Thus Shukracharya's daughter Devayani, was given in marriage to Yayati and Shukracharya's daughter Kritwi to Anuha. Independently of marriage alliances, stories are told where Rishis, who were born in royal houses, or where Rajarishis, became by their sanctity and devotion, entitled to be called Brahmarishis. One Priyamedha was elevated, and Shini, Gargya, and Trayaruni were also so promoted to the status of Brahmarishis, and their progeny to that of Brahmins. Also Mudgala and Gritsamada, who were before kings, became thus Brahmins. The Brahmins, on their side, felt no scruple in learning the Dhanurveda or archery; Agastya Muni, as is well known, was skilled in Dhanurveda, and conquered the non-Aryan King Ilvala, and the Kalakeyas, who were pirates on the sea-coast. Agniveshya was also noted for his skill in archery, and he was the teacher of Dronacharya himself a great Brahmin commander in the wars of the Mahabharata. His son Ashwathama, and his brother-in-law Kripa were similarly renowned. Instances where Brahmins caused the ruin of the day by their curses are, no doubt, more frequent than those where kings cursed the Brahmins and brought about their ruin. As illustration of the first class, we may mention stories about King Nahusha and Vena Raja Nahusha, as is well known, had by reason of his superior merits become the occupant of Indra's throne, but he made the Brahmins carry him in a palanquin, and Agastya Muni resented the ill-treatment and cursed him, which led to his downfall. King Vena was similarly dethroned. Similarly, Vashistha's curse against Sahsrarjuna enabled Parashurama to lop off his numerous hands. Vashistha is also mentioned as having cursed Raja Kalmashapada, and Raja Trisanku became Chandala in consequence of the curse. On the other hand, Vashistha himself did not escape unharmed. There is, besides, the story of Ambarisha, who was persecuted by Durvasa, and in the result Durvasa had to entreat Ambarisha to grant him pardon and withdraw the Sudharshana which perpetually followed him and gave him no rest. As regards the women, numerous stories are told by their remaining unmarried throughout their lives, and of their engaging themselves in the pursuit of devotional exercises or in the study of philosophy. The story of Amba, who remained unmarried all her life, is well known. She wanted to marry with Shalva, but he would not take her and she would not accept the choice made by Bhishma for her. The daughter of Kunigarga also remained unmarried during life. Gargivachaknavi, Vadavapratitheyi and Sulabhamaitreyi—all these are historical names of women who passed their lives in celibacy and engaged in discussions on philosophic subjects in the court of Janaka.

Perhaps, the most instructive of these ancient stories is that which is connected with the rivalry of Vashistha and Vishvamitra. Both these names occur in the Vedic hymns, and though their rivalry is noticeable even in these early hymns, they furnish no authority for the legend which gathered round their names in the period which succeeded the composition of the hymns. Vashistha is a great exponent of Brahmin orthodoxy. The legends seek to make out that Vishvamitra was not by right a Brahmarishi. He was only a Rajarishi, and aspired to be a Brahmarishi. Vashistha would not support him in this ambition, and that accounted for their strife. Throughout the story Vishvamitra represents the view of those who try to admit the non-Aryans into the Aryan community and seek to elevate them. The story of Trisanku, for instance notwithstanding its exaggeration, has a moral of its own. Vashistha had without justice condemned Trisanku to be a Chandala simply because he aspired to go to heaven by the force of his merits. Vishvamitra took up his cause and performed the Yagnya, because Trisanku had saved his wife and children during a great famine. The result was that Trisanku was accepted in heaven notwithstanding the curse of Vashistha, the story of Suna-sepa, who was the son of a Brahmin, and was purchased as a sacrificial victim to be offered to Varuna in the place of the king's son, who was first promised, is also full of the same liberality on the past of Vishvamitra, who saved the Brahmin's life by his mediation. The result of the conflict between Vashistha and Vishvamitra was complete victory on the part of the latter, for Vashistha admitted Vishvamitra's claim to be a Brahmarishi. Vashistha's line was continued by his grandson, Parashara. Krishnadvaipayana, Vishampayana, Yagnyavalkya, Shukra Muni and Jaimini, all belonged to the orthodox side. Vishvamitra's family was connected by alliances with that of Bhrigu, Jamadagni and Parashara. The great Rishis who colonised Southern India were undoubtedly Agastya and Atri, who with their wives Lopamudra and Anasuya occupy a prominent place in the story of the Ramayana. King Rama stopped in their Ashram and Valmiki's description of these Ashrams presents a picture of these holy settlements which does not lose its charm even at the present day. These settlements were the pioneers of civilization in Southern India. There were similar establishments in other parts of India, on the borders of the civilized kingdoms. The Rishi, with his wife and his numerous pupils, kept herds of cows, cultivated the land, and founded colonies or cities, and helped the Rajas from the north to establish their power in the south. Jamadagni's story of the conflict with Kartavirya, and the subsequent wars between Parashurama and the sons of Kartavirya, no doubt, refer to such expasion of power. King Rama himself was helped by Agastya in the final struggle with King Ravana. Parashurama is said to have similarly carried on a war with the Rakshasas, which was put an end to by the mediation of Vashistha. The early Rishis were great both in peace and in war. In this respect the Rajarishis were as great as the Brahmarishis. Risabhadeva, for instance, had one hundred sons, of whom nine devoted themselves to meditation and philosophy and eighty-one followed the Karma-marga, and the remaining ten ruled over kingdoms. King Janaka was great as a sovereign ruler, and greater still as a saint. Vamadeva was noted for his piety, devotion and knowledge, which came to him in his mother's womb. The Brahmin Rishi Balaki was taught higher philosophy by Ajatasatru, the Raja of Kasi. It may be seen that there was no monopoly of learning in those early times and Rajas and Brahmins sat at the feet of each other to learn wisdom. There was, in fact, no permanent division of functions between the two orders and, therefore, they were somewhat like the temporal and spiritual lords we know of in England. They could interchange place, and did in fact, so interchange them in numerous instances.

This brief account of the time when the Rishis flourished in this country naturally leads to the inquiry as to how it was that in course of time Brahmin Rishis came practically to monopolize the title and deny it to the Rajas. The story of Vashistha and Vishvamitra furnishes some clue to a solution of this difficulty. The great names of Agastya and Atri, Vashistha and Jamadagni, Bhrigu and Bharadwaja, Parashara and Vamadeva, Vaishampayana and Yagnyavalkya, Valmiki and Vyasa, Kapila Muni and Shuka Muni, naturally carried influence with all classes of people. The Rajarishis were not much known for their authorship, and when these old families succumbed to foreign conquerors in the early period of the Christian era, the new Rajput, or Jat, conquerors had no hold on the popular mind, and the Brahmins retained or increased their hold on the affections of the people. The Puranic literature which had its birth about this time confirmed this superiority of the Brahmins, and the result was that the term Rishi came to be applied only to Brahmins, as being the only literary or cultured class of the time. Their predominance continued unchecked, except so far as the Vaishnava movement came to the relief of non-Brahmin classes. The Vaishnava movement has struck its deepest root in the Punjab, where the ten Gurus, from Nanak to Guru Gobind Singh, have effected a change the like of which no other part of India can exhibit. The Granth Sahib has taken the place of the old Vedas and Puranas, and the Gurus and their descendants occupy the place of the Brahmins. Since the establishment of the British rule new forces have been in operation, and the road is now again open by which the best men of all classes might aspire, as in the past, to be the true Rishis of the land. A movement which has been recently started in the Punjab may be accepted as a sign that you have begun to realise the full significance of the need of creating a class of teachers who may well be trusted to take the place of the Gurus of old. The chief point, however, that is to be considered in this connection is, who should be these Gurus of the future. It is with this view that I have endeavoured to place before you a brief account of the true Gurus of the past, namely, the Rishis who were both Brahmarishis and Rajarishis, only distinguished from one another by their individual inclinations and abilities. We must keep that ideal before us if we mean to prove ourselves the worthy descendants of our earliest ancestors. Of course, the teachings and the methods and the subjects taught in these days must be made to suit our new exigencies and environments, but the spirit animating the teaching must be the same as that which led the first settles to cross the Vindhya Range, and establish their colonies in the South. By reviving our ancient traditions in this matter we may hope in the near future to instil into the minds of our young generations lessons of devotion to learning, diversity of studies, and personal loyalty to the teacher without which no system of school or college education can ever bear any fruit. This, however, is not all. In addition to these lessons, our new teachers must know how to introduce their pupils to a correct appreciation of the forces which are at work in the wider world outside, and which, in spite of temporary checks or seeming reverses, represent all that is best in human efforts for the elevation and happiness of man. Our teachers must enable their pupils to realise the dignity of man as man, and to apply the necessary correctives to tendencies towards exclusiveness, which have grown in us with the growth of ages. They must see that our thoughts, our speech, our actions are inspired by a deep love of humanity, and that our conduct and our worship are freed, where necessary, from the bondage of custom and made to conform as far as possible, to the surer standard of our conscience. We must at the same time, be careful that this class of teachers does not form a new order of monks. Much good, I am free to admit, has been done in the past and is being done in these days, in this as well as other countries by those who take the vow of lifelong celibacy and who consecrate their lives to the service of man and the greater glory of our Maker. But it may be doubted how far such men are able to realize life in all its varied relations, and I think our best examples in this respect are furnished by Agastya with his wife Lopamudra, Atri with his wife Anasuya and Vashistha with his wife Arundathi, among the ancient Rishis, and, in our own times, by men like Dr. Bhandarkar on our side, Diwan Bahadur Raghunatha Rew in Madras, Maharshi Debendra Nath Tagore, the late Keshab Chander Sen, Babu Pratap Chandra Mazumdar and Pandit Shivanath Shastri in Bengal, and Lala Hansa Raj and Lala Munshi Ram in your own province. A race that can ensure a continuance of such teachers can, in my opinion, never fail, and with the teachings of such men to guide and instruct and inspire us, I for one, am confident that the time will be hastened when we may be vouchsafed a sight of the Promised Land.

RAJA RAMA MOHANA ROY

It has been arranged that after service this day, I should speak to you a few words about the life and teachings of Raja Rama Mohana Roy. All of you are aware that this day, the 27th of September, is the anniversary of his death. He died while he was on a visit to England; and his remains were buried there by loving friends. He died in 1833; we are in 1896. We are, therefore, cclebrating in this place on this occasion the sixty-third anniversary of the death of this great man. Among the orthodox community, this particular fortnight—the dark half of the month of *Bhadrapada*—is dedicated by a very ancient and a very useful custom to commemorate the death of our departed ancestors. Each man and woman tries during these fifteen days to remember the debt of gratitude he or she owes to those who gave them birth : and though in this Samaja this practice has no place and we may not follow the outward observances, the sense of filial love and duty, which moves thousands of people in all parts of the country to show their gratitude for the debt due to our ancestors—has a significance and a truth which we cannot afford to ignore. This is then the sixty-third anniversary of the death of a person who might well be called one of the fathers of the Brahma Church. I say one of the fathers, and advisedly. Because I hold, as I have said on many other occasions, that we, the members of the Brahma Samaja can claim a long ancestry, as old as any of the sects prevailing in the country. The Brahma movement was not first brought into existence in 1828; we are representatives of an old race; as old as the Bhagavat Gita and the Bhagavata Purana; much older still, as old as Narada, Prahlada, and Vasudeva and the nine sages who visited *Janaka*. From that time there is a continuity of *Sadhus* and saints down to the present day. Raja Rama Mohana Roy, as I said, was thus one of the fathers of the Brahma Church but he was neither the first nor the last. For even in these modern times we have had the founder of the Swami Narayana sect, Keshava Chandra Sen, and Pandit Dayananda Saraswati; which fact shows that the old fire, that animated those who have made this land the sacred birthplace of many religions and religious movements, has not been burnt out. Before, however, I come to speak about Raja Rama Mohana Roy's life and teachings some of you will be interested, I believe, if I draw your attention to the fact that while the anniversaries celebrated in the case of Gods and birthdays in the case of men are allowed to be buried and for the most part forgotten, we find that it is the anniversaries of the deaths of great men that are honoured all over the world. There must be some meaning in this custom so universally prevalent among Christians, Mahomedans, Parsis, Buddhists, and Hindus; it could not well have been a mere accident that, while the *Jayanties* of gods and incarnations are the days of their births, in the case of men we celebrate the time when they leave us. There is a very good and sufficient reason for this difference. No man, till death takes him away from the temptations of this world, can say to himself, nor can it be said of him by his friends, that the man's life's purpose has been accomplished. A Greek Philosopher was asked a similar question. He said, 'wait till that particular man dies before you sing any song about him.' The life that we lead here has a serious purpose; it is to be guided by discipline, and discipline is, as you know, always a hard master. Out of the hundreds of thousands who start in the race of life, those who reach the goal are but few. Temptations lie in the way, and the difficulties that we experience disable many of us, and it cannot safely be said till a man's death that his life's purpose has been accomplished or that his is a life worthy of the purpose for which he was sent into this world. That is the reason why in the case of men it is the anniversary of death that is commemorated by those who remain after him. No man can be called great who has not, to the last hour of his life, fulfilled the responsibility which greatness implies; and this brings us to the consideration of the question, what constitutes the greatness of the men we love to honour after their death. When we celebrate the anniversaries of our own ancestors, of our fathers and grandfathers, mothers and grandmothers, the question is not whether they are great or whether they are not great. To every one of us our fathers and mothers are always objects of reverence as the ancestors who gave us birth, and whatever may be their failings, the mere fact that they are persons to whom we owe all that we have, constitutes a debt of gratitude which we are bound to discharge by celebrating their memories at least once a year in a more solemn manner than we may be disposed to do on other occasions; but when we make a public commemoration of our great men, the question naturally arises: 'What is it that constitutes greatness in the sense in which you and I and everybody else understand the word? What is it that constitutes this greatness of character?' There are various views held on this subject. To such of you as are interested in this study. I would recommend a very careful perusal of some or the English authors, especially Carlyle on 'Heroes and Hero-Worship' or Emerson on 'Great or Representative Men.' These two books will place before you all that might be said on this question: 'What is it that makes a man great, so that we should be anxious to keep green his memory from year to years?' One view, that is Carlyle's view, is that sincerity of purpose and earnestness of conviction make a man great. Every one of us can feel that there is a good deal of truth in that observation. All of us are more or less acting parts in the theatre of this world. Every one of us, be he small or great, be he learned or unlearned, each of us has a small stage: on that he struts and strides, moves about and goes on, persuading others as he also persuades himself that he is not playing a part but that he is playing the reality. However, when he is shut up in his own chamber, when nobody sees him, then you find that every one of us is disposed to wonder and to laugh at the way in which he moved in this theatre. For the most of us there is no reality about it. Sincerity of purpose and earnestness of conviction certainly go a long way to make a great man's character. If we are wanting in one thing more than another it is in this sincerity and earnestness. In the case of great men, that is, men who are worthy of being so reckoned, you will find that this element of greatness is more or less found in a much larger measure than in the ordinary run of men and women who constitute human society. We may be sincere and earnest on occasions; but habitual sincerity of purpose and habitual earnestness of action are a gift, a possession, and a treasure that are denied to most of us. You may take up the life of any man whom the world classes as great; and you will find in a large number of such men this trait of character. Take the case of Luther. In his time there were more learned and even better men than himself, such as Erasmus and Melancthon, who were equally gifted and equally endowed. But what was wanting in them was the earnestness of conviction and sincerity of purpose which were found in Luther. We are all of us more or less speaking under constraint, moving under constraint; we know that there is no outside control over us, yet we make our own constraint; and we find that full freedom of movement is not left to us. That is not exactly what constitutes a great man. I will give you another instance of this trait of character in great men. There was a son of a Mahomedan butcher, aged ten or eleven. His father told him to follow his own trade. When, however, the knife was given him and he was told to use it in the way in which his father was using it, he said: 'I am not going to use this knife on this poor dumb animal, till I know how it feels when applied to the sentient parts of my own body, till I am satisfied on this head, I will not use the knife.' And so saying he used the knife on his own person first; and feeling that the pain was insufferable, he gave up that trade, he gave up the associations in which he was born, and left the world and retired and thus became the great Mahomedan-Hindu saint of Maharastra, Shaik Mahomed of Shrigonda. That is one of the traits of character which makes a man great. However, it is not mere sincerity and mere earnestness that go to make a man great. He must be original. He must have imagination which brings him into contact with the Infinite and the real. Such men are called geniuses. Things strike them in a way in which they do not strike us. We are so familiar with things that we can scarcely realise the inner spirit in them; somehow or other there is an obtuseness about us which prevents us from seeing things as they are. For instance, there is a story told of Dayananda Saraswati as regards the circumstances which led him to leave his home and become a *Sanyasi.* He was, as you know, a great man; there is no denying it, whatever may be our differences with him. Among the men of the present generation few men can be named alongside him. When a boy he was sent by his father to perform worship in a Shaiva temple during the night of a fasting day. The father's command was that the boy should sit up all through the night, and see that the water-pot which was hanging over the god was always filled and that water was continuously dripping over it. So the boy of ten or twelve went to the place and sat the night out. At about midnight he found that he was more or less getting sleepy; he could not keep his hand steady and prevent his eyes from closing involuntrily; he tried all manner of means, but still he was dozing; and he found that some of those dirty creatures which are always found in dark and close temples sat unconcernedly over the Linga, and disturbed the flowers. As soon as he heard the noise, he got up and found that the water was falling on the rates instead of over the idol. Well, that is a very common experience of us all, but it suggested to him a new line of thought which made him leave his home. It suggested to him that the dumb mechanical worship had no power in it and that the spirit must approach the Soul of the world in some other way than this. This is only one instance. But it shows how great men are original. Originality or imagination, like sincerity of purpose, is thus an essential trait in human greatness. There is a third element again. Not only must a great man occupy a higher plane of thought and action but he must have an attraction about him. I cannot be called magnetic, or any other physical form of attraction, but there is such an attraction about him, that it inspires in those about him the same spirit which he feels of self-sacrifice and public devotion. Any man who stands by himself single and whose example and teachings have not succeeded in penetrating into the hearts and intelligences of other people in such a way that these hearts and intelligences are bound to become part of him, cannot be called a great man.

Truthfulness, great impulses, moral aims, resourcefulness to attain those aims by the bond of love and fellowship—these are the traits of character which go to make a great man, and those in whom they are best developed are the greatest of men. You have all read accounts of the life of *Buddha*. He had such a hold upon men's minds that wherever he went hundreds and thousands followed him as the Great Teacher, so that they ensured the permanent success of the movements which he inaugurated—a most unparalleled success in the world's history. Take again the story of the prophet Mahomed. A poor, illiterate man, he did not dream of religion in his youth, and yet at forty he goes into retirement, incessantly moves about in such a country as Arabia to find that he is persecuted and has to fly for life; but there was such an attraction among men and women towards him that in the course of ten or twenty years he was able to dictate terms to the largest and the most powerful potentates of the day. Here, then, you have a general idea of what constitutes greatness. Earnestness of purpose, sincerity in action, originality, imagination and, above all, the power of magnetism—we might call it vital or spiritual magnetism—these are the qualities which go to make a man great. I have thus given you my own conception of what a great man is. He is not the rihcest man, nor the most intelligent man, nor the most cultivated man, nor the most successful man, but a great man is he who, whether he be poor or rich, learned or unlearned, in the profession or out of the profession, successful in life, or unsuccessful in life, the great man is he who combines some of those virtues that I have just attempted to draw your attention to.

Having said this much we shall turn to see whether in Raja Rama Mohana Roy some of these virtues can be found in a way to justify our regard for him as one of the greatest men that India has produced during the last two centuries and as one of the fathers of the Brahma Church movement. His was a very simple life. He was born in 1774 and he died in 1833; he thus lived for about sixty years; a time which many of us here are now nearing, and some of us have exceeded. He was born a Brahmin. On his mother's side he belonged to the *Shakta* sect, which is the orthodox sect on the Bengal side. On his father's side he came from a family which was well-known for its *Vaishnavism.* So the *Shaktha* and *Vaishnava* blood joined together in a sort of mutual reconciliation in producing this great man who was destined to accomplish work which this union of a *Vaishnava* father with a *Shakta* mother typified. In those old days when schools and colleges did not exist, this boy at the age of twelve left his village and went to Patna to study Arabic and Persian, which were then the Court languages. At sixteen he went to Benares and there studied Sanskrit for four years, not to be a Pandit, but to understand the real significance of the old learning. He thus became an Arabic, Persian, and Sanskrit scholar, without knowing a word of English till that age.

His familiarity with the Arabic and the Sanskrit philosophy enabled him at the age of sixteen to conceive a dislike to the idolatrous practices which in those parts of Bengal have reached an exaggerated form, with which most of us here are not familiar. There are idolatries and idolatries. But the Bengal system of Kali worship is something of which even we have no idea. This was the sort of idolatry which he denounced at sixteen. We might well compare notes as to what we did at sixteen with such a record. Were any of us lighted up with the fire that burnt in his heart? His father got vexed with him; and he had to leave his home. He went outside of India as far as Thibet and there he became practically familiar with the Buddhistic system. He knew Musalman philosophy, he knew the Sanskrit philosophy, and in the four years' time that he spent in travelling he became familiar with the Buddhistic philosophy.

After four years' travelling his father got reconciled with him and allowed him to return home. There at twenty he commenced to learn English, completing that study at about twenty-five. Till forty he spent his time in the service of the English Government. He did not rise to any very good position; but was, I believe, the Head Cleark or *Shirastedar* to the District Judge or Collector in several places. At forty he retired from the service and for the first time came to Calcutta. Till then he had not taken any part in any of the public movements. He lived twenty years more. From 1814 to 1833, his life was of incessant work which far exceeded in measure the labour of many hundreds of people like ourselves. He was at once a social reformer, the founder of a great religious movement, and a great politician. These three activities were combined in him in such a way that they put to shame the performance of the best among us at the present time. Raja Rama Mohan Roy's services to the country were not confined to any particular department of human activity. He waged war against polygamy. He first denounced the practice of *Sati* in 1818 when our Presidency of Bombay came under British rule. From that time to 1828 this crusade was carried on continuously for ten years. But not having obtained success he went on this same mission to England in 1830 when he was called to give evidence before a Parliamentary Committee that was sitting there. He was also entrusted by the Emperor of Delhi with some political mission. This crusade against *Sati* represents the most prominent side of his social activity.

As regards his attempts to revive the pure Monotheism of the Upanishad period, it may be noted that after coming to Calcutta in 1814, he established a rudimentary form of the Brahma Church in a spot where people might meet to discuss and also pray, and join in prayer. From 1814 to 1828, this work was carried on with unflagging enthusiasm, and brisk controversy was kept up not only with the orthodox defenders of Hinduism, but with the Christian missionaries. He called upon both Christians and Hindus to return back to the wisdom of their ancient sages. In the two volumes which are published of his life you will find that nearly one whole volume is devoted to the Raja's publications and pamphlets addressed to the Christian missionaries. The rest of the volume is devoted to his expositions of the *Vedantic* and *Upanishad* philosophy. He was reading and writing, preaching and protesting, refuting and discussing all these twenty years. But while he was doing all that, he did not abstain from studying the political wants and needs of his time. In those early days, when the Charter of the East India Company was about to be renewed in 1833, he was called from India and he went to England to give most useful evidence before that Committee. Unfortunately, the climate did not agree with him and he fell a sacrifice in his country's cause, among strangers in a foreign land, far away from his dear home.

Here ends a brief exposition of the life of this great man. He started the Brahma Samaja movement and that Samaja is his living memorial. He made efforts for the abolition of the practice of *Sati*, and though he did not live to see the result, the Government felt itself compelled by the labours of this great man to take measures to stop *Sati* by legislation five years after his death. People here are not quite familiar with the enormity of this practice of *Sati* in those days. I know there are some men who still say that it was a wrong step to stop *Sati* or to abolish it. You will have some idea of the enormity of this evil from one of the pamphlets Raja Rama Mohana wrote and the petitions he submittet to Parliament. In one of those pamphlets figures are given for fourteen years, and in the Lower Provinces of Bengal alone there were eight thousand cases of *Sati*-burning during the fourteen years, or an average of six hundred per year. There was not a single family which had no case of *Sati*-burning in the last century. These *Sati* sacrifices were not voluntary; but women were pressed to immolate themselves. Once a woman said 'yes' in her agony of grief, her relations made it impossible for her to change her mind. If Government had not stopped it we should have had these horrors repeated before our eyes to this day. If the credit of putting an end to these horrors belongs to any man, that credit must be given to Raja Rama Mohana Roy. *Sati*-burning was not the only horror men inflicted on themselves in those early days, but men and women used to drown themselves, or jump down from lofty precipices into the waters below and thus invite death in a hundred other forms. If there is credit due to any man for having turned the national current in the right direction in this matter, that credit is due to Raja Rama Mohana. Of his political activities I shall not say anything from this platform. Anybody who wants to know what true patriotism is, had better study the evidence that he gave and the letters he wrote to men in power over sixty years ago—long before our era of Congress meetings and Conferences.

We shall now turn to the religious movement to which he devoted his chief attention. This Atmiya Sabha of 1814, was developed in the course of fourteen years into the Brahma Samaja, established in 1828. All who wish to know what the Brahma Samaja is, not merely what it is reported to be, cannot, I believe, do better than read the Trust Deed in which are stated by that great man his views about the noble objects and aims of the Brahma Samaja movements. The spirituality, the deep piety and universal toleration which are manifest in every word of this document, represent an ideal of beauty and perfection which has not been realized by his successors, and it may yet take many centuries before its full significance is understood by our people. The future destiny of the Brahma Samaja is concealed in the womb of time. We cannot say it may not fail. We hope it will succeed. But what its founder intended it to be is not a question which we can afford to dispute. I shall tell you what he intended it to be, and request both those who belong to the Samaja, and those who are outside its pale, to consider whether his conception of it was not as noble as any which the highest among us and in other lands have ever been able to form. What Raja Rama Mohana felt was that we had in India a nation, gifted with a religious history transcending all the records of every other race. Here was a nation, which was gifted, was well endowed, was spiritual in all its real aspirations. This nation had gradually ascended to the conception of the purest form of Monotheism that the world has yet seen. In the *Upanishads* and in the *Bhagavat Gita* it had developed—not by a mere impulse, not by the command of any single prophet, but by the slow process of growth and evolution—a system of the purest form of Monotheism that man can conceive. The higher thought of the nation had learned to place its trust in a Universal Spirit, the One without a Second, in whom all lived and moved and had their being, who was the Cause of all, the Lord of all, the Friend of all, the Guide of all, the most fatherly of fathers, and the most motherly of mothers. One age after another constructed the edifice, laying brick upon brick and layer upon layer, and storey after storey rose. Well, this highest conception was not only confined to Pandits, Philosophers and Shastris, but it was the common property of every class, the very lowest of the low, men who were socially not much respected nor very respectable, the poor villager, the hunter, the gardener, the fisherman, the weaver, the goldsmith, the barber, the shopkeeper—they all shared this common faith equally with the Brahmins, the Pandits, and the Yogis.

While Raja Rama Mohana was struck with this unversal prevalence of the monotheistic principle, he was deeply pained at the thought that this exalted faith was turned to no practical account, because it was associated with external observances and rites which were in entire discord with it. These external rites and observances made the nation worship all manner of gods and goddesses, elemental, mythological, tribal and local divinities, with the most grotesque features and the wrost inhuman associations. This polytheism had also grown side by side with the higher teaching of the Upanishads, that God was One without a Second, and of the Bhagavat Gita, that He alone was to be worshipped. This contrast between the monotheistic spirit and the polytheistic observances strikes every student of our religious life as a puzzle which baffles the understanding. You can well imagine how it must have struck a great soul like that of the Raja who from his very boyhood had been brought up an iconoclast and waged war with idolatry of all kinds. He brooded and thought over it, and he worked, and suffered for it in a way of which we have no conception. The question that he put to himself was, how does it come to pass that Monolatry does not go hand in hand with Monotheism in India, when in other countries where the monotheistic principle is less exclusively professed, monolatry has been for two thousand years and more the prevailing practice? This is the question I request you to consider each for himself. I offer no solution of it myself to-day; because though I have been thinking about it for a long time I have not yet been able to find a rational and consistent solution of the difficulty. The question, you will recollect, is not of idolatry or non-idolatry. That difference relates to the method of devotion and not to the object of worship. The difference to which I have drawn your attention has a deeper source and requires our most anxious consideration. In most cases idolatry is only a consequence of this practical polytheism which prevails in the land and which leads men against the teachings of their own higher reason to think that one Supreme will does not govern all the operations of nature, but that many gods and goddesses, good and bad deities, or *Devatas*, are permitted to influence the operations of nature and the well-being of man in a hundred different ways, and it is these subordinate powers which must be propitiated each in its own way and on its own day. It is this ceaseless distraction of the mind between the devotion to the One Supreme Lord of all and the claims of the multiple small agents of good and bad influences which is the real evil. There is image worship among the Roman Catholics and there is saint worship and *Pir*-worship among Christians and Mahomedans, but on the whole they do not detract from the monolatrous character of the devotions of these people. With us this limit has been overstepped with the consequent debasement that we see all about us. Rama Mohana Roy naturally felt pained at this modern debasement, and with a view to bring into accord our practical devotions with our monotheistic faith, he gathered together kindred souls who felt with him on this point and established the Brahma Samaja. He did not regard the Brahma Samaja faith as a new Dispensation, or a new declaration of God's purposes. He aspired only to establish harmony between men's accepted faith and their practical observances by a strict monolatrous worship of the One Supreme Soul, a worship of the heart and not of the hands, a sacrifice of self and not of the possessions of the self. There was nothing foreign in its conception, origin, or method. He wanted men and women to cherish their own ancient treasures of faith and to secure their freedom from the bondage of superstition and ignorance. This was the work which the Brahma Samaja was intended to carry out. It is not for me to say how far that promise has been fulfilled. If it has not been fulfilled, the blame is not his but ours. To us the same problem presents itself to-day, as it did to him early in the century. And it is a problem on the right solution of which our destiny here and hereafter greatly depends. In connection with this anniversary I beseech you to take the great lesson to heart and try to work out its solution in such a way that the integrity of your soul may be restored. When this correspondence between the head and the heart, this concord between the flesh and the spirit is established, Indian monotheism will be a great power in the land, uniting 250 milions of men and women in a bond which shall be indissoluble. The historical differences of national creeds will continue to exist like the different styles of architecture. The Christian Church will not look in outward appearance like a Mahomedan mosque or an Aryan temple, but the differences of style and form will not interfere with the spiritual unity of purpose. When this is accomplished, another great idea, the union of all religions, which Raja Rama Mohana Roy cherished deeply in his heart, will be realised, and with it people in all lands will say with one voice 'Thy Kingdom has come and Heaven has descended on Earth.'

Since this address was first delivered there are evident signs of the awakening of thoughtful minds in all countries to the necessity of securing the co-operation of all nations towards this great end. And the best evidence of it was furnished by the great Parliament of Religions held at Chicago in connection with the great Columbian exposition, the smaller Unions among Christians themselves, held at New York, (U.S.A.) and Paris, (France) this year. The great World's Temperance Union is a similar sign of the the times. We may note also the fact that the missionaries from this country have been actively working both in America and in Europe to familiarise the people in those parts with the higher spiritualism of our ancient land. Also the Theosophical movement, which represents men who profess all the known religions and yet feel that they can co-operate together in this common elevation. All these indications may be regarded as the early dawn, which will before long usher in, full blaze, the Sun of Righteousness and Glory which will unite all nations in a common brotherhood.

3

Role in Freedom Movement

Ranade took deep interest in the political and constitutional developments in our sub-continent. His rule on the platform of the Sarvajanik Sabha deficts a romantic saga of his career. He suggested several reforms in the revenue system of India, and advised useful modifications in the land system. He also sponsored the promotion of local self-government. He also suggested simultaneous examinations of Civil Services both in England as well as India. He always appreciated the efforts of the founders of Indian National Congress like A.U., Dadabhai Naoroji, Gopal Krishna Gokhale, D.E. Wacha, Pheroze Shah Mehta and others.

It was as First Class First Grade Subordinate Judge that Ranade came to Poona in November, 1871. The post carried with it a salary of Rs. 800 a month. It was only an *acting* appointment at first, but he was confirmed in the position in 1873. Excepting one, it was the highest office to which a subordinate judge could ordinarily attain, but he was appointed to it at the very outset of his legal career and when he was not yet thirty years old. His jurisdiction in this office extended over all civil suits, of whatever value, and against all persons except the Government. The Government showed its confidence in him by giving him authority to hear appeals from the decrees of the second class subordinate judges—and he was probably the first subordinate judge to be invested with appellate powers. Mr. Mankar, himself once a sub-judge, says of him,—"His judgments, remarkable for patient and minute inquiry, exhaustive treatment of every case that came before him, careful examination of every document filed in it, lucid statement of facts, just appreciation of evidences, elaborate expositions of the various bearings of the question at issue, and cogency of arguments adduced in support of the decisions finally arrived at, often won the admiration of the High Court.'

When Ranade came to Poona, he found that there had been inaugurated there in the previous year a society called the Sarvajanik Sabha. The object of the society was to represent to Government the needs and the wishes of the people, and its membership included a large number of persons of position and influence—landed-proprietors, bankers, merchants, retired Government servants, lawyers, professors, and most of the ruling chiefs of the Southern Maratha country. Ranade found in this society a means of expression for that social conscience which burned within him, and a good instrument for furthering his purposes. He became a member immediatly after his arrival in poona, gathered the reins of its affairs into his own hands, and for the following twenty-two years was the life and soul of it. The original founder of the Sabha was Ganesh Wasudev Joshi—affectionately called "Uncle Sarvajanik"—and he and Ranade worked hand in hand, Joshi being the executive power in the society and Ranade the brains. The Sabha played a very important part in the awakening of Western India, and in creating a public opinon upon political, social, and economic matters.

Gladstone, in 1871, appointed a Parliamentary Committee which inquired into Indian finance.[1] In the following year the Sarvajanik Sabha, with a view to obtaining a report

1. Known to history as the Fawcett Committee. Dadabhai Naoroji gave evidence before it, endeavouring to demonstrate the great poverty of India and the very high incidence of taxation.

that would be supplementary and perhaps corrective of that of the Parliamentary Committee, resolved that it would on its own account make an investigation of the material conditions of the whole of the Maharashtra[1] district. This report was published in 1873 in the form of a small book. As Mr. Phatak points out, Ranade, by arranging for the investigation and by writing the report, taught his countrymen an important lesson, showing them how to diagnose their own troubles in an independent manner, and how to make suggestions for remedy, instead of waiting idly and obsequiously for Government to do everything. The report laid the blame for the distress existing in the Ahmednagar and Sholapur districts at the door of the land policy, and as a result the Government henceforward took a keen and not always favourable interest in the Sabha's activities.

It may be noticed in passing that the Parliamentary Committee lasted for four years and came to an end with the fall of Gladstone's Cabinet. Ranade accomplished the formidable task of making an epstome of the 3,500 pages of its four volume report. His epitome after being revised and supplemented was published in 1877, under the title of *A Revenue Manual of the British Empire in India.* Ranade had been invited to go to England to give evidence, but the abrupt ending of the Committee prevented his visit from taking place.

In 1874, Ranade, through the Sabha, sent to Parliament and to the chief Government officials and to the newspapers copies of a petition regarding Responsible Self-Government. The petition proposed that India should have representatives in the Parliament at London and that Indian questions should

1. Maharashtra is the name given to an area of 100,000 square miles, stretching inland from the middle portion of the west cast of India. It is rougnshly tringular in form—the sides of the triangle being: (1) the coast-line from Daman to Karwai, (2) a line running from Daman to a point somewhat eastward of Nagpur, (3) a line running from that point beyond Nagpur to Karwar. The population of the area is abcut 30 millions. (See M.G. Ranade's *Rise of the Maratha Power*, pp. 19-20).

be settled with their consent. The number of representatives was to be eleven, and everyone who paid at cast fifty rupees in taxes was to have the right of voting in the election of the repesentatives. To show that popular opinion favoured the demand, he secured thousands of signatures from among the people. Ranade of course was not so simple as to imagine that Government would at once grant the demand. To his mind the chief value of such efforts consisted in the fact that they were first steps in the people's political education. The general condition of the country was one of political slumber, with here and there a few minds beginning to be awake. Ranade's aim was to get the ideas of self-government underlying his polition considered and discussed, so that the ferment of national aspiration might enter into the dull mass of the life.

An outbreak of mob violence accompanied with burnings and robberies which became known as the Deccan Riots, occurred in June, 1875. The victims of the attacks were chiefly the *savkars* (i.e., the village money-lenders), and the general opinion was that the motive was to destroy the savkars debt-records and to take revenge on them for their cruel and heartless treatment. The Government apparently lent its countenance to the idea that the bad conduct of the savkars was responsible for the ourbreak. But Ranade and other members of the Sabha felt convinced that the real root of the trouble was the Government's system of land-taxation. The other leaders of the Sabha wanted to make this opinion known to Government, but Ranade counselled caution. He reminded his friends that they were in the Government's bad books, on account of the attitude the Sabha had adopted towards a recent affair which had ended with the deposition of the Gaikwad of Baroda. He pointed out that if, while the disturbance was in process, they exonerated the savkars and blamed the Government's land-policy, the Sabha might be suppressed and all its potential usefulness destroyed. In accordance with the advice, the Sabha waited until after the trouble had died down, before sending its representation to Government.

Being now thoroughly suspicious of the Sabha Government took steps to discover who exactly were it leaders and what their real intentions were. Mrs. Ranade recounts a rather amusing affair, in which her husband brought about the discomfiture of a secred agent who was sent to Poona to investigate.

He was a Bengali gentleman, and when he came to poona he endeavoured to make himself popular by keeping open house. The secretary of the Sabha was among the many poople who were attracted to the company of this stranger of the cultured mind and winning manners, and who flocked to enjoy his abundant hospitality. But Ranade, suspecting that the man was a spy, arranged to have his movement watched. It was then discovered that the stranger's letters were not delivered by the postman, but that he called every morning at the general post-office himself. It was also established that his correspondence seemed to be chiefly carried on with a Government secretary at Calcutta or at Simla. These facts began to be whispered abroad, and the number of persons frequenting the hospitable house began to diminish. The stranger evidently guessed that his purpose was discovered, for one day, not long after, the Poona folk found that he had disappeared, leaving no trace behind him.

In connection with the great Delhi Durbar of 1877, a meetting of Poona citizens was held under the auspices of the Sarvajanik Sabha, and a loyal address, the draft of which had been prepared by Ranade, was sent up form it of the Queen's Government. The address besides assurance of loyalty and expressions of consideration for the Queen's health and prosperity, contained some complaints and requests—and to these latter some of the Anglo-Indian newspapers took strong exception. Ranade's answer was that the British Government ought to follow the immemorial custom of Indian rulers and grant some striking boon at times of great rejoicing. He urged that the great occasion of the Queen's assumption of the new title of *Empress of India* should be marked by the gift of responsible self-government. He followed this up by an impressive statement of the fact, which his great contemporary, Sir Pherozeshah Mehta, also used offen to dwell on, namely, the impossibility of Europeans entering into the Indian mind as Indians themselves can. He further pointed out that though the Muslim emperors were tyrannical and despotic, they yet understood a very important principle of Imperial rule, and that was the trusting of the native princes, and the giving to them of responsibilities in war and in peace. He desired the formation of a Council of Representatives and a Chamber of Princes, believing that in these institution both princes and people would find a unity of aim, their outlook would be broadened, and their minds sharpened. "Uncle Sarvajanik" carried these aims to more concrete expression by sending an open letter on the subject to the princes, and by meeting with many of them at the Delhi Durbar, and so trying to awaken them to a knowledge of their duty.

The year 1877 was one of dreadful famine in the Deccan and thousands of peasant folk were at the doors of death. Ranade was deeply moved by the state of affairs, and working through the Sarvajanik Sabha he was able to render very valuable service in the catastrophe. What the Sabha did was to organise and to carry on an intelligence service in the famine areas. It sent representatives to make inquiries on the spot. These men were able as a rule to get close to the people and to elicit the real facts interrogating the *kulkarni*,[1] the postmaster, the school-master, and other such persons of the villages. Their reports were sent up to the Secretary of the Sabha. The work of selecting the Sabha's famine-inquiry agents and of allotting them their spheres of labour was entrusted to Ranade. On the basis of the agents' reports, he wrote papers giving detailed information regarding the famine conditions, and these were regularly forwarded to Government over the signature of the Sabha's secretary. His papers also reviewed the Government's famine activities, and were frank in criticism as well as generous in praise. The inquiry

1. The village officer whose duty it is to keep the accounts of the cultivators with the Government.

work raised the Sabha greatly in the estimation of Government, and many Government officials highly commended its efforts. But, later on, the Sabha again fell into disfavour, in connection with a strike of people employed on relief work which it was suspected of having instigated.

It was difficult to combine whole-hearted help with frank and independent criticism, but Ranade was particularly expert at steering the Sabha between the Scylla and Charybdis of uncritical acquiescence and unbridled impatience. When, for example, the Government officials accused the Sabha's report of exaggeration, he induced it, instead of hotly rebutting the charge, simply to insist that its investigators had collected their information with great ability, and that if there was anything improper in their reports it represented the opinions of the people in the famine-stricken areas. Mr. Phatak is probaly right when he asserts that if the guidance of the Sabha affairs had not been in Ranade's hands at this time of would have suffered the disciplining at the hands of Government that actually befell when it was again pursuing famine activities, in the year 1897. On that occasion a hotheaded agent of the Sabha got it into trouble by an action that was officially stigmatized as "tending to cause unnecessary trouble to the administration, to induce landholders to bring on themselves coercive processes, and to be injurious to the public interests," the result being that "the Poona Sarvajanik Sabha as at present constituted must therefore cease to be recognised as a body which has any claim to address Government on questions of public policy." If Ranade's hand had still been at the helm at that time, the Sabha would never have foundered on such a rock.

When the stress of the famine was over, Ranade, in order to put his views before the Commission that had been appointed to investigate the best remedies for meeting famine, wrote a paper, entitled " Famine Administration in the Bombay Presidency." In it he warmly gave Government credit for following certain sound principles and methods, declaring that this had "justified the confidence felt by the people in their rulers and greatly contributed to the acknowledged success of famine management in this Presidency." Then he went on "to hold up the weak points of the system before the bar of public opinion," and with a great array of facts and figures, he challenged the comfortable official conclusions as to the percentage of the population affected by the famine and as to the percent, age of deaths resulting from it.

THE JOURNAL OF THE SARVAJANIK SABHA

Land Problem, Local Government, Native States, and Education

In 1878, the *Quarterly Journal of the Sarvajanik Sabha* began its life of nineteen years. Ranade was closely associated with it up till 1893. In many an issue as much as two-thirds of the contents were from his pen, and in its pages he marshalled his ideas on many a political, social, and religious theme. The following Notice to Subscribers which appeared in the first number will explain the nature of the *Journal*.

"A desire has been expressed by several European and Native well-wishers of the Poona Sarvajanik Sabha that its proceedings should be published regularly in the form of a quarterly publication so as to be easily available for purposes of reference. The Managing Committee of the Sabha have accordingly resolved to try the experiment of such a periodical publication of the proceedings of the Sabha. Besides publishing the proceedings it is proposed to take advantage of such a publication to insert independent communications, reviewing and discussing the more important political question of the day. There are many topics upon which public opinion has to be created and formed before any formal action can be taken in respect of them by the Sabha. Such topics will find a fitting place in the independent section of the proposed quarterly . . . . The Journal will consist of about 48 pages royal octavo to be priced at Rs. 4 per annum, and it will be published in the months of July, October, January, and April."

This is a fitting point at which to try to enter into the general trend of Ranade's mind, by reviewing some of his central thoughts, as they can be gathered from the pages of the *Sarvajanik Sabha Journal.*

A considerable number of Ranade's contributions to the *Journal* deal with India's agrarian problem. Seventy-five per cent of India's Population is agriculturist, and the great majority of these agriculturists are small-farmers, who live a hand-to-mouth existence, half-strangled in toils of indebtedness, and falling an easy prey to ruin in times of famine or drought. It is not surprising therefore to find a man of Ranade's patrioic and humane nature much concerned with the various aspects of the land problem. We find him, in 1879, writing on "The Agrarian Problem and Its Solution," and on "The Deccan Agriculturists' Relief Bill"; in 1880, on "The Law of Land Sale in British India"; in 1881, on "Mr. Wedderburn and His Critics on a Permanent Settlement for the Deccan," and on "The Central Provinces Land Revenue and Tenancy Bills," and on "Land Law Reforms and Agricultural Banks"; in 1883, on "The Emancipation of the Serfs in Russia," "Forest Conservancy in the Bombay Presidency," and "Prussian Land Legislation and the Bengal Tenancy Bill'; in 1884, on "Proposed Reforms in the Resettlement of Land Assessment," "A Protest and Warning against the New Departure in the Land Assessment Policy," and "The Ecomomic Results of the Public Works Policy"; in 1890, on "Netherlands India and the Culture System"; and, in 1891, on "The Reorganization of Rural Credit in India".

From a study of these papers we discover that Ranade held several strong convictions regarding India's land problem, and these we shall now endeavour summarily to set forth.

(1) *The Wretched State of the Indian Agriculturists.* From many a page of Ranade's writings we get the impression that Indian agriculture is a thing of great possibilities, on which might be reared a strong, contented, and flourishing populace, but which somehow seems to be cursed with a withering disability. In his "Land Law Reforms and Agricultural

Banks," after having made a characteristically carefal survey based on the 1872 Census, he presents the following picture:

"We have thus a poor soil (he is referring particularly to the Deccan) afflicted with scanty and irregular rains, inhabited by a sparse population, for the most part agricultural and uneducated, with no openings for labour save an exhausted soil, with average holdings of less than ten acres per each head of family, burdened with a payment of State demand which represents one third of their net gains, forced to be content with a hand-to-mouth subsistence represented by a maximum of Rs. 60 for a family, and involved in heavy bonds of debt under circumstances beyond their control to a numerous mass of small creditors, largely foreign in their domicile, and not prepared to take up cultivation of land on their own account. These are the client features of the social and economical condition of one people which it is necessary to bear in mind, while discussing the question of the best method of relief."

(2) *The Causes of the Agriculturists' Condition.* Ranade refuses the facile explanation that this distressing state of affairs exists "because the Indian *ryot*[1] is an improvident, spiritless and ignorant peasant, whose condition has been wretched all along and can never be improved"; and the Commission that investigated after the Deccan Riots supported him in that refusal. But in any case, thriftlessness and ignorance and lack of spirit are *results* and not causes—as Ranade himself indicated when he drew attention to the change in the character of the French peasantry after the end of the 18th Century.[2] They are defects whose roots can be traced back to faulty social institutions and to unsound economic arrangements.

Ranade sees three main causes of India's agrarian troubles. The first lay in existing *System of Rural Credit* which was

1. Ryot is the Anglicised name for a present agriculturist.
2. See "The Reorganization of Rural Credit" and "The Emancipation of the Serfs in Russia."

carried on by a vast number of petty village money-lenders, under laws that offered great facilities for extortion. The people were nearly all struggling under a burden of ancestral debt, and paying enormous rates of interest of from 25 per cent. to 75 per cent. Moreover the rural economy, under the prevailing circumstances, made these money-lenders indispensable, for the State had a rigid land-revenue system, whereby the ryot had to pay a certain sum in cash at a fixed time, and as that time was not generally coincident with the time when the ryot realised his produce, he had to borrow from the moneylender to pay the State demand—a condition of things that was of course aggravated in time of scarcity of famine. The result was that the land tax was really to a large extent paid by the money-lender on behalf of the ryot, who was constantly involved in ruinous debt. The whole system thus tended to be uneconomical and wasteful.

The second cause was the *Lack of Capital*—a deficiency that inevitably made the agriculturist's position poor and precarious. There is, he says, "an utter paralysis of industry in rural India, due to the poverty of the resources of the classes engaged in the production of wealth."

The third cause, and in Ranade's view the most important one, because the other two really arose out of it, was the *Government's of Land Policy*. The State's monopoly of land and its right to increase the assessment at its own discretion were, he declared, the two most pre-eminent obstacles in the way of the country's growth in material prosperity. The result of the Government's claim to be the ultimate owner of all the land was that the assessments tended to be screwed up, and the payment of land revenue became a crushing burden that killed all enterprise and initiative. He maintained that :

"The only guarantee against excessive enhancement, which is found effective where land is held in private right, is the competition of landlords among themselves. There is no place for this guarantee under the Indian system, because the land is the monopoly of the State, single and individual. The absence of such a check has resulted in wholesale enhancement all over the country to an extent of which the Government itself is now ashamed."

The burden and the rigidity of the land tax lead to borrowing and to the evils of indebtedness. The uncertainty of the State impost and the unsatisfactory position of the ryot as semi-proprietor, prevent a ready flow of capital to the agricultural industry.

(3) Having thus diagnosed the disease, Ranade with a clear voice declares the remedies. They are,—juridical reform to help the ryot to avoid the evils of debt; banking and loan facilities to encourage the flow of capital into the agricultural industry; reform of the land tenure system so as to do away with the uncertainty and the burden-someness of the temporary settlements.[1]

Ranade saw a great many of his ideas with regard to juridical reform embodied in the Deccan 'Agriculturists' Relief Bill of 1879. Its aim was to remove the legal encumbrances that were depressing the ryot. It did this by empowering the Courts to go behind the actual contract; where there was a mainifest unfairness; by requiring that every bond to which a ryot was a party should be written by or under the supervision of the village registrar; by extending the period of limitation of suits so that the creditor did not have to renew the bond or file a suit every three years; by giving wide scope to the principle of conciliation; by authorising village *munsiffs* to try suits of less than ten rupees; by disallowing compound interests by abolishing arrest and imprisonment for

1. Where the system of *temporary* settlements is in operation, the land is subjected to a thorough economic survey every 30 years or so and the amount of annual revenue payable by that land is decided is accordance with the results of the survey. Under the *permanent* settlement, the amount of revenue payable has been fixed in perpetuity.

debt; by restricting the liability of land to be sold for unsecured money debts; and by restricting the liability of heirs to pay ancestral debt.

Ranade cordially welcomed the Bill, though he was doubtful of the wisdom of interfering with the obligation to pay ancestral debts, and though he saw that one effect of the Bill would be greatly to reduce the ryot's power of obtaining loans from the money-lenders, while he would nevertheless have to get money somehow if the land revenue system remained as rigid as heretofore. For twelve years (1881 to 1893) Ranade was, as a Special Judge under the provisions of the Act in which the Bill issued, an administrator of its purposes. But he always insisted that the relief intended would be achieved only if the Bill were worked in conjunction with a more liberal land revenue policy.

We find Ranade dealing with the question of the creation of better banking and loan facilities for the agriculturists as early as 1881, pleading that Government should encourage and even guarantee private effort wherever it is willing to undertake the loan business on terms that would leave a proper margin for the ryot's subsistence. He saw that the crying need of capital in the agricultural industry was a matter that urgently required to be dealt with, for the industry was hampered, impeded, and depressed by the lack. He saw too that the credit system which was in vogue in rural India was utterly demoralising and harmful in its effects. His mind turned as was its wont to discover what had been done to meet similar situations elsewhere, and we find in his paper on "The Reorganization of Rural Credit," written in 1891, that he examines what has been done for rural credit in a number of European countries where conditions are comparable to those of India, namely, in Hungary, France, Italy, Belgium, Switzerland, and Germany. He finds that in these countries the introduction of a system of credit adapted to the special needs of the agricultural classes has worked wonders, and he urges that similar success may be expected in India. In this connection we can see how Ranade was in the van to progress, leading thought and moulding public opinion. It was in 1892 that the Madras Government began to think about appointing a special Commissioner to inquire into Cooperative Banking in Europe and the possibilities of its application to India, and it was in 1895 that the report of that Commissioner, Sir Frederick Nicholson, was published. Ranade died before the Indian Co-operative Credit Act of 1904 was passed, but we are probably right in assuming that his clear diagnosis of the disease, and his unfaltering exposition of the lines of remedy, helped to bring about the introduction of the Co-operative Credit Movement into India, with all its beneficial results and wide possibilities.

Ranade never tried of insisting that the agrarian problem was insoluble without a reform in the land revenue system. "We have," he writes in 1881, "for the last fifteen years, in good and evil report, exposed the failure of the present system, and advocated a permanent settlement of land as the only alternative open to Government, by the side of which reform all other agencies sink into insignificance." The change required is to give the owners of land complete and independent proprietorship. "Let each man's land," he says, "be as much his absolute property as his house or clothes." And again. "The elments of national prosperity are wanting in a country whose principal resource is agriculture, and that agriculture is in the hands of a thriftless and poverty-stricken peasantry, who are weighted down with heavy charges, and whose life and labours are not cheered by the charm and strength inspired by a sense of property."

In maintaining such a position Ranade had of course to meet the claim, often put forward, that according to traditions going far back beyond the days of British rule, the State in India is the universal landlord, and that its land-revenue is really a *rent* and not a tax. But he vigorously rebuts that claim.

In its final shape Ranade's proposal for a permanent settlement took the form which can be gathered from the following quotation:

"Our own proposal is that the permanent assessment claimable from all soils should be once for all fixed at a proportion of the gross staple produce, the proportion being based upon the principle of dividing the net profits in *kind* half and half between the Government and the private holder. This *kind* payment so fixed should be unchangeable for all time, whatever improvement the private holder may affect in his land. As however the Government cannot conveniently receive the *kind* payment, its disbursements being all in cash, we would commute the *kind* payments into money values, and those money values would be liable to periodical changes according as prices permanently rise or fall over a great part of the country."[1]

Ranade felt that Government's unwillingness to grant anything in the nature of a permanent settlement was due to its fear of expreriencing a scarcity of revenue if it let go its hold on the unearned increment of the land. Accordingly, he is always careful to point out that extension of the permanent settlement would so develope the resources of the country that both the earned and the unearned increment would greatly increase, and as a result the direct and indirect taxes would come in time to yield a greatly enhanced return. But he also thought that the unearned increment theory is "one of those hobbies that has been ridden to death in this country, involving the Government and the people in common confusion and ruin." He sees two great benefits that would result from the permanent settlement. The first is that private capitalists would he encouraged to invest their capital in the land:

"All improvements in husbandry suggested by science and experience presuppose a great expenditure of capital to be invested in the land. The magic of property can alone induce people to incur such expenditure. Neither

1. "Protest and Warning against the New Departure in the Land Assessment Policy"

private savkars nor joint stock land banks will venture capital to sink wells, or to use manures, or throw dams across streams, unless the tyots to whom these advances are to be made possess full proprietor rights over the lands. If land banks have succeeded in other countries so well, most of the success must be undoubtedly laid to the credit of the fact that the peasants in those countries are not tenants of the State, but own the lands they cultivate in absolute right."[1]

The other great benefit is that the hand would come into the possession of persons who were able to make an effective use of it:

> "The thrifty ryot will maintain his place and extend his operations and rise to a better position, while the indifferent and lazy ryot will make way for better folk who will take his place to the great advantage of the general interest. The change will not be sudden but a slow organic growth, and the new order of things will develope the best interests of all classes without any shock to the vested interests."[2]

Ranade felt that the Government land policy was struggling to keep up a poverty-stricken peasantry in possession of the soil, and was preventing the natural union of capital and land. The money-lender does indeed often become the virtual owner of the land, the ryot sinking to the position of serf to his creditor, but the money-lender has no wish or intention of working the land himself. "The monied classes," writes Ranade, "having at present no interest in the land, cannot occupy the position nor enjoy the status nor discharge the fuctions of landlords. The absence of such a class retards progress in all directions. The Presidency of Bengal enjoys this advantage over the rest of India, and this circumstance

1 "Land Law Reforms and Agricultural Banks."
2. "The Agrarian Problem and its Solution."

alone accounts for its prosperous and progressive condition."[1] With the adoption of his land policy proposals, he looks forward to a time when "there will grow up all over the country a provident and thrifty class of landlords whose interest it will be to make the most of the resources of the soil and of the great public works constructed by the Government"; and the political and social advantages of such a change would, he said, be even more important than the economical ones.

The Government of Bombay never exactly adopted the land policy which Ranade so vigorously urged, but in 1884 it decided to take steps to reform the assessment laws, and the line along which it proceeded was to introduce a large element of permanency. The classifications of soil that had been evolved were accepted as fixed once for all; no enhancement of tax was to be made on account of improvements made by the holder; changes of assessment were to be made only on consideration of such things as rise or fall in the general level of prices, benefit accruing from the building of railways and similar public works; and limits to the possible enhancement at any one time were set.

In the foregoing paragraphs, we have set out Ranade's main contentions regarding the agrarian problem, but he also pointed out many other things that he regarded as requisite to agricultural prosperity. Of these we shall just give the bare list: spread of education; the revival of industries and the diversion of some of the surplus labour from the land; a diminution of taxes and of the extravagant cost of Government; foresight in forest conservancy, and especially avoidance of the injury to agriculture wrought by denuding of trees the mountains, hills, uplands, and river-banks.

In the year 1870, local self-government had become one of the great questions of the day. For a decentralising system of provincial finance had been introduced by a Government

1. "The Agrarian Problem and its Solution."

resolution which expressed the hope that thereby opportunities would be afforded for "the development of self-government, for strengthening Municipal institutions, and for the association of Natives and Europeans to a greater extent than heretofore in the administration of affairs". The wide purpose of political education which the Resolution had in view was in exact harmony with the trend of Ranade's mind, and in the pages of the *Sarvajanik Sabha Journal we find* a number in articles from his pen urging the careful and vigorous development of the local self-governing institutions. It was a characteristic of Ranade's mind always to bring to the elucidation of a problem the light of historical analogies. In accordance with this characteristic, we find among his contributions to the discussion of this question a paper entitled "Local Government in England and India," in which he carefully describes the rise and the present condition of the local government institutions in England, pointing out the lessons of warning and of example that they afford for India.

In 1881, the Government of India further improved the financial position of the Provincial Governments, and instructed the Provincial Governments similarly to endow local bodies from Provincial resources, and to make these bodies more powerful and useful. Departments which the people were likely to understand and to administer well were to be made local. Thus the administration of primary education, medical charity, minor public works, registration of vital statistics, model farms, vaccination, and sanitation were to be handed over to the local bodies.

It is of interest to notice that Ranade was of opinion that the revenue derived from spirituous liquors and narcotic drugs should be deprovincialised and handed over to the Municipal and Local Boards. He says,

> "Certainly no Government officials can be in a better position to take care that people do not abuse their liberties in the matter of intoxicating drinks that the people themselves, especially when these people have by tradition a religious horror of this vice...We also hold

that a limited and clandestine consumption is a lesser evil than a widespread legalized consumption. Each community will have the power of controlling the further growth of this pest of western civilisation and we doubt not that in such hands the license fees and other duties would be raised to such a pitch as to render indulgence in spirituous drinks and narcotic drugs an extremely costly luxury. There would not be and very heavy loss to revenue, and even if there were a slight loss, surely a Government which, in its solicitude for the welfare of its subjects, has actually repealed *in toto* the import duties on cotton goods, ought certainly to be prepared to sacrifice the interests of revenue to what is unquestionable a nobler object, namely, the emancipation of the people from moral degradation and ruin. The anti-opium party in England would give a more practical direction to their agitation if they would take up this question, and first of all force the hands of the Indian Government to abstain from trading in the vices of their own subjects, or to speak more accurately as being nearer the truth, to abstain from gradually initiating their own subjects into vices for which they have inherited no natural propensity."

Ranade's mind was essentially constructive, and accordingly when he saw that the Government was concerned to develope and extend local self-government, he set himself to sketch the changes that required to be made in the constitution and the powers of the local bodies, if the Government's intentions were to be realised. Looking forward to a time when the two basal units of representative government in India, namely, the Municipality and the Local Board, would have been placed on a firm footing, and when the way would be open for making the Legislative Councils also representative in their turn, he outlined a new constitution for the Bombay legislative Council. His scheme, while allowing to Government a working majority in the Council, provided for the inclusion of twelve non-official representatives, who were to be elected by the members of the Municipalities and of the

District Committees. Commenting on his scheme, Ranade declares that its leading feature and in his opinion its greatest recommendation is that,

> "While in the present state of progress in India, it will give an adequate representation to the people in their Government, it will be far from democratic in its character and results. This double process of election is equivalent to filtering as it were the popular suffrage through intermediate bodies. The masses of the people themselves are, in the present state of their civilisation, incapable of choosing the fittest men to be their representatives in the Legislature, but those who manage the local affairs of these masses, and who possess their confidence, ought undoubtedly to be in a position to choose as deputies for the people generally the fittest to be their representatives in the Legislature...With such a consultative Council of notables at hand, Government will feel that it wields its enormous strength with an easy conscience and its present responsibilities will be greatly lightened."

That comment reveals Ranade's. caution. In view of recent developments under the Montagu-Chelmsford Reforms, his suggestions seem very mild and timid. But the official attitude has changed enormously since these days, for at the conclusion of his paper Ranade declares that he is why aware that the majority of his proposals will be denounced as "visionary and radical," by the bureaucratic mind!

India, however, was then entering into the liberal regime of lord Ripon, and the reforms for the extension of Local Government were zealously advanced. In May, 1882, there appeared a Resolution dealing with the reform of Local Government, of which Ranade said that "a State paper more liberal, life-inspiring, and instinct with true statesmanship can hardly be conceived, and has certainly not been seen for many years in India." The recommendations of the Resolution went father in some directions than Ranade and the Sarvajanik

Sabha had been inclined to go, and we get another interesting example of the cautious nature of Ranade's mind in the counsel of wariness that he gives to the authorities. He says,

"The sudden and sweeping introduction of extreme measures, must always be deprecated in the interests of a healthy and natural growth of free institutions; for such extreme measures, if prematurely and suddenly introduced immediately after a very repressive policy, are calculated to demoralise a people instead of elevating them... Ours is the last pen which would willingly support the continuance of a system of official control and dictation; but a calm redection of the real state of things compels us to raise our voice against the sudden and sweeping introduction of an important reform, even though we do so at the risk of indurring the displeasure and taunts of a small minority of well-intentioned but, none the less, over-enthusiastic people.

...The primary object of the Government of India's scheme is to give political and popular education to the people, but efficiency in the local administration cannot be lost sight of. Efficiency and economy in local administration is in fact one of the elements of political education which has to be taught as much as anything else, for no education in the art of self-government can be of the slightest permanent value which does not provide at the same time for efficiency and economy in local administration."

In the following year the Bombay Government introduced two bills to bring into effect the ideas expressed in the Resolution of 1882. Ranade discussed them carefully in the pages of the Sabha's *Journal* with a keen eye for anything that he thought was unsound, or that would stultify the object in view, and especially for anything that would interfere with the financial independence of the Municipal Committees or the Local Boards.

The Sarvajanik Sabha took a warm interest in the Native States, and we find in the *Journal* congratulatory addresses sent on various festive occasions to the Gaikwad of Baroda, the Maharaja of Mysore, and other rulers. In addition to the congratulations, the addresses usually contained a good deal of very straight advice regarding the responsibitities of Princes and the right methods of governing. In 1882, when the young Gaikwad was on the point of assuming the full rights and privileges of sovereignty, the Sabha deemed it its duty, respectfully to submit for His Highness's consideration a few suggestions regarding the best form which the administration of Baroda under His Highness's rule should assume. The suggestions were really the work of Ranade, who had in 1880 published in the *Journal* a paper entitled "A Constitution for Native States." He begins by pointing out that great effort is often made to train the future rulers in those qualifications which their British guardians deem essential for turning them out cultivated and polished gentlemen. But he insists that "no amount of mere personal accomplishment in the young rulers will cure the defects of the system of absolute rule which prevails everywhere, and the temptations of which prove in too many cases so overpowering as to wash off the varnish of education in a few years, and leave the State none the better, often much worse, for the care taken of its Chief during the minority. Our own impression in that as much, if not more, care should be bestowed upon the training of the State and the People in the arts and habits of expecting and securing responsible rule and well-ordered power, as is now lavished upon the education of the Princes, and in teaching them good manners." It is objected that Indian peoples do not manifest the power, habits, and public feeling "which alone can awe a mischievously inclined ruler, and stop him in the race of vice and cruel exactions," and that a *paper* constitution would be useless. But Ranade answers that this function of the people can be discharged by the British authority, "whose representative already wields great powers, and has generally the good sense requisite to make him a useful control, and this fear will be efficient as a sanction till the more genuine home-growth of native public opinion learns to respect itself and enforce obedience." Ranade would have the State adopt a constitution, and the Chief would have to pledge himself to respect it : "Any grievous and long-continued departure from this pledge, should, upon the representation of the subjects, be visited after warning by the Viceroy and local Governors representing the Paramount Power, with the penalty of deprivation under circumstances under which, in a free State, public opinion would have sanctioned and enforced deposition." The constitution that he outlines in marked by his usual clear-headed and competent treatment.

In browing over the pages of the *Sarvajanik Sabha Journal* one comes across many passages that throw light upon Ranade's religious position, and upon his desire for such social reforms as the raising of the age for marriage and the abolition of enforced widowhood. As we shall have occasion farther on to look at his views on these matters, we shall pass them by now. But before turning from our endeavour to see the outlook of Ranade's mind by means of his writings in the *Journal*, we must take some native of what he wrote on educational matters.

Always critical of the centralising of power and the increasing of official control, Ranade delighted to see local resources being utilised and developed. This characteristic is revealed in a paper which he wrote in 1882, called "Primary Education and Indigenous Schools." The opening paragraph is typical of Ranade's readiness to make his contribution to the practical needs of the hour, and also of his tendency to look at a problem under the light of past experiences and of established facts. After having reminded his readers that the Bombay Committee of the Education Commission was soon to commence its labours, he proceeds :

"It is time that we should pass in review the various systems of elementary education which have been in operation in omicient parts of British India during the last 25 years, and live contrasting their results furnish the ground-work of fact on which the authorities more directly concerned with the practical working of this department may be expected to proceed in its future reorganisation consequent on the labours of the Education Commission—the main object of whose inquiry is to ascertain the present state of elementary education throughout the Empire, and the means be which this can everywhere be extended and improved."

He then goes on to make a strong plea on behalf of the indigenous schoolmaster, defending him against the common charges of ignorance, laziness, lack of discipline, and wrongness of method, and suggesting that the official authorities give too much importance to a crammed book knowledge of the elements of grammar, geography, and history, while other subjects which are of much more importance in practical life are little attended to. He reminds us also that the class which has now to be reached is the agricultural community forming the backbone of the population :

"They require to be better fed and clothed and housed before they can be asked with advantage to educate themselves. A knowledge of the rudiments of reading and writing sufficient for their daily life is all that can be expected at present, and this knowledge the indigenous system of schools provides satisfactorily and cheaply. A few picked boys might be helped by free scholarships to pass through the higher grades of instruction, but for the majority the simplest rudiments will suffice for many generations to come."

Ranade calculated that 14,000 more schools were required in the Bombay Presidency, and that to provide these on the prevailing system would require an annual expenditure of fourteen lakhs of rupees. But on the system he proposes he declares that a school could be provided for every village with a population of over 200 souls at an annual cost of only four lakhs. He would incorporate the existing indigeous schools "by extending a small capitation grant for every boy in regular attendance, and an additional grant on the payment by results system for every boy whom these send up for the free scholarship exams." In the next place he would "encourage the establishment of more private schools either by the class from which the indigenous schoolmasters come, or from certificated teachers who should be licensed to open schools on their own account, and make their own arrangements for receiving payments in *kind* or money trom the villagers, the amount so derived being subsidised by a State gratuity, ranging from 2 to 5 rupees a month, according to the numbers attending the school and its results at the free scholarship exams." And he declared that hundreds of trained and certificated young men who now complain of a want of occupation would voluntarily devote themselves to the work of instruction on these terms.

There was considerable talk about that time of withdrawing State help from higher education in order to be able to do more for primary education. Ranade's opinion was against such a step. He felt that it would greatly retard the progress of the country, if that were done before the richer classes had increased in numbers and in appreciation of the responsibilities of their position, and had begun to endow institutions in the way the richer classes in other countries have done. He wrote,

"It is the middle, or rather the hereditary literary and mercantile classes, about 10 per cent of the whole population, which appreciates the present system of instruction, and in the work of Indian regeneration the real leadership belongs to this class of society. Until they are permeated with the leaven of new ideas, it is useless to expect any general or lasting progress. They alone can furnish the teachers who will undertake the work of popular education. India's present circumstances, social and economical, require that those agencies should be allowed to operate freely in all directions, and it becomes as much the duty of Govrnment to help the middle classes to obtain higher education as to assist the lower to secure primary instruction."

The well-known observation that the style is the man readily occurs to the mind after a perusal of Ranade's writings. He imparts his ideas by means of sentences that are massive, well-balanced, and heavily weighted with meaning. He never scintillates and he seldom surprises, but he maintains a consistently high level of clear, dignified, and sonorous prose. We do not find flashes of splendour and brilliance of coloured lights, but we get steady and illuminating brightness. There is little or nothing of poetic rapture or emotional glamour, but frequently there occurs a vivid stroke of realistic metaphor, as for example in this sentence, "Proposals for reform should not err on the side of over-leaping their mark, any more than they should try to set up dead carcases in the seats of life and power." Where there is a warmth of passion in his writing, it nearly always comes as the sequel to an accumulation of convincing facts. His closing paragraph is often an appealing climax in which ideas, marshalled with scientific restraint, seem at last to burst into into a glowing flame. He was capable of slight inelegancies of diction, which suggest that his attention was mainly concentrated upon the thought to which he was giving expression and that, beyond a certain point, he did not greatly concern himself with the form of the expression. The only thing that might betray Ranade's foreign-ness to the English language is an occasional slightly unidiomatic use of a preposition—and such occasions are extremely rare. When we remember that English was not his mother tongue, we cannot but be astonished at the power with which he could express his ideas through that medium. Courteous and kindly as his nature was, Ranade could yet on occasions hit out hard, and he then reveals himself as a master of restrained invective. The following passage, besides being interesting as giving his idea of the qualities required in a ruler, illustrates his ability in this direction :

"Large-hearted sympathy, a generous scorn to catch sectional applause, great moderation of views, honest consistency of purpose, a firm hold of certain large lines of policy, a sense of dignity in asserting independence when great interests require the sacrifice, an even balance of mind in the presence of troubles—these are the attributes which go to make successful rulers of men. Their entire absence in the retired

Governor conspicously marks him but as a costly failure, who by his self-seeking and ex-aggerated laudation of his own acts has degraded the noble standard of duty in the Indian service which scorned to flatter race pride and left its deeds to speak in glorification of the doers."

In the seventies of the nineteenth century, a few political associations had come into existence in different parts of the country. These included the British Indian Association and the Indian Association Calcutta; the Bombay Association, replaced by the Bombay Presidency Association of Bombay; the Sarvajanik Sabha of Poona; and the Mahajana Sabha of Madras. But none of these associations was organised on an all-India basis. Many of the problems they discussed were of an all-India nature, and hence the necessity of forming a nation-wide political organisation began to be felt. The railways had by now connected all cities of India; and the Delhi Durbar of 1877 had suggested to many Indians who attended it, like Surendranath Banerjea, Jamshedji Jeejeebhoy, Vishwanath N. Mandlik and Naoroji Furdoonji, the feasibility of organising all-India conferences and associations. Surendranath Banerjea had already founded the Indian Association in Calcutta in 1876 with the view that it would be the centre of an all-India movement. The Association took up the issue of the reduction of the maximum age of Indian candidates for the I.C.S. examination, which was an attempt to practically close the door to Indians. "The underlying conception, and the true aim and purpose of the Civil Service agitation was the awakening of a spirit of unity and solidarity among the people of India," said Surendranath. To obtain support for the cause, Surendranath travelled in northern and western India, visiting all important cities, from Lahore to Banaras and from Ahmedabad to Poona. As described earlier, at Poona he was guest of Ranade. His mission met with good response. Further attacks on the interests and self-respect of Indians forced the need for an all-India political organisation. Abolition of cotton cloth) import duties in 1877, at the request of British cloth manufacturers, had alienated the commercial and industrial classes in India who were hit hard. There were increasing instances of racial discrimination in awarding punishment for crime. The Ilbert Bill controversy made it obvious that race-distinction was part of the official policy; the triumph of English residents in India in this controversy also served to demonstrate to Indians the value of organised agitation. Along with educated Indians, even a few fair-minded Englishmen felt that these policies should be stoutly opposed. Two such Englishmen were William Wedderburn and A.O. Home. A distinguished British official in India, Hume had resigned from service in 1882 and settled down at Simla. His appeal no educated Indians to volunteer themselves for national service, and his call for sacrifice and unselfishness in order to attain freedom and happiness had made a great impression. On his initiative, the Indian National Union was formed. In March 1885, the Union sent invitations to leading politicians from all Provinces to attend a conference of the Indian National Union to be held in Poona in December. Owing to the out-break of cholera in Poona, the venue was later changed to Bombay. In the meanwhile, Surendranath Banerjea's Indian Association of Calcutta, together with two other organisations had independently issued similar invitations for a 'National Conference' at Calcutta. It was too late to cancel these invitations, and hence a conference was held in Calcutta too. The two conferences voiced the same grievances and aspirations. From the next year, the leaders of both these conferences worked in the same organisation. At the Bombay assemblage, the name adopted for the organisation was the Indian National Congress. It was attended by seventy-two delegates and a number of visitors.

Being a Government servant, Ranade could not officially associate himself with this organisation. In those days, however, the Government allowed much latitude to its servants in these matters. Besides, in the early years of the Congress, its politics was not intolerable to the Government; the majority of British officials greatly disliked it, but not so much as to crush it down. A few fair-minded officials, including the Viceroy, Lord Dufferin, even supported its aims and objects. Official rules prevented Ranade to be a delegate and openly participate in the deliberations of the Congress. But he could be a visitor, and he could take part in all informal discussions. All the delegates from Western India—W.S. Apte and G.G. Agarkar from Poona, Dadabhai Naoroji, K.T. Telang, Pherozeshah Mehta, D.E. Wacha, B.M. Malabari, N.G. Chandavarkar from Bombay and editors of the newspapers in Poona and Bombay—were his friends and close associates in public work; they held him in high esteem. Hume, who had visited Poona in 1884 and 1885 in connection with organising the Congress, once said that Ranade was an uncommon person whose constant thought and concern were for the welfare of his country; and he had the highest regard for Ranade. That Poona rather than Bombay was originally fixed as the venue of the first conference itself shows how much influence Ranade wielded on the organisers. For, except Ranade, there was none in Poona who was of the stature of the Bombay stalwarts. It is reported that while the conference at Bombay was discussing as to which name should be chosen for the new organisation—National Union, National Conference, National League, National Assembly for National Congress—it was Ranade who suggested the name that was finally adopted. The resolutions of the first Congress were settled at a private meeting held at the residence of Principal Wordsworth of Elphinstone College and attended by other officials who included Sir William Wedderburn, Mr. Ranade, and Rai Bahadur Lala Baij Nath of the province of Agra. Mr. Ranade went farther and took part in the deliberations of the open session. His speech, however, had to be off the record. Mr. R.M. Sane, in his reminiscences, relates how, while the resolution for the abolition of the Indian Council was being discussed, Ranade detected an inaccuracy in a statement, and rose from his chair among the audience to speak and correct the error. He was so engrossed with the subject that he forgot that he was officially debarred from speaking in the meeting. In the Congress, Ranade was important enough to send, in 1895, a telegram to Surendranath Banerjea offering him the Presidentship of the Congress at

Poona. "I replied the same day thankfully accepting the offer... Mr. Ranade was, in regard to all public movements in the Western presidency, the power behind the throne. A public servant, loyal to the Government, with that true loyalty, not born of personal motives, or of passing impulses, but having its roots in the highest considerations of expediency and the public good, he was the guide, philosopher and friend of the public men of the Western presidency; and all public movements, were they political, social or religious, bore the impress of his masterly personality," said Surendranath Banerjea Immediately after the first Congress, a deputation consisting of Manmohan Ghosh, R. Mudaliar and N.G. Chandavarkar proceeded to London; it carried a manifesto entitled "India's Appeal to the English Electors", which was mostly written by Ranade. These facts and incidents leave no doubt that, although official records are and must be silent on the point, Ranade was one of the few founders of the Indian National Congress.

As Ranade was debarred from making speeches in the Congress, one cannot infer from the official proceedings what his reactions were to political events. But one can safely say from the fact that he attended every Congress and offered his views to concerned leaders individually that he was enthusiastic about the aims and objects of the Congress and was in general agreement with its resolutions. As is well known, the objects of the Congress were: to promote personal intimacy and friendship amongst public workers in all parts of the country; to develop sentiment of national unity, to put on record the opinions of the educated class on social questions, and to determine the lines of work for the political workers during the ensuing year. The chief resolutions passed during those early years included demands for the abolition of the Indian Council, for the admission of some elected members into the Indian and Provincial Legislative Councils and for widening of their powers, and for simultaneous examinations in England and India for the I.C.S., and the raising of the maximum age of candidates for them. In support of these demands, Ranade had been writing and speaking for some years past.

Ranade desired that this annual gathering of 'public workers in all parts of the country' should deliberate not on work in the political sphere alone but in the spheres of social reform and economic progress as well. At the very first sitting of the Congress in Bombay, he exerted himself to gather support for the holding of an Indian Social Conference annually; and the first one was held in 1887 in Madras immediately after the Congress session in the pandal of the Congress itself. This practice continued for some years, a large number of delegates and visitors used to stay to join the annual Social Conference in which Government servants like Ranade could fully participate. In the economic sphere, there existed a need for an association for industrial development. Ranade corresponded with Hume if the organisers of the Congress could be induced to take up this activity, and Hume seemed doubtful. Ranade then independently organised the Industrial Association of Western India with the help of Messers. G.V. Joshi, Javerilal and D.E. Wacha. The first Industrial Conference was held in 1890 at Poona.

It is in Ranade's address at the annual Social Conferences that we see the philosophy which was at the back of his politics. Notwithstanding his striving for a larger share for Indians in shaping laws and policies of the Government, Ranade was an ardent advocate of the maintenance of British connection. He regarded it as providential. He had a religious belief in God's Providence. According to him, it was the benign Providence which had brought the Mohammedan rule into India, as a result of which the contact between Hindus and Mohammedans "brought about a fusion of thoughts and ideas which benefited both communities"; and he proceeded; "Both Hindus and Mohammedans lack many of those virtues represented by the love of order and regulated authority. Both are wanting in the love of municipal freedom, in the exercise of virtues necessary for civic life, and in aptitudes for mechanical skill, in the love of science and research, in the love of daring of adventurous discovery, the resolution to master difficulties, and in chivalrous respect for womenkind. Neither the old Hindu nor the old Mohammedan civilisation was in a condition to train these virtues in a way to bring up the races of India on a level with those of Western Europe. And so the work of education had to be renewed, and it has been now going for the past century and more under the *pax Britannica* with results which all of us are witnesses to in ourselves."

Fierce wrangling was started on the question : should precedence be given to work for India's political progress or to that for her social reform? Extremists on one side, particularly the British officials, would like Indian leaders to exclude politics and devote themselves solely to social reform. Those holding extreme view, on the other side, represented by Tilak, would like them to concentrate on political progress and ignore the problem of social reform. All spoke in the name of nation's progress. Ranade, on high philosophical grounds, attached equal importance to both. He said in 1990 : "You cannot have a good social system when you find yourself low in the scale of political rights, nor can you be fit to exercise political rights and privileges unless your social system is based on reason and justice." This was Ranade's reply to extremists of both the sides. Work for social and political reform must go on simultaneously. This also partly explains why Ranade would postpone demand for India's independence to a future date—what chances of success were there for an independent democracy while the social system was full of injustice?

Ranade had faith in a great political future for India, and it was this which inspired him in all public work. He said: "With a liberated manhood, with buoyant hope, with a faith that never shirks duty, with a sense of justice that deals fairly to all, with unclouded intellect and powers fully cultivated, and, lastly, with a love that overleaps all bounds, renovated India will take her proper rank among the nations of the world, and be the master of the situation and of her own destiny. This is the goal to be reached—this is the promised land. Happy are they who see it in distant vision, happier those who are permitted to work and clear the way on to it, happiest they who live to see it with their eyes and trend upon the holy soil once more. Famine and pestilence, oppression and sorrow will then be myths of the past."

CONFLICT WITH TILAK (1885-1895)

During the decade from 1885 to 1895, Ranade's noble work for the country found the greatest obstacle in an individual, who also is entitled to respect as a builder of modern India, Bal Gangadhar Tilak.

Tilak was fourteen years younger than Ranade, and brought up in circumstances bordering on poverty. As a student of the Deccan College at Poona, Tilak exhibited qualities of genuine love for the acquisition of learning,intellectual energy, independent thinking, industriousness, determination and courage. Ranade's bold effort in arranging through the Sarvajanik Sabha for the defence of Malharao Gaikwad of Baroda, the Sabha's memorials on public grievances, and Phadke's ill-fated rebellion to liberate the country were events which struck the imagination of the College youth, and turned their thoughts to the conditions of the people and the country. While studying for LL.B., Tilak met Agarkar who was struggling with terrible poverty—he could not afford to have more than one shirt—and yet, when he took the B.A. degree, he decided to turn his back on money and happiness, resolving to dedicate his life to the service of the country. Tilak developed similar ideals; and the two friends for hours on used to discuss how best to achieve them. While they differred on the relative importance of social reform or political progress, they agreed that only proper education, imparted by Indians themselves and inculcating the spirit of patriotism, was an important prerequisite for the upliftment of the nation. They decided to renounce all prospects of personal advancement, which for graduates in those days were vast, and devote themselves to the real education of the people. They began to think of establishing schools on lines similar to the missionary institutions. They turned to Ranade for advice. Ranade was then at Dhulia. He wrote to them that they better think well before starting a new school, but he wholeheartedly appreciated their resolve to take up national work, adding that 'the country would not be emancipated unless it had, like America, its national Press, national education and national church'. At this time they came to know that Vishnushastri Chiplunkar was thinking of resigning from Government service and starting a private school in Poona. Chiplunkar had, while serving as a teacher in Government school, started in 1874 a magazine called *Nibandhamala* through which he poured forth his burning patriotism and infinite pride of everything Indian. Along with the Christian missionaries he also attacked social reformers who used to find fault with the institutions of Hinduism. Tilak and Agarkar joined hands with this selfless and patriotic idealist, and the three comrades started the New English School in 1880. They established a new tradition of selfless work, in contrast to the public work which till then was done by well-off persons—either well-placed Government servants or more or less successful members of learned professions. Their group widened a bit in numbers; and, in order to extend true education to general public, they started two weekly papers, the *Kesari* in Marathi and the *Mahratta* in English. They also conducted a press. Boldly championing the cause of the oppressed, they ran into difficulties with the Dewan of Kolhapur whom they charged with administering dangerous drugs to the Maharaja. Tilak and Agarkar were prosecuted for defamation. Meanwhile, Chiplunkar passed away. As those on whom the accused depended for evidence appealed to them not to disclose their names, they tendered apology. But neither this apology nor the brilliant advocacy of their lawyer, K.T. Telang, saved them, and they were sentenced to four months' imprisonment. This raised them greatly in the esteem of the public; and when they came out from the tormenting Dongri jail in 1882, they discovered that they were regarded as heroes. The Tilak-Agarkar group started the Fergusson College in 1885, in which the two became Professors. For running the institutions, including the College, the group established the Deccan Education Society. In the meanwhile, the Malabari proposals had thrust into foreground the question whether social reform should take precedence over the political. Agarkar was editor of the *Kesari*. and Tilak of the *Maharatta*; their old difference of view points, which till now lay burried, began to show itself in the editorial comments and policies. In 1886, the Society severed its connection with both the newspapers which were looked after by one V.B. Kelkar. A litrle later, Tilak took up the responsibility for the publication of the *Kesari*. Agarkar soon started his own weekly paper, *Sudharak* (meaning, the Reformer); he was assisted by G.K. Gokhale, who had recently joined the Fergusson College as Professor and a Life Member. Tilak and Agarkar were equally merciless in controversy; this widened the gulf between them. Besides, there were differences regarding the administration of the institutions. Moreover, Tilak, by temperament, was a difficult person; the majority of his colleagues rightly or wrongly felt that he was haughty, assertive, arrogant and aiming at self-glorification. Tilak resigned from the Society in 1890, and *ipso facto*, ceased to be a member of the teaching staff. He continued to look after the *Kesari*, which was no longer connected with the Society.

Without denying the desirability of social reforms like widow remarriage and women's education, Tilak persistently criticised the reformers' efforts for some reason or the other. He criticised them for sponsoring the Poona Female High School because its social atmosphere under a European Head Mistress was Westernised; he criticised them for partonising Pandita Ramabai's Sharadasadan because its head was a Christian lady and it surreptitiously carried on proselytising activities; he criticised them for supporting the Rakhmabai case on the ground that the lady was self-willed and attacking the very institution of marriage; and he criticised them for defending the Age of Consent Bill on the ground that they were invoking State interference in a matter which was purely social. These points of criticism were not without foundation; and where he entered into academic controversies regarding interpretation of Sanskrit texts, his learning and analytic powers could not but evoke admiration. But Tilak was open to blame on two counts. First, like a typical opposition party in a parliament, he was exposing defects without doing anything positive or suggesting anything constructive to promote social reform, as if his motive was more to discredit the reform party than to help reform itself. In the second place, while opposing the reformers, he set at naught ordinary rules of decency and, by the scurrility of his attacks, made the life of the reformers awfully unpleasant.

Impertinence ran through even his learned rejoinders to the reformers' arguments. Bhandarkar and Telang were great Sanskrit scholars of international repute and Ranade was a veteran, highly respected for soundness as well as originality. And yet during the Age of Consent controversy. Tilak doubted the depth of Bhandarkar's knowledge. Of Telang, Tilak said that he was too busy as a lawyer to go thoroughly into the scriptures, and so his interpretation was undependable. That was a slur on Telang, the author of a scholarly treatise on the *Ramayana*. Controverting Ranade's plea that the old scriptures were more-liberal towards women than the prevailing laws, and hence laws should be liberalised, Tilak concluded his reply by saying about Ranade, "Oh! What an argument! What a magnificent display of stupendous learning! Indeed, there is no comparison between Manu and the *Mahabharata* on one hand and Rao Bahadur Ranade on the other". After the passing of the Age of Consent Bill,Tilak, in his fury, wrote in the *Kesari* that Ranade, Bhandarkar and Telang were not the leaders of the people; on the contrary, they were men who had brought destruction on the people. "They must be cut off, as a diseased limb of the body is done away with!" At one place Tilak described these three leaders as 'wicked men adorned with learning'.

Not even once did any of these three gentlemen reply abuse with abuse. The strongest words that were uttered from their side came from *Bhandarkar* : "I have been carrying on literary controversies since 1864 but never did I hitherto meet with an opponent who treated me with such studied discourtesy as Mr. Tilak has been doing. This circumstance has rendered my task disagreeable and even painful." The patience and even the forgiveness with which Ranade bore these vituperations of Tilak reveal the magnitude of this personality.

By his persistent and vociferous propoganda, however, Tilak succeeded in undermining the esteem in which Ranade and others were held among the literateclasses of Maharashtra. That Tilak himself was a great scholar greatly helped this process. Ranade was no longer the unchallenged leader of educated Maharashtra. Henceforward there was only the Ranade party, opposed by the Tilak party. Reformers of society are always in a minority and generally not liked; but due to Tilak, the Maharashtra social reformers became, in the eyes of the literates, objects of ridicule and hate. But the literates themselves were a small minority in the whole populace. Moreover, the poison did not extend beyond Maharashtra.

In politics, Ranade was most highly respected in Western India. Tilak entered politics, and there too he struck a new note. He joined the Sarvajanik Sabha. He started attending the Indian National Congress in 1889. He also attended the two sessions of the Indian Social Conference in 1890 at Calcutta and in 1891 at Nagpur. These were the years during which the controversy of social reform was developing fast. In the 1890 session of the Congress, Tilak conveyed to the President a resolution passed by the orthodox Shastris requesting him not to allow the Social Conference to be held in the pandal of the Congress. But he did nor make any speech in favour of this resolution; and as no other Province or leader raised any objection, the Shastris' resolution was ignored. Provincial Conferences (Political) began to be held; Tilak took part in these too. In 1891, the Bombay Provincial Conference was held in Poona; it passed a resolution, initiated by Tilak and opposed by the social reformers' group, expressing dissatisfaction against the Government for having passed the Age of Consent Bill against popular opinion. Thereupon, G.K. Gokhale, who had been, along with Tilak, one of the Secretaries of the Provincial Conference, resigned that post. In the 1892 Provincial Conference, Tilak was again elected Joint Secretary along with Sir Dinshaw Edulji Wacha and Chimanlal Setalvad. In 1893, Ranade was appointed High Court Judge. He could no longer participate in politics even as freely as he did while he was an ordinary Judge. Moreover, he shifted to Bombay. However, in Poona a group of public men who held him in high respect continued to ask his advice and act according to his instructions. Gopal Krishna Gokhale was Ranade's disciple. Gokhale joined the Deccan Education Society in 1886 and was the colleague of Tilak and Agarkar. But in the matter of social reform he fell in with the views of Agarkar. Master of the English language, he wrote the English section of Agarkar's paper *Sudharak*. Ranade noticed his zeal for public work, intellectual capacities humility and reverence for superiors; on the other hand. Gokhale developed great admiration for Ranade. Gokhale once said, "He (Ranade) was to many young men scattered all over the country like the central sun from whom they derived their tight and warmth. . . . to those young workers who were privileged to come in intimate personal contact with him, his word was law and his approbation their highest earthly reward." In 1890, Gokhale was elected Secretary of the Sarvajanik Sabha.

In the beginning, there were no political differences between the Tilak and Ranade groups. Tilak participated in all political associations like other members, and supported resolutions generally agreed upon. But the first difference arose over the attitude to be taken about the Hindu-Muslim riots which occurred in 1893. Communal clashes in Junagadh created a tension in Bombay and later in Poona and other towns. Tilak was of the view that the Muslims encouraged by the Government were to be blamed for these riots. But the Ranade group thought it tactless to emphasise the responsibility on any one community or the Government.

Just about the time of these riots in 1893, Tilak hit on the idea of reorganising the festival of Ganesh. Till then it was a household function : Tilak proposed to make it a public function. The community celebrations would last for ten days; the people would gather to worship the deity in a religious spirit; and these gatherings would witness artistic displays, listen to devotional music, hear under the guise of religious discourses learned lectures on the political and economic problems of the day. This religious movement caught on. Tilak's followers utilised it to spread the spirit of love of religion and of the country. It served to build up Hindu solidarity, as a reply to the British policy of favouring the Muslims and instigating the latter to be aggressive. This whole approach was disapproved by the Ranade party; they would keep worship as a purely personal affair, and organise the solidarity of all national-minded Indians including patriotic Muslims.

By opposing the Ranade group, earlier in respect of social reform and now with regard to Ranade's appeal for self-restraint, Tilak emerged as a representative and leader of the average literate Hindu of Maharashtra, while the Ranade group was relegated into a minority. In both these battles, the Government was also attacked by Tilak. For, when the reformers advised the Government to pass the Age of Consent Bill, the Government, far from being indifferent, actually passed it in defiance of public opinion. In the Hindu-Muslim conflict also, Tilak had aimed his powerful shafts at the Government. In Maharashtra, therefore, a mistaken belief developed that the Government and the Ranade group were somehow on one side and Tilak and the people were on the other.

Tilak stood as a candidate for election to the Bombay Legislative Council and won, against two candidates, one of whom was supported by the Ranade party. The two parties contested for power in the Sarvajanik Sabha. In July 1895, the Tilak party captured it, electing its own office-bearers, but allowing G.K. Gokhale of the Ranade party to continue as Secretary. Gokhale, being alone in the hostile committee, resigned after a year. The Tilak party could claim that it alone represented the opinion of the Poona public. This claim was soon exposed. When Ranade went to Poona during the Divali vacation, he founded a new association, the Deccan Sabha, to give scope to his followers for public work. At this,

Tilak was furious. He said that, like Bacon, Ranade was learned yet mean-minded.

Tilak, Gokhale and Gadgil were Secretaries of the Reception Committee of the Indian National Congress which was to be held in Poona, in 1895, under the Presidentship of Surendranath Banerjea. Gokhale and Gadgil and a majority of the Reception Committee members belonged to the Ranade party. An important duty of the Secretaries was to collect funds for holding the Congress. The orthodox section in Poona led by Sardar Balasaheb Nath and S.V. Date began to agitate for withholding donations unless an undertaking was given that the Social Conference would not be allowed to be held in the Congress pandal. Although personally Tilak agreed with them, he appealed that the success of the Congress was most important, and that donations should be liberally given without preconditions. However, a big meeting was arranged by the orthodox party, which was addressed, among others, by Tilak and his friend, Namjoshi. Resolutions were passed demanding a re-constitution of the Reception Committee with Tilak as the Secretary and desiring that the connections between the Social Conference and the National Congress should be completely severed. This raised internal squabbles as a result of which Tilak resigned from the Secretaryship of the Reception Committee. He was now free to express his personal opinion against the Social Conference. S.V. Date, a rich and stout man with a vulgar tongue was leading the orthodox party. He had a fancy for Tilak and gave a veiled threat that it the Social Conference was to be held in the Congress pandal his people might create a riot and burn the pandal itself. A leading social reformer, who was returning home after seeing a play, was hit with a stick on his head. Tilak issued an urgent appeal to Congress Committees of all places, that they should pass in Committee meetings as well as in public meetings, resolutions opposing the holding of the Social Conference in the Congress pandal, and forward the resolutions to the Congress Working Committee. Accordingly, several Congress Committees did so. Fearing disturbances, most newspapers in India advised the Congress not to press its majority view, and separate the venue of the two gatherings. Personal requests of Surendranath Banerjea and others led Ranade, the Secretary of the Social Conference, to announce that it would not be held in the Congress pandal. The Tilak party and the othodox party together thus won a victory.

Enough has been said in the foregoing pages to bring forth the sublimity of Ranade's endeavours in the cause of the country. It would be wrong, however, to regard Tilak, his bitter opponent, as lacking in patriotism or as an opponent of social reform or as an unscrupulous seeker of popular leadership. In patriotism, Tilak was second to none; in readiness to suffer for his country, he was unsurpassed; his courage in freedom's battle was an inspiration to millions. But he held fast to a view about the situation of the country which was fundamentally different from Ranade's and inevitably they were thrown into conflict with each other.

As against Ranade's restlessness at the prevalence of iniquitious and cruel social customs, by the side of which political subjection was insignificant, Tilak, following Chiplunkar, held that there was nothing basically wrong with our society, and that it was the foreign rule which was galling. While Ranade desired that work for political and social progress should go on side by side, Tilak was impatient for political emancipation and patient regarding social reform. Tilak recognised the existence of social evils, to which reformers had pointed, and in his personal conduct he was a reformer. He sent his daughters to school to learn English; he did not marry them until they were sixteen; he did not observe untouchability and caste distinction in his household. He congratulated Bhandarkar on having his widowed daughter remarried and Karve on having married a widow. What he objected to was not social reform but a movement for social reform. Political work must not only precede social reform work; the latter must be held in abeyance until political progress reached the point of national independence. According to Ranade, political progress was a matter of evolution; Tilak saw, though he did not express this in the early stages, that progress towards national freedom would require national resistance, in which all people must stand united; and social reform, in the very nature of things, must divide society into opposed groups of reformers and conservatives. To Ranade's plea for State legislation in social matters, Tilak had several objections: The evil which the Age of Consent Bill sought to remove was not so *serious* as *Sati* or infanticide. The Government whose intervention was sought was a foreign Government which we should not approach as beggars for help. Lastly, social reform legislation was obviously unpopular; would a democratic legislature of free India have ever passed it in 1880? Though not expressed in these words, this was Tilak's line of thinking. If it is thus understood, many of his apparent errors also can be explained and even excused. From their admiration of Western culture and persistent condemnation of Indian society he inferred that the programme of social reformers was only an imitation of Western customs, which, to him was anathema; in vain Ranade tried to prove to him and those like him that the proposed measures of reform were to follow customs prevailing in our own society in its glorious days. It was abhorrent to him that a minority of our countrymen like Malabari and Ranade should unite with the foreign Government in enacting the Bill to which the majority was obviously opposed; and this infuriated him. It was thus that he saw noble servants of the nation like Ranade with a prejudiced vision and regarded them as adversaries. Ranade, however, was clear in his vision and lofty in his stature. Writing to a friend in Madras about the bitter and acrimonious opposition which Tilak was conducting against him, Ranade simply said, "It is a genuine struggle between earnest men."

STATE LEGISLATION IN SOCIAL MATTERS

The discussions raised by the publication of Mr. Malabari's Notes on Infant Marriage and Enforced Widowhood have been notably distinguished for the warmth and freshness of light thrown upon many of our most cherished social institutions. As is usual in the case of all discussions on social evils, much declamation and invective have been employed on both sides, to supply the place of calm and critical investigation, and the merits of the questions really at issue have been obscured by clouds of words and figures, and empty boasts of self-satisfied complacency. These questions really reduce themselves to two points of inquiry,first, whether or not the institutions assailed produce on the whole more of evil than good, and secondly, whether the evil that is in them admits of a speedier and more effective remedy than is implied in the advice of those who would let things alone, and would drift along with the stream of events, but neither exert themselves, nor permit others to make an effort, to regulate the current and make it run steadier and stronger in the desired direction. One the first point, taking the general sense of those who have spoken out on both sides, there appears to be a general agreement. The dispute here is confined to the alleged extent of the evils, which are freely admitted to be real. On the second point, the difference of views in radical, and there does not appear to be any great likelihood of an agreement ever being arrived at which will satisfy both parties. When one sees how men, who had grown grey in the denunciation of these evils, turned round immediately a suggestion was made for practical action, and joined the orthodox majority in their praise of the existing arrangements, the 'Political Rishi's' warning about the defects of Hindu character seems to be more than justified. There appears to be no ground for hope, under such circumstances, of seeing any genuine reform movement springing up from within the heart of the nation, unless that heart is regenerated, not by cold calculations of utility, but by the cleansing fire of a religious revival. However, there is really nothing strange in all this outcry. There will always be, and there always have been, as Lord Ripon in another connection observed, a clean and an unclean party in small municipal, as well as in large social, arrangements. If the population of our cities were entirely left to themselves, and each man's or woman's vote was as good as another's, the good sense of the men of light and leading would no doubt prevail in the end, but, in the earlier stage of discussion and argument, we should doubtless hear many an appeal to the glory of our ancestors, their long life and vigour, maintained, it might be proudly observed, in spite of, or in the absence of, municipal conservancy. Even in European countries, there are anti-vaccination doctors; Shakers, who take no medicine, but leave the body to cure itself; physical science pedants who still question the truth of the motion of the earth round its sun centre, and its motion round its own axis. A love a paradox is a weakness which clings to many great minds, grows with their other excellences like a parasitic excrescence. Leaving these unnatural developments aside, it is clear that there is a chance of producing a reasonable conviction among, not the vast majority of those who do not think, but among the considerable minority, who in every country lead public opinion by informing it and setting it in proper form before the community in general.

Viewed in this light, there is abundant reason for hope that an historical study of these institutions will dispel many a false conception of the antiquity and sanctity of the existing arrangements.

The early celebration of child marriages, the forcible disfigurement of widows and absolute prohibition of remarriage in the higher castes, the occasional and local practices of polyandry and polygamy, are all admittedly corruptions of recent growth unknown to the best days of our country's history. The late lamented Hon. Rao Saheb V. N. Mandlik, C.S.I., who speaks with an authority which few will dispute, has freely admitted that the Hindu girls' marriageable age is twelve, and that the corresponding age for boys has been reduced from time to time as the period of Bramacharya studies, was more and more curtailed. Taking the most narrow acceptation of the Grihya Sutra rules, this period could not well be legally curtailed below twelve years, thus making the marriageable age for boys twenty years. In regard to the question of widow marriage, it is admitted by the orthodox leaders of the opposition that the prohibition forms part of the Kali-Nishedha, or prohibitions intended for the Kali Yuga only. The writings of Manu and Yajnawalkya show, what the Puranas and Itihasas confirm that monogamy is the natural condition of Aryan life and that both polygamy and polyandry are disreputable excrescences. Nobody can, under these circumstances, contend that, on the strictest interpretation of the texts, the local usages which obtain at present agree with our best traditions of the past. Those who advocate a return to the old order of things are thus in good company, and are not foreign imitators.

We have to consider, next, how it came to pass that the Aryan population, in course of time, departed from the vigorous and healthy usages of their ancestors. Such an enquiry alone will enable us, who now aspire after a higher life, to trace our way back without risk of failure or disappointment. The Hindu community has always been self-contained, if not original, in its grasp of social matters, and no analogies drawn from Christian or Mahomedan nations can have any convincing force, unless they are supported by reasons and associations of our own venerable past.

The rise and fall of female rights and status in Hindu Aryan Society has a history of its own, at once interesting and suggestive in its analogies with the corresponding developments in the institutions of another kindred stock, the Roman Aryans, who have so largely influenced European ideas. Both began by a complete subordination of the women in the family to the men, and of the men themselves to the head of the family. In early Vedic times, the woman was, like the deformed or the sickly member of a family, devoid of rights, and being incapable of self-protection, was disentitled to share the inheritance. The succession in a united family after the death of its chief went to the surviving male members, his sons and brothers, and, in their default, the more distant agnate males.

The earlier Sutrakars, Baudhayana and Apastamba, clearly reaffirmed this exclusion from inheritance and asserted the perpetual subjection of every woman to her father, her husband, and her son. Gradually, however, as the Aryans settled in the land, and the necessities of war gave place to the gentler virtues and victories of peace, the earlier Smritis found admission by express texts for the wife, the mother, the grandmother, daughter, and the sister, and finally to the female relations of the male Gotraja Sapinda. It is hardly necessary to follow this growth step by step. Corresponding with this recognition of the claims of family affection, a chivalrous regard for women, and for their personal comfort and liberty, was asserted in other ways. The women took equal part with the husbands in solemn religious rites, and as queens took their places in great religious sacrifices and the deliberations of State, on occasions of display and power. They were permitted at their choice to remain single and unmarried and neither the father nor the mother would interfere by exercising their power of choosing husbands for them. They were poets, philosophers, and Rishis, and composed hymns, wrote works and studied and argued with men on equal terms. This went on for many centuries, and the proofs of it are too numerous in all our early writings to admit of any hesitation on the part of even the most hostile critic. Marriage was optional with man as well as with woman. The texts of the marriage ritual, the rule for selecting brides or rather bride-grooms, the practice of Swayamvara in mature age, the liberty to be married again on the death, or absence, or incurable impotency, of the first husband, both before and after con-summation, the strictness of the monogamous tie, all these privileges were conceded to women in the natural growth of things.

Thus far, there was no break of continuity, and all was smooth sailing. The analogies between the Roman and Hindu developments were complete so far. In course of time, the Aryans, like the Romans, having overcome their enemies, fell to fighting among themselves, and long and murderous wars between Brahmins and Kshastriyas devastated the land. Under the pressure of these complicated difficulties, the strong love of the active virtues of fighting and hunting, chivalrous regard for women, and the enjoyment of the innocent pleasures of life generally, gave way to a philosophy which regarded life and being itself as a pain and a calamity, the bustle of the arts of peace and war as a vanity of vanities. And naturally weak woman, from being the soul of chastity and virtue, came to be described as a snare and a burden. The gods, who had cheered the conquering and militant Aryans with their countenance, retired with the Rishis to the Himalayas and beyond. They could no longer be seen, and gave way to a fatalastic belief that man was the slave of his own miserable *Karma*, and must bear it patiently till he learned how best to throw off this mortal coil. The great excess of bad passions which had deluged the land with fratricidal blood demoralized society, and lowered the status of women in the family, the State, and in the social arrangements generally. The Aryan ideals lost their charm, and a lower type of character and morality asserted its predominance as the down-trodden races, which had been driven to the hills, issued from their haunts, and fell upon the demoralized and disunited Aryan kingdoms on all sides. At the same time, a new race of invaders from Central Asia, partly Scythian and partly Mongolian in stock; entered India by the North-West, and the North-East, drove before them the old Aryans, and established their power and colonies in the Punjab, Sind, Rajputana, Central India, Bengal, Guzerat, and even in parts of Maharashtra. This process of the upheaval of non-Aryan races, and the invasion and settlement of barbarian Scythian and Mongolian conquerors, was in active development for many centuries, and these ethnic and political forces have profoundly modified the institutions and usages of modern India. They brought to the surface races of men with a lower civilization more patriarchal, and, therefore, less chivalrous ideals of life. Polyandry, has always been a normal institution of the non-Aryan or Scythian and Mongolian races. It derived new dignity from the rise to power of these backward races. The woman's lot has always been one of dependence and misery in barbarous countries. It could not be otherwise here. Woman in these ruder races was bartered in marriage as a moveable chattel or slave. She was burned with the deceased lord, with his bows and arrows, his horse and weapons, to provide for his comfort in another world. When these races rose to power, the better minds were driven to seek shelter in asceticism and abandonment of the world which had for them no charms and only misery, life-long and unrelieved; and instead of being the deity of peace and goodwill in the family, woman became the symbol of corruption and vice. Optional celibacy and Swayamvara were under these circumstances out of the question. The old state of pupilage and dependence was re-affirmed. Late marriages, and the liberty of second marriage to widows, were denounced, though here and there they were allowed to associate with the husband's surviving brother for the purpose of procreating children for him. The well-marked four-fold divisions of life lost their meaning and their sanctity, and baby and child-espousals could not but come into foshion. and bring in their train polygamy and concubinage. Things thus settled themselves on this lower level of barbarous usages. Gradually, the better and the Aryan portion of the community recovered from the surprise and discomfiture, and the dark clouds of the Middle Ages of Indian History, the dreaded Kali Yuga of the Puranas, began to clear up.

Political and ethnic agencies of great power have wrought the evil, and we cannot afford to lose sight of this fact in our attempts to elevate the status of the female sex. Fortunately, the causes which brought on this degradation have been counteracted by Providential guidance, and we have now, with a living example before us of how pure Aryan customs, unaffected by barbarous laws and patriarchal notions, resemble our own ancient usages, to take up the thread where we dropped it under foreign and barbarous pressure, and restore the old healthy practices, rendered so dear by their association with our best days, and justified by that higher reason which is the sanction of God in man's bosom.

The next question is, as stated above, a more difficult one to deal with. How this gentle revolution is to be effected without breaking with the past, is a problem which admits of difference of views. There are two schools of thinkers among those who have discussed this subject. One set would utilize all the active and passive agencies which tend to encourage and vitalize reform; the other set would leave things to take their own course, fiim in the confidence that the passive agencies at work would secure all our ends just as we desire, slowly but surely. Those who feel the full force of the ethnical and political causes mentioned above, and also feel how necessary it is at certain stages of man's progress to secure the assertion of right ideas by the highest sanctions, advocate to some extent the help of State regulation, as representing the highest and most disinterested wisdom of the times, working to give effect to the other tendencies, concentrating and popularizing them. Those who are not sufficiently alive to these considerations would trust to education and the gradual development of better ideas by their own internal force, to achieve all that we desire. It is needless to state that the publication to which these remarks are prefaced is intended to strengthen the hands of the first set of thinkers and to show, by the example of what occurred in the past, that timely State regulation is not attended with the mischiefs which people attribute to it, and that it co-ordinates and vivifies the healthy action of the other agencies. It becomes, in this connection, necessary to consider briefly the several objections urged by the advocates of the let-alone school in their order of relative importance.

The first objection urged on this head is that these are social questions, which it is not the duty of the State to regulate. We answer that this argument is not open to those who welcome, as the vast majority of this class of opponents freely do, State regulation for the abolition of *Sati*, of infanticide, the suicide of *jogees* on the banks of the Ganges, and self-torture by hook-swinging before idol shrines, or to those who propose compulsory education, and compulsory vaccination, and sanitary precautions generally. Individual liberty of action is no doubt a great force, but this liberty has its limitations imposed by the fact that no man's liberty should encroach upon the liberty of those who surround him. Whenever there is a large amount of unredressed evil suffered by people who cannot adopt their own remedy, the State has a function to regulate and minimize the evil, if by so regulating it,the evil can be minimized better than by individual effort and without leading to other worse abuses. The State in its collective capacity represents the power, the wisdom, the mercy and charity, of its best citizens. What a single man, or a combination of men, can best do on their own account, that the State may not do, but it cannot shirk its duty if it sees its way to remedy evils, which no private combination of men can check adequately or which it can deal with more speedily and effectively that any private combination of men can do. In these latter cases, the State's regulating action has its sphere of duty marked out clearly. On this, and on this principle alone, can State action be justified in many important departments of its activity, such as the enforcement of education, sanitation, factory legislation, of state undertakings like the postal service, or subsidies given to private effort in the way of railway extension and commercial development. The regulation of marriageable age has in all countries, like the regulation of the age of minority, or the fit age for making contracts, been a part of its national jurisprudence, and it cannot be said with justice that this question lies out of its sphere. The same observation holds true of the condition of the widow rendered miserable in early life, and thrown helpless on the world. More legitimately than minors, the widows are the wards of the nation's humanity, and to the extent that the evil they suffer is remediable by man, it cannot be said that this remedy may not be considered by the State as fully within its proper function.

The next argument urged on the other side is that the evil is not so great as some people think, and that it really needs no state action. There can be no doubt that, to some extent, Mr. Malabari has laid himself open to this side attack. The evils of child-marriage, and enforced widowhood, and unrestricted polygamy, are not guantitatively, and calculating them by satistical returns, so great as Mr. Malabari described them to be. But this does not go to show that, after making due allowance for all exaggerations, the residue of unredressed wrong which calls for remedy is not sufficiently great to justify action. Much the same thing was said when it was proposed to prohibit Sati or Infanticide. Wherever there is undeserved misery endured in a large number of cases there is ground for state interference, always supposing that the interference will lead to the redress of the wrong, better than any individual effort can accomplish.

A third way of stating the the same objection is that the parties who suffer do not complain of it, and strangers have, therefore, no business to intervene. This is a very old line of defence. It was urged as an argument against the abolition of slavery, as well as against the laws which rendered Sati and Infanticide crimes, and validated widow marriages. Perhaps, the worst effect of injustice is that it depresses the down-trodden victims to such an extent that they lick the hand of the oppressor. The slaves fought no the side of the Southern planters against their Northern liberators. No wonder then, if the helpless women and widows side with the orthodox majority. If the State contemplated forcible action in spite of the wishes of the victims, the argument might be urged with some effect. But nobody in his senses can, or does, contemplate any such method of procedure. Widows and children are not the proper persons who can seek their own relief under the wrong that is done to them, and to society, and this argument therefore, falls to the ground.

Fourthly, it is urged that, admitting the fact that such regulation falls within the province of State action, and that these evils, after making all allowances for exaggeration and the apathy of the victims, are still sufficient to justify State action, if such action can remedy the wrong without leading to other and greater abuses, and that it is not proper to wait till the victims rebel—it is urged that a foreign Government cannot be trusted with this power. This jealousy of foreign interference in social matters is not altogether a bad sign, and if the interference was of foreign initiation, the force of this argument would be irresistible. In this case, however, the foreign rulers have no interest to move of their own accord.

If they consulted their selfish interests only, they would rather let us remain as we are, disorganized and demoralized, stunted and deformed, with the curse of folly and wickedness paralysing all the healthy activities and vital energies of our social body. The initiation is to be our own, and based chiefly upon the example of our venerated past, and dictated by the sense of the most representative and enlightened men in the community, and all that is sought at the hands of the foreigners is to give to this responsible sense, as embodied in the practices and usages of the respectable classes, the force and the sanction of law. These considerations weighed with our leaders in the past, when they welcomed this co-operation in the abolition of Sati and Infanticide, and also in the recognition of the validity of widow marriages.

If we are to abjure such help under all circumstances, we must perforce fall back behind the Parsis, Mahomedans, and Christians, who have freely availed themselves of the help in recasting their social arrangements. The Parsis through their Panchayat secured to their community the benefit of the Parsi Marriage Act, and their Matrimonial Courts with Parsi delegates to assist the Judge. The Khojas have been striving to secure similar concessions for their own community. The Nayars, in Malabar, have very recently had the benefit of an improved Marriage Law extended to them by legislature. The movement of proper regulation of religious endowments, in respect of which public opinion is almost unanimous, may be cited as an illustration of the readiness of all classes of people not to object to State Legislation at the hands of foreign rulers. Further, as it is likely that foreign rule will last over us for an indefinite length of time, we reduce ourselves, by accepting this policy, to the extereme absurdity of shutting out a very useful help for many centuries to come. In such matters, the distinction of foreign and domestic rulers is a distinction without difference. It has a meaning and significance when foreign interests override native interests, but when the foreigners have no interest to serve, and the initiative is to be all our own, the recognition of State help is not open to the stock objection urged by those who think that we forfeit our independence by seeking such regulation on lines approved by us.

Fifthly—It is further urged, in deprecation of State action, that in this matter we must not lose sight of the fact that institutions, like constitutions, must grow and cannot be made to conform with foreign ideals to order. There is, no doubt, some force in this observation, and it would be a fatal objection if the argument for ehange were based on the ground that we must copy the foreign exemplar. The remarks which have been made above are, however, a sufficient answer to this allegation. The change is sought not as an innovation, but as a return and restoration to the days of our past history. Those who advocate it justify it on the authority of texts revered, and admitted to be binding to this day. The intermediate corruption and degradation was not of the nation's seeking. It was forced upon it by the predominance of barbarous influences, and by the intolerance of ruthless conquerors. That force having ceased to be operative, we must now return to the old order of things, if we are to grow to our old proportions. The history of the suppression of Infanticide and of Sati shows that these institutions, which had grown as excrescences upon the healthy system of ancient Hindu Society, were checked, and could be checked, only by the strong arm of Law, and once they were denounced as crimes, they disappeared from the face of the country. Before Government made up its mind to deal finally with these evils, the usual arguments that institutions grow, and cannot be made to order, were urged, and the duty of religious neutrality was held up in terrorem to frighten the timid and arouse the passions of the ignorant and the prejudiced. The diseased mal-formations of the body cannot, and should not, be dealt with in the same way as its normal and healthy developments. The sharp surgical operation, and not the homoepathic infinitesimally small pill, is the proper remedy for the first class of disorders, and the analogy holds good in the diseases of the body politic, as also in dealing with the parasitical growths of social degeneration.

Sixthly—The apprehensions against State legislation expressed in some quarters might have been most reasonable if, as a fact, Hindu Society was really not governed by any law, and it was proposed for the first time to regulate these matters by subjecting them to the controlling action of the State. The fact, however, is that law, a written law, and a very stringent one too, does regulate these matters, and it is enforced much in the same way as other laws by our Courts of Justice. The courts are bound to give effect to that law, and decree personal rights and disabilities in strict accordance with it. What is now proposed is to substitute the more ancient and righteous law for a later degenerate off-shoot of that law, cancel the travesty of law which is condemned by all, at least more amenable to reason, and utilize the force of State sanction as a final support. No private understanding can prevail against the coercive power of unjust law as it is now enforced. The new law proposed is itself not a foreign importation, but is only a revival of the ancient law of the country as laid down in the texts, and all that the Government is called on to do is to revert from the times of corruption to the times when Hindu Society was more healthy and vigorous.

There is another incidental and an important advantage likely to accrue in consequence of the change proposed. All progress in social liberation tends to be a change from the law of status to the law of contract, from the restraints of family and caste customs to the self-imposed restraints of the free will of the individual. Nay, more, the confusion caused by inconsistent Smriti texts and judicial authorities on ancient Hindu Law and custom furnishes the strongest argument for a definite improvement based on ancient lines by way of codification on the subject by the legislature. There is not a custom, however absurd, which cannot be defended by some strong text of ancient law. The usual practice of reconciling texts, intended for different ages and countries, and the loss of the spirit of true criticism, have benumbed the power of judgment. The liberation from superstitious thraldom, which will result from the changes proposed, is not likely to be the least of its benefit. It will be necessary to be very circumspect in graduating the change desired to meet exactly the extent of the evil crying for redress. The past century or half a century has effected a change in national sentiment, which, if not recognized to the extent it has gone, will only lead to a catastrophe and revulsion of feeling that will be simply irresistible, and may involve the ruin of many interests dear to the nation's heart.

There is only one more objection which we think deserves a passing notice. It is said that all previous legistation was directed against positive crimes, or was only of a permissive nature, while the evils now sought to be remedied are not crimes, and the remedies proposed are not of a permissive character. On the first point, we must urge that the practices now complained of are in some respects far more criminal than those which State action has checked. Sati was committed under temporary insanity caused by grief, while infanticide was in too many cases dictated by a similar mad impulse. They both offences not committed in cold blood, and their effects spent themselves in a single act of violence, which inflicted the greatest shock on the perpetrator himself or herself. In most cases enforced widowhood and disfigurement, the destruction of home sanctity by polygamous connections, the stupidity of baby marriages, are not impulsive acts, they are done in cold blood, and they inflict lifelong and undeserved misery on helpless victims, while the offenders suffer but little. So far as their moral heinousness is concerned, they are inflictions of injustice without any redeeming features, and the criminal responsibility of the nation is beyond all reprieve.

As regards the question of permissive *versus* compulsory legislation, we have no patience with those who can find consolation in empty words. The remedies proposed are in their nature permissive, and need give offence to nobody. It the law lays down strictly that no polygamous connection shall be entered into except for reasons specially permitted by the ancient law of Manu, we fail to se how such legislation is more compulsory than permissive. When the law lays down than no widow may disfigure herself except of deliberate choice, and at a fit time of life, say after she is twenty-five years old, where indeed is the compulsion? When the law lays down that marriages shall dot be celebrated below a certain age, at least twelve for girls and eighteen for boys, under penalty that earlier celebrations will not meet with the recognition of the Civil Courts in cases of disputes, where again is the compulsion?

We have thus noticed and answered all the usual objections urged by those who honestly support the continuance of the existing order of things. The question of principle is one which must first be argued out in all its bearings. Once the principle is recognized, the details of legislation may safely be left to the common sense of the community. It is with this view that the compiler of this publication has addressed himself to the task of placing before the public, in an acccssible form, the literature of the subject in the shape of the debates that took place when the Widow Marriage Bill was just introduced in the Legislative Council thirty years ago. The arguments then urged and refuted have a curious family likeness to those we have at present, and just as the apprehensions then entertained were disappointed, so surely we trust to see that all our ignorant prophecies will be falsified. The directions in which the marriage law needs reform have been already briefly indicated. Diwan Bahadur Raghunath Rao has already sketched out a draft Bill in which some of the reforms urgently required are set forth in full detail. The late Maharaja of Burdwan submitted thirty years ago a scheme for abolishing polygamy. The views of those who have given thought to the subject on this side of India may be briefly thus summarized.

We would, to start with, fix twelve and eighteen as the minimum ages of marriage for girls and boys. These periods are in full keeping with the most approved practice, and the more respectable orthodox sentiment of the present day. Even Rao Saheb V.N. Mandlik has stated twelve years for females as a permissible limit, and for boys we do not think he will regard eighteen years as an unreasonable limit. Marriages contracted before this age should be discourged, not by pains and penalties of the criminal law, but by the attendant risk of making them liable to be ignored, as in the case of contracts entered into by minors, liable to be ignored or set aside in case of disputes in the Civil Courts for sufficient reasons. Marriage, unless consummated should not be recognized as a perfect union before the limits laid down above are reached. Before such consummation, the girl should not be recognized as having become one with the husband in Gotra, Pinda, and Sutaka. This is the ancient law, and our revival of it will do away with the superstition which paralyses the action of parentsin dealing with the misery of child widows. We would on no account permit disfigurement except after twenty-five years,when the widow may be presumed to be able to realize the circumstances of her position, and can choose deliberately the celibate course of life. Under no circumstances should one wife be superseded by a second connection, except under the safeguards recognized by Manu and other writers. The widow's forfeiture of her husband's estate as a consequence of her second marriage should be done away with, and her life interest in her husband's inheritance should remain intact, whatever her choice of life might be. The marriage of a widower above fifty with girls below fourteen should be strictly prohibited as being opposed to the most approved Smriti texts.

These are the several changes which the advocates of Reform seek to accomplish, not all at once but in due progression. They are fully aware that the details of legislation will not be easily settled, without suggesting many difficulties and doubts which will have to be provided against. The time, however, for suggesting these details has yet to come. We think the discussion has now reached a stage when all sides may well agree in asking for a Commission of Inquiry. Such a Commission, composed of representative Natives, and Europeans, on the model of the Education Commission, will pave the way for practical suggestions. Its inquiries will give point to the discussion, and tend to preserve the interest that has been aroused in all quarters.

It is admitted on all hands that Ranade did a very big work in the political education of India, and also that his efforts along the less obtrusive lines of political agitation were very effective. For the last quarter of the nineteenth century his was the inspiring and dominating mind at the back of most of the political movements carried on by Indians. He was among the "seventy-two good men and true, the foremost amongst India's intellectuals"—to use the words of Mr. H.P. Mody—who "on the fateful morning of the 28th December, 1885, sat down together to carve out a future for their country." The Indian National Congress which then came into being proved a great instrument for rousing the national consciousness and for guiding the national movement. Mr. A.O. Hume has the honour of being regarded as the Father of the Congress, but he was accustomed to call Ranade his "Political Guru." By his weighty and well-informed utterances, Ranade stimulated thought and moulded opinion on such burning political questions as the Vernacular Press Act, the Arms Act, the Civil Service Examinations, the Central Asia Question, etc. His advice was eagerly sought by all sorts of political leaders.

He saw that though India was not in a position to male its will directly effective, yet much could be done indirectly by bringing pressure to bear on the British Parliament. Already in this way alteration of the Press Act, and satisfactory adjustment of the expenses of the Afghan War had been secured; and Ranade always urged that full use should be made of existing means of getting their wishes respected, without sitting idly waiting for the day when they would have power to choose their own representatives. The policy he advocated was that the Indian Nationalists should form a connection with the British Liberal Party, win its sympathy, and through it get Indian grievances brought before Parliament. He saw that under the British system it was only by having a question made a party matter that a proper hearing for it could be secured. It was in pursuance of this policy that, in 1876, he collected money to assist the candidature of Henry Fawcett, a politician whose warm and helpful devotion to the cause of India was a dominant feature of his career. Again, in 1885, Ranade took much interest in the preparation for the work of a deputation of Indians who were being sent to bring Indian affairs to the notice of the British electorate, and he himself composed the rough draft of a leaflet that was to be distributed among the electors.

In 1885, the new law for Local Self-government was brought into operation. Ranade thought it a step in the right direction and, indeed, he felt that it was to some extent the fruit of his own efforts, made through the Sarvajanik Sabha. Therefore, when he discovered that his old friend, Mr. Kunte, was vigorously lecturing against the new Act, he was much grieved. Fearing that Kunte's efforts would have the result of delaying the introduction of self-government in the district, he resolved to counteract him.

One day he went into a hall in Poona where Kunte was lecturing and sat among the audience. Thereupon Kunte, to mark his annoyance, turned his back on the sadience and went on speaking vigorously for a time. When he had finished, Ranade went up and sat near him. After the meeting had ended he asked Kunte to come for a drive with him in his carriage, but he angrily refused and went to his own carriage. Ranade quietly followed him and said, "Very well, if you will not come in my carriage, I shall go in yours,"and so he did. In silence they drove off. During the drive their differences were composed, and from the next day, Kunte's lectures against the Act ceased.

It is of interest to note that G.K. Gokhale, one of the great men of Indian public life, witnessed this incident and was much impressed with the part that Ranade played in it. Two years later he was introduced to Ranade, and from that time onwards—Gokhale was then twentry-one—there existed between the two a close association, which had far-reaching effects upon the younger man. Ranade was quick to realise the possibilities of Gokhale, and he set himself to develop them. Bikhale always claimed to follow the spirit of Ranade. he called him his Guru, would never sit down in his presence, he held him in an almost religious reverence. He right for about twenty years in the Fergusson College, at Poona, under the Deccan Education Society, working in accordance with the principles of the Society, in a missionary spirit, and for a mere subsistence allowance. Then, in 1902, but of a strong of impulse of duty, he gave up teaching, in order, as he declared, "to embark on the stormy and ancertain sea of public life". He became a member of the imperial Legislative Council in that year, and in and through that body made his influence felt in quite a remarkable was. Throwing himself with immense vigour and thoroughness into the efforts for India's political, social, and industrial advancement, he soon became the recognised exponent of Indian aspirations. In 1905, he started the *Servants of India Society*, the object of which is to "train national missionaries for the service of India and to promote by all constitutional means the true interests of the Indian people." His long and intimate association with Ranade tempered the steel of his mind and character for the great tasks to which he was destined. From Ranade he learned to found himself upon realities and to accept the way of hard study, and he imbibed his master's width of view, balance of mind, and moral fervour.

In June of 1885 a banquet was given to Ranade by the Poona citizens to celebrate his appointment to the Legislative Council. Some of the speakers on that occasion urged him to give up Government service, and to devote all his time to the popular cause, telling him that he could serve his country better if he were free from all the restraints of an official position. But Ranade made it clear that he was not of that opinion. On the other hand, Ranade was several times offered high posts in Native States. In 1896, when replying to a third invitation given to him by the Baroda State, he wrote : "In my relation with the British Government, I have always been known as one who, while serving in the post that he has successfully filled, has at the same time never bartered his freedom for any personal consideration." The friends whom Ranade consulted had strongly advised him not to accept an appointment in a Native State, because to do so would stop his free expression of opinion.

There are three things that cannot but impress memselves upon the mind of anyone who studies Ranade's political writings and addresses. These are : (1) his frank recognition of his country's weaknesses, (2) his fearless exposure of Government faults, and (3) his hearty approval of the British connection.

He deplores Indian lack of unity and inability to work harmoniously together for common ends. He deplores the lack of enterprise and perseverance, and the tendency to be too easily elated and too easily depressed. He thought that the people were too prone to shout catch-words of which they did not really understand the significance. Speaking in 1893, he said :

"We bandy about the words freedom and independence, but of their meaning many have no clear idea. Freedom means making laws, levying taxes, imposing punishment, and appointing officials. The true difference between a free country and an unfree one is that in the former before punishment is given a law must have been made; before taxes are levied, consent must been secured; before making a law opinions must have been taken."

He saw among the people of his day a tendency to turn their eyes too much to the past, and to extol extravagantly and without proportion the days of old. He saw that there was danger of this attitude becoming an opiate, deadening the mind to present duty. He therefore urged the need of hard, self-denying work, in place of mere vapouring about the glorious days of yore. "We should learn to be men, stalwart puritan men, battling for the right, not indifferent nor sanguine, trustful but not related serious but not dejected. This is the change in character that has to be accomplished."[1] Reverence for the past, Ranade held, was not in itself a bad thing, quite the contrary, but it must be combined with activity and vigour. He urged also that discrimination ought to be exercised in our homage to the past. The part of India's past which is worthy of all honour is the time when science, literature, and philosophy flourished, and when the Empire of the Indians extended from Java to Mongolia. But the last 1,500 years had brought India to its present evil condition, and Ranade declared that there was no sense in honouring it and no obligation to do so. He said that now and again, during these 1,500 years, gleams of the ancient power and purity had appeared, but in the present the glory had altogether departed. He urged that the men of the present must seek to do their duty with strength of purpose, perseverance, resolution, and joy, and thereby restore to India the greatness that it possessed in the very ancient days. We cannot break with our past altogether, he said, and we should not want to do so, for it is a rich inheritance of which we have no reason to be ashamed. But, while respecting the past, we must ever seek to correct the parasitical growths that have encrusted it, and sucked the life out of it.

With equal faithfulness Ranade dealt with Government actions and policies in his writings and addresses. He criticised the land administration, and indicated what he regarded as better methods; and in a similar way he dealt with many other particular matters. He reviewed very frankly the administrative records of Viceroys and Governors. He felt that the Government in India tended to be too much centralized, and too little adaptable to the varying local circumstances. "One code, one law, one measure, the same taxation, the same routine forms, a fondness for uniformity as an end in itself—this is the besetting sin of the administration."[2] On many an occasion he uttered candid words about the faults into which the

1. Address entitled "The Telang School of Thought," Bombay.

2. Speech on Lord Repon's Local Self-Government Scheme, 1884.

members of a ruling race are always prone to fall, and the complete prevalence of which would be fatal to all real advance. His clearest statement on this matter was given at the time of the controversy on the *Ilbert Bill.* This was a Bill introduced in 1883 to give Indian District Magistrates and Sessions Judges the right to try European British subjects, and empowering Local Governments to extend the right to other officials belonging to certain specified classes. The European community was fiercely indignant at the Bill and tried to stampede the Government into abandoning it. Ultimately the Bill was passed, but it an amended form, which substantially whittled down its scope. When the commotion had subsided, Ranade wrote an essay giving a summary of the affair and a statement of his own opinion. He said :

"The educated minority of the native population with their free press, and their associations unconsciously sympathized with by the mass of their countrymen, represent the soul of Indian Liberalism, and their strength lies in the justice of their claim. Arrayed against them are the mighty forces of the official hierarchy, supported by the non-official phalanx of their countrymen here and the great reserve of power and prejudice stored in the large vested interest of their mother country. These are the liberal and conservative forces at work in India . . . . This prejudice and aversion is the native and besetting sin of all conquering races. The Spartan had his Helot, the early Roman patrician had his Plebeian subjects, the later Roman had his Latin and Italian allies, the American and West Indian planter had his Negro and his Chinese settler. In our own country the regenerate castes had the mass of the aboriginal population under their foot and put them down with a severity which has reacted on themselves with terrible vengeance. The British population in India has arrogated to itself the distinctive position of a superior caste, and history but repeats itself in their cry for power and privilege, and their contempt for the conquered and subject population."

In spite, however, of his keen consiousness of many defects in the attitude, policies, and actions of the ruling race,

Ranade never ceased to be a loyal upholder of the British connection. He discerned a great moral purpose at work in India's long and chequered history. He said:

"I profess implicit faith in two articles of my creed; this country of ours is the true land of promise; this race of ours is the chosen race. It was not for nothing that God has showered His choicest blessings on this ancient land of Aryavarta. We can see His hand in history. Above all other countries we inherit a civilization and a religious and social polity which have been allowed to work their own free development on the big theatre of Time. There has been on revolution, and yet the old condition of things has been tending to reform itself by the slow process of assimilation."

He shows how Buddhism was outlived and conquered by an imbibing of its excellencies and rejecting of its errors. He shows how the Muhammadan repression was outlived, the people emerging all the better for the hardy discipline in suffering that it went through under that domination. Their character was strengthened in directions in which it had been deficient; their manners and tastes were refined, and they were advanced in many practical accomplishments. But the most lasting benefit of the contact came through the higher tone given to the religion and thoughts of the people. "Caste, idolatry, polytheism, and gross conceptions of purity and pollution," Ranade declares, "were the precise points in which the Muhammadans and the Hindus were most opposed to one another."[1] And he shows that the reforming sects which arose within Hinduism from the fifteenth century onwards "had this general characteristic that they were opposed to these defects in the character of our people." Summing up his philosophy of Indian history, he declares:

"The history of this great country is but a fairy tale, if it has not illustrated how each invasion from abroad has

1. Speech at the Social Conference, Lucknow, 1899.

intended tc serve as a discipline of the chosen race, and led to the gradual development of the nation to a higher ideal if not of actual facts, at least of potential capabilities. The nation has never been depressed beyond hope of recovery, but after a temporary submerging under the floods of foreign influences, has reared up its head—absorbing all that is best in the alien civilization and polity and religions."[1]

He sees the British connection as the coping stone of this long disciplining process, referring to it as "the discipline afforded us by the example and teaching of the most gifted and free nation in the world, whose rule guarantees to us a long continuance of these favourable conditions."[2]

"Both Hindus and Muhammadans," he said, "lack many of those virtues represented by the love of order and regulated authority. Both are wanting in the love of municipal freedom, in the exercise of virtues necessary for civic life, and in aptitudes for mechanical skill, in the love of science and research, in the love of daring and adventurous discovery, the resolution to master difficulties, and in chivalrous respect for womankind. Neither the old Hindu nor the old Mahammadan civilization was in a condition to train these virtues in a way to bring up the races of India on a level with those of Western Europe, and so the work or education had to be renewed, and it has now been going on for the past century and more under the *Pax Britannica* with results—which all of us are witnesses to in ourselves."[3]

Ranade believed that in God's providence Britain had been entrusted with a great mision in India. "The sole *ratlonale* of British rule in India," he once wrote, "is its capacity and its providential purpose of fostering the political education of the country on the largest scale in civil and public activities."[4] Even in days of political reaction and of popular disappoint-

1. Speech at the Social Conference, Lucknow, 1899.
2. *Ibid*, Allahabad, 1892.
3. Speech at the Social Conference, Lucknow, 1899.
4. *Sarvajanik Sabha Journal*, Vol. VIII, No 3, 1886.

ment, he held fast to his trust that God's providence was over all, and that the good sense and innate justice of the British character would acknowledge the rightness of India's claims. In words bright with the colours of the Old Testament, he pictures the goal whose attainment would be the fulfilment of Britain's mission and of India's aspirations:

"With a liberated manhood, with buoyant hope, with a faith that never shirks duty, with a sense of justice that deals fairly to all, with unclouded intellect and powers fully cultivated, and, lastly, with a love that overleaps all bounds, renovated India will take her proper rank among the nations of the world, and be the master of the situation and of her own destiny. This is the goal to be reached—this is the promised land. Happy are they who see it in distant vision; happier those who are permitted to work and clear the way on to it; happiest they who live to see it with their eyes and tread upon the holy soil once more."[1]

The Dust raised against Ranade by the Tilak group rose thick and high, but not so high as to be wafted to other Provinces. Propaganda against him was done mostly in Marathi papers and in meetings in Maharashtra. Irreverence for him was confined to Maharashtra. In no other place objection was raised to the holding of the Social Conference in the pandal of the Congress. On all-India political work. Ranade continued to exercise just the same influence as before. His wise counsel was sought and respected by great political leaders all through his life-time. He continued to take part in the shaping of the resolutions of the National Congress before they were moved in the open session. In 1899 at Lucknow, when the Congress session was over and its President, Romesh Chunder Dutt, made a speech in the Social Conference, he said: "I feel further honoured in taking part in these proceedings because, as we know, they are conducted by that honourable gentleman, Mr. Justice Ranade. . . We in Calcutta respect him as you in Lucknow do". Srinivasa

1. Speech at the Social Conference, Calcutta, 1896.

Sastri once wrote, his figure "could always be seen in the intimate discussions of the subjects committee of the Congress. Every difficulty was referred to him. At every crisis he would interpose with his great authority and the Congressmen of those days, giants though they were proud to acknowledge that many a time Mr. Ranade kept them straight on the road of progress." Mud-slinging in Poona did not in the least tarnish Ranade's image in the eyes of India.

In Poona itself there was a large group of Ranade's admirers. The ablest of them, Gopal Krishna Gokhale, was also one of those who was most devoted to him. He was Ranade's disciple. The way in which Ranade as preceptor guided, instructed and trained Gokhale, and the manner in which the latter reverentially accepted the discipline imposed by his preceptor is unique in the history of political work in India. Gopal Krishna Gokhale was born in 1866. After doing his B.A., he became in 1885 a teacher in the New English School, founded by Chiplunkar, Tilak and Agarkar. A year later he became a life member of the Deccan Education Society. As a Professor in the Fergusson College, he revealed essential qualities of a good teacher—a grasp of the subject, fluency of speech and correct expression. In the ideological quarrels between his colleagues, Tilak and Agarkar, he found himself in agreement with Agarkar, the nationalist and social reformer. Ranade then was in Poona. Agarkar highly praised Gokhale while speaking to S. H. Sathe, a prominent worker of the sarvajanik Sabha. Greatly impressed by Gokhale's intelligence and character, S.H. Sathe introduced Gokhale to Ranade probably in 1889. Ranade was always on the look out for young men who had potentialities of becoming public workers: and he had the capacity of drawing out their hidden qualities. On the other hand, Gokhale, only twentythree years old, was only too glad that he had the privilege of working under the guidance of this doyen among public men. Most willingly Gokhale carried out the tasks entrusted to him by Ranade. With closer acquaintance, Gokhale's respect and Ranade's affection grew until they culminated in a preceptor-disciple relationship. At first, Ranade asked Gokhale to prepare mere abstracts of documents or reports on public questions and later to prepare drafts of memorials to be sent by the Sarvajanik Sabha to the Government. Before asking him to prepare any of these drafts, Ranade used to discuss with him the points to be included, and the general nature of the draft; after it was prepared, Ranade used to go through it and make suggestions and corrections. Gokhale had to rewrite the draft in the light of these remarks. Of couse, all this work was voluntary and unpaid. Never did Gokhale resent or feel reluctant or complain; he carried out the instructions of the master so that the master was satisfied. Ranade, even on the best of Gokhale's performances, did not shower praise; 'that will do' was all that he said. The satisfaction of this great man was all the reward which Gokhale got, and that was enough for him. The more Gokhale knew Ranade, the more he saw the qualities of true greatness in him—saintliness, patriotism, comprehensive understanding of all aspects of human life, scholarship, sound thinking, sincere teaching and zealous work. From a speech he made on Ranade, it is evident that these were the qualities which impressed Gokhale.

In 1890, Gokhale was elected Secretary of the Sarvajanik Sabha; he also became editor of its quarterly journal. Ranade had maintained a high standard of the journal issued by the Sabha: and the Sabha had acquired a reputation for reliability of facts, comprehensiveness of views and soundness of conclusions. Ranade gave training to Gokhale to develop in him the critical faculty, balanced mind, the capacity to see both sides of a case, industry in going through all relevant facts and figures, and the appropriate style of writing. 'There must be vigour in thought, not in language', Ranade had taught Gokhale; and Gokhale changed his style accordingly. In 1889, Gokhale attended, for the first time, the Congress session in Bombay; he actively participated, seconding a resolution which recommended simultaneous holding of I.C S. examination in India and in England. Next year, he decided to study intensively economic statistics pertaining to India. Ranade directed him to his friend and able scholar of Indian statistics, Ganesh Vyankatesh Joshi. In a letter of introduction to Joshi, Ranade wrote: "During the last six month that he (Gokhale) has been working with me I have formed very high opinion of his great powers and abilities, his readiness to do his best under all circumstances. He is essentially an honest—intellectually as well as morally—student, and I am sure you will find in him a worthy collaborator." He spoke at successive sessions of the Congress, exhibiting all the qualities in which Ranade had trained him—study of facts, logical thinking, graceful but restrained language.

The controversy over the holding of the Social Conference in the Congress pandal in Poona in 1895 when Gokhale was the Secretary, the capture of the Sarvajanik Sabha by the Tilak group resulting in Gokhale's resignation, and the formation of the Deccan Sabha by the Ranade group are some of the incidents which have already been narrated in an earlier chapter. Soon after, a Royal Commission, with Lord Welby as Chairman, was appointed to inquire into the administration and management of expenditure in India. This gave an excellent opportunity to Indian leaders to place before the influential circles the injustice done to their country; but their facts and arguments had to be irrefutable. Along with seasoned oplitical leaders like Wacha, Surendranath Banerjea and G. Subramania Aiyar, Gokhale also was sent to give his evidence in London. Under the guidance of Ranade and G.V. Joshi (both of whom were outside Poona), Gokhale prepared his evidence, the final copy of which had to be prepared on the ship. Gokhale was then a youth of thirty and the elders felt anxious, especially as they had not seen the final draft. Ranade wrote to Dadabhai Naoroji and Wedderburn in England requesting them to go through it and make suggestions to Gokhale where necessary. Gokhale's draft was read by them and they found it perfect. Gokhale's evidence, written as well as oral, was a great success, in spite of severe heckling by some hostile members of the Commission. Glowing compliments were showered on him by several persons, including Wedderburn, Dadabhai, and Caine. Gokhale passed on these encomiums from competent judges to G.V. Joshi, and proceeded to write:" All this praise belongs to you after Rao Saheb (i.e. Ranade)." And to Ranade, Gokhale wrote: "If you find time to go through the statement and feel satisfied, I shall have received the only reward I care."

The tremendous success of Gokhale's evidence before the Welby Commission was marred by an unfortunate episode. During Gokhale's stay in England, an epidemic of bubonic plague had broken out in Poona, and the Government had taken drastic measures to root it out. Reports got circulated that the British soldiers, while engaged in carring out these measures, had committed many acts of high handedness, including rape. Indignation rose to a high pitch; and some friends conveyed these reports to Gokhale. Gokhale thought it his duty to give them publicity in the British Press. The Bombay Government quickly declared that there was no substance in the reports. Gokhale had to prove them or apologise. On return to India, he found he could get no proofs—in such matters it was extremely difficult in India to get proofs—and Ranade advised him to offer a public apology. Gokhale was in great mental agony. The Anglo-Indians poured forth their fury for having made irresponsible allegations, and the Tilak group fiercely attacked him, charging him with cowardice in not fighting it out and having risked jail. Ranade stood by him throughout this period of trial and gave him comfort. Gokhale was hesitating to attend the session of the Congress in Amravati, but Ranade counselled him not to feel dejected and to fact the public with strength that comes from the conscience within.

Gokhale imbibed the fundamental ideas of Ranade on Indian politics and economics; he carried on, after the death of his master, the Ranade tradition. In politics that tradition is summed up in a passage from the manifesto of the Deccan Sabha, which was from the pen of Ranade himself. "Liberalism and moderation will be the watchwords of this association. The spirit of liberalism implies a freedom from race and creed prejudices and a steady devotion to all that seeks to do justice between man and man, giving to the rulers the loyalty that is due to the law they are bound to administer, but securing at the same time to the ruled equality which is their right under the law. Moderation imposes the conditions of never vainly aspiring after the impossible or after too remote ideals, but striving each day to take the next step in the order of natural growth by doing the work that lies nearest to our hands in a spirit of compromise and fairness." A close look at the quotation will show that the followers of the Ranade tradition were distinguished from pure 'Loyalists' by the word Liberalism and from 'Extremists' by the word Moderation. The whole of Gokhale's political thought in subsequent years conformed to the principles contained in this passage.

But Gokhale followed not only the precepts but also the example of his master. Like Ranade, Gokhale was, above everything else, a patriot. It was Ranade's patriotism which impressed him most. "The first thing that struck any one who came in contact with Mr. Ranade," said Gokhale, "as underlying all his marvellous personality, was his pure, fervent, profound patriotism. In all my experience, I have met only one other, so utterly absorbed, day and night, in thoughts of his country and of her welfare, and that is Dadabhai Naoroji. To him India's past was a matter of great, of legitimate pride; but even more than the past, his thoughts were with the present and the future, and this was at the root of his matchless and astonishing activity in different fields of reform." Besides intense, forward-looking, constructive patriotism so described by him as residing in Ranade, Gokhale also imbibed from his master the qualities of gentleness, forgiveness, patience, and constant introspection before blaming others for faults.

The elevating influence which his Guru-exercised on Gokhale is described by himself as a spiritual experience. "It is no exaggeration to say that younger men who came in personal contact with him felt as in a holy presence, not only uttering 'nothing base' but afraid even of thinking unworthy thoughts, while in his company. The only other man who has exercised a similar influence on me in my experience is Mr. Dadabhai Naoroji."

Ranade was both the profound theoretician and the prime organiser of the social reform movement. "For 20 or 30 years," writes W.B. Patwardhan, "he (Ranade) was practically the life-breath of the reform movement. He organized the movement, focussed the various forces and spasmodic activities of individual reformers; he shaped it anew, and reconciling it with the past soldered it with all that was noble and precious in our heritage."

In each of his annual addresses before the Indian National Social Conference from 1888 to 1900, as has been said earlier, he gave a brief account of what was done in the previous year in all parts of India to promote social reform, and also urged, on sociological and moral grounds, further efforts. Ranade took appreciative note of every effort, however small, even if done by otherwise conservative persons. Thus, if a generally conservative caste association passed a resolution recommending curtailment of expenditure on marriages, or if a body of the orthodox Pandits signed *vyavasthas* which slightly relaxed hindrances in the way of free admission of men who had been to foreign countries, these incidents were mentioned in the address. The general effect of these annual reports was to give hope to individuals who were likely to be dejected by the overwhelming opposition to the movement. It also consoled those who personally suffered mental persecution.

The difference between social reform and social service is not always easy to see, and Ranade' list of 'reforms' contains some which it would be appropriate to include under 'services'. In 1894, at Ranade's initiative, a questionnaire regarding social reform was circulated to ascertain the sense of enlightened persons about the more important questions which affect our vital social interests'. The questions included, among their subjects, compulsory education, school playgrounds, school boarding houses, libraries and gymnasia, and the beggar problem.

About these, there could be no difference in principle between 'reformers' and 'non-reformers'. But it is interesting to note two items in Ranade's social reform programme, namely, avoiding religious disputes between Hindus and Mohammedans and removing the ban on the re-entry into the Hindu fold of those previously converted to other religions. Anxiously Ranade asked his correspondent: "Would it not be possible for the leaders of the two communities in your town to form a committee with a view to fix the customary usage and to settle the disputes amicably when they arise, and keep up the good feeling between them both?" In his annual summaries of social work, he did not fail to mention approvingly if there occurred any reconversions into Hinduism. 'In the Central Provinces a Native Christian was taken back into his caste by the leading Pandits in Jabalpore.' 'The Arya Samaj has distinguished itself by the re-admission into their community of repentent converts to other religions'. The motive behind this approval was definitely not the desire to increase the number of Hindus; it was, to uphold the right to profess the faith of one's choice. If a Christian or Mohammedan chooses to join the Hindu faith, to debar him is to deny him the right of freedom of religion. Curiously enough, what deprived him of this right were the injunctions of the Hindu religion itself! When he found a leading paper of the orthodox party advocating reconversion, he felt the support coming from 'unexpected quarters'. "Nothing could be more pathetic, nothing more profoundly true than the appeals made by this exponent of conservative opinion to the Hindu community generally to drop their ancient spirit of exclusiveness, and receive with open arms those who may desire to come back to the old religion, and thus ward off the danger of national suicide, which otherwise is inevitable." Ranade, however, would plead for permitting re-entry into Hinduism, not on the ground of prevention of 'national suicide', but on another ground, namely, the claims of conscience, or "free liberty in the matter of this interchange of faiths". On this ground, presumably, he would approve of conversion to any religious faith, not to the Hindu alone, provided, of course, it was demanded by conscience.

Ranade analysed the efforts made to bring about social reform and enumerated four methods. The first was the method of tradition, that is, the basing of reform on the old texts. The reformer took the old texts as the basis, and interpreted them in a new way so as to support a social reform. Ranade, averse to make a complete break with the past, made considerable use of this method. In about 1870, he wrote an essay, 'Vedic Authorities for Widow Marriage', and in 1888, 'The Shastric Texts on the Subject of Infant Marriage'. The second method was that of appealing to the conscience of the people, to their innate 'sense of right and wrong, good and bad, sinful and virtuous'. The third method was to enforce reform by means of penalties, imposed either by the caste or by the State. Ranade appreciated this method—in fact, there were two methods, enforcement by the caste through social boycott and enforcement by the gorvernment through legislation—because, in his opinion, in either case it was a constraint imposed by the wise upon the ignorant in their common interest. But this method Ranade would advocate only where absolutely necessary. 'It is a coercive method, which should not be resorted to, until other ways have been tried.' It was thus, only reluctantly, and because he was convinced of its necessity, that he joined in the advocacy of the Age of Consent Bill. The fourth method about which Ranade was even more reluctant, was the rebellious method, that of the reformers separating themselves from the rest and forming a new camp. 'This has its merits too, but many more demerits, the chief among which latter is the breaking of continuity !'

Though with some reluctance, Ranade admitted the method of State legislation as a means of social reform. In the context of Malabari's proposals, he ably defended this view against the objections of those who would eschew this method altogether. To the objection that it was not the duty of the State to regulate social matters, he reply was that the State could not shrik its duty to remedy evils 'which no private combination of men can check adequately or which it can deal with more speedily and effectively than any private combination of men.' To the argument that the evil was not so great, as some people thought, Ranade said that much the same thing was said when it was proposed to prohibit *Sati* or infanticide. To another objection that the parties who suffered did not complain of the evil, Ranade reminded that the same argument was used against the abolition of slavery. It was argued that the foreign government which ruled India could not be trusted with the power of regulation of our social customs. Ranade had several arguments to rebut this view. First, the foreign government had no interest in changing our social customs for the better. Secondly, the initiative in social reform legislation was to be our own; 'all that we seek from this foreign government is to give the force and the sanction of law to the practices and usages which we, or rather the most enlightened among us, consider desirable.' Thirdly, "If we are to abjure such help under all circumstances, we must perforce fall back behind the Parsis, Mohammedans and Christians who have freely availed themselves of the help in recasting their social arrangements". And fourthly, "As it is likely that foreign rule will last over us for an indefinite length of time, we reduce ourselves, by accepting this policy, to the extreme absurdity of shutting out a very useful help for many centuries to come." To the objection that social reform legislation imposed innovations to conform with foreign ideals, Ranade replied that the change was sougth not as an innovation, but as a return and restoration to the days of our past history. The proposed legislation was justified on the basis of revered religious texts. Injunctions prescribing evil practices were introduced in a later period of natural decay. "We must now return to the old order of thing...All that the Government is called on to do is to revert from the times of corruption to the times when Hindu society was more healthy and vigorous."

Ranade's approach was sociological. He was keenly conscious of the inter-relations between political, social, economic and cultural aspects of national life. When the Tilak group argued that conferences and organisations were necessary for politics but not at all so for social reform, Ranade said: "The integrity of any human being cannot be broken up into separate spheres of activities." Growth was either all-sided, or not at all. A nation could not have an advanced social system while it was politically backward, nor a politically advanced system while it was economically and socially backward. Nor could it have an advanced social, political and economic system while its religious ideals were at a low level. "No man can be said to realise his duty in one aspect who neglects his duties in the other directions."

This was his reply to those who were politically progressive but socially conservative. But there were others who were socially so progressive that they wanted radical reforms at one stroke; and Ranade had to caution them against being too rash. The power of the long-formed habits and tendencies must not be ignored. "The true reformer has not to write upon a clean slate. His work if more often to complete, the half-written sentence. He has to produce the ideal out of the actual, and by the help of the actual. We have one common stream of life flowing past us, and we must accept as valid the acts which were noted in the past, and on the principles of the past, and seek to turn the stream with a gentle bend here, and a gentle bent there, to fructify the land; we cannot afford to dam it up altogether or force it into a new channel...We cannot break with the past altogether; with our past we should not break altogether for it is a rich inheritance, and we have no reason to be ashamed of it."

With a marvellous sociological insight. Ranade saw that in India a social change was coming, and he beckoned the people to work for it. He saw that the British conquest of India did not mean only a change of rulers; it meant a change in the environment. Insecurity of pre-British times had gone, and peace and order prevailed; isolation was destroyed by railways and steamships; caprice of autocratic princes had disappeared and rule of law prevailed. If the environment had thus changed for the better, was it not natural that the social structure too might undergo a change to suit it? Social reform in India, according to Ranade, was but the process by which society was adapting itself to the new environment. It was thus not only desirable but inevitable.

This view not only indicated the scholarly vision which Ranade had; it also gave confidence to the struggling social reformers who were assured, by implication that time was on their side.

During the past several centuries deterioration and decay was continuing. The change of environment brought about by the British contact would prove stimulating and vitalising. It was this revival, this new life, that would sweep off the evils that had crept in during these long years. Reform, therefore, would first mean reform of ideas, and only afterwards, reform of social institutions. "Now what have been the inward forms or ideas which have been hastening our decline during the past three thousand years?" he asked. Then he proceeded to point out four such ideas, which must be discarded in favour of new ones. First, the feeling of isolation and superiority over other groups, or the caste feeling, which should be replaced by a feeling of equality. Second, a blind submission to the authority of sacred books, which should be given up in favour of freedom of thought. Third, a sense of helplessness against fate or *Karma*, which should be replaced by a faith in the strength of the moral force within us. And the fourth, the nation that all human life was an empty dream or *Maya*, making us tolerate evils of this world like poverty and tyranny; this notion should be replaced by the view that human nature was noble and dignified and that mankind had a great future. The only way to remove the deformity of our social structure was to place ourselves under the discipline of better ideas mentioned above. Reform of social institutions "are reforms only so far, and no further, as they check the influence of the old ideas, and promote the growth of new tendencies."...

Reform, therefore, was not so such a matter of outward forms, the social institutions, as of inward development. The thing to be reformed was our own self, heart and head and soul: our prejudices were to be removed, our superstitions were to be eradicated, our courage was to be strengthened. Social reform was in essence, moral reform. "This or that particular reform...the removal of this or that particular defect or vice is not and should not be the only end and aim of the agitation to improve our social condition. The end is to renovate, to parify, and also to perfect the whole man by liberating his intellect, elevating his standard of principle for which they are endured."

Reformers in any society are few. They meet with indifference, derision, active opposition, or even persecution from the majority. The role of the reformers is as noble as it is unhappy. "Strength of numbers we cannot command, but we can command earnestness of conviction, singleness of devotion, readiness for self-sacrifice in all honest workers in the cause. Even though these workers may be few in number, they will in the end succeed in overcoming opposition. We have above all to learn what it is to bear and to forbear—to bear ridicule, insults, even personal injuries at times, and forbear from returning abuse for abuse. In the words of the Prophet of Nazareth, we have to take up the cross not because it is pleasant to be persecuted, but because the pain and the injury are as nothing by the side of the principle for which they are endured."

4

The Assessment

Ranade was a great reformer who always engaged himself in socio-economic and political activities in our subcontinent. Born in a middle class family, he earned an all-India status among his contemporaries who were fighting for swaraj. His wife reminsced about her husband thus :

DAYS AT NASIK

As I said before, we were transferred to Nasik. Only three of us wont, accompanied by a house-boy and coachman. There were no women with us, either from among the relatives or servants. Nasik is a place known for women cooks, so we thought we would easily get one. But it turned out otherwise. More than a month and a half elapsed and yet no cook was available. I was not used to housekeeping, so I would easily get confused and perplexed, with the result that even the simplest of jobs often became a mess. My husband noticed all this, but he never said a word to show displeasure even if there was too much salt or chillies in what I had cooked. In my confusion and excessive anxiety that the dishes should turn out well, I sometimes put a double measure of salt and at other times forgot to put any at all. But even then not a word or irriration escaped him. However incapable a person may be, it was as if he had taken a vow to treat everyone indulgently. After he had his food and went to the courts, I would sit down for my meal and then I would feel miserable for the excessively salty or utterly saltless stuff I had cooked. I would firmly resolve to be very careful about the evening meal and not to forget anything.

If I did succeed in preparing a good meal, then he would say good-humouredly to my brother-in-law, "Aba, you seem to be enjoying the vegetable now. But in the afternoon, although there were more dishes, you did not touch anything. Why was that ? Was anything wrong with them ?"

Aba would reply, "The vegetables in the afternoon ? Ah—one of them was saltless, the *bhajiyas* were too salty. The curry and one vegetable were tolerable. So I ate that."

Then, my husband would say, "A student should not even notice whether the food is salty or saltless or too hot. He should eat whatever is given. Do I ever find fault ? I quietly eat what is available and go about my business."

Sometimes I would be bold and say, "If I were told, I could add some salt; but I discover the blunder only when I sit down to eat myself and then I feel thoroughly ashamed."

"How can that be helped ? It is better to find this out by one's own experience rather than be told about it. It makes one more alert and attentive. I bought a cookery book for you today. You can study the book and try out a recipe every day. All the ingredients should be measured out carefully and the dis prepared with an unflurried mind. If it turns out nicely, well and good ! If not, it will at least be a good pastime. Everything is possible, if only one tries attentively."

For the first few days after I got the cookery book, I used to try out a new recipe every day. Sometimes it turned out well; at other times, it failed, even if I tried again and again. After a good many days, I lost interest. We also got a good woman to cook and I found more leisure for my studies. I had by now completed reading the first Howard

Reader and started studying the second one. My husband found two or even more hours to help me read my lesson and to put questions on word meanings and spellings and also teach me a new lesson. He would teach me for about an hour and a half in the morning. Then, after a walk in the evening, he would ask me to read Marathi newspapers for abaut an hour before dinner. After dinner, till about ten or half past, he would ask me to read aloud the books received for the Dakshina Prize Committee from Poona. This was our routine.

He was usually awake by about four o'clock in the morning. Then he would ask me to recite from Kekavali or other *aryas* or *shlokas* or passages from the Navaneet or Prarthana-Sangeet. Sometimes he would himself begin chanting a Sanskrit *shloka* or hymn, and explain the meaning to me and get me to learn it by heart. He would ask me to repeat *shlokas* learnt earlier and test how much of the meaning I could remember. This continued till day break. Then I would get busy in the kitchen getting ready the provisions, vegetables, chutneys, salads and butter-milk. I would serve out the first helping and we would all have our food together, with free, pleasant talk. The cook would serve the rest of the food. When my husband had gone to the courts, I would begin preparing some snacks for the afternoon. They had to be sent to the office and two or three kinds had to be prepared everyday. It easily took me about two hours. At a quarter to two, I would pack the tiffin-carrier and send it with the brahmin. Then I would sit down for my lessons. By half-past four I would have by rote all the words in the lesson with their spellings. He used to ask me the spellings and meanings first and then make me read the lesson. If I could not, he would be angry. His anger was not of the usual type. He did not scold or shout at you or use bad words. He sat silently, sadly with just a sigh at the most. He would be like that for a very long time. An ebullient person scolds and shouts, perhaps uses a bad word or two and that is the end of it. In a few minutes such a person laughs and talks again. It is as though there had been no occasion for anger at all.

But my husband was not like that. He would never be irritated by trifles. But if he did get cross at something, his anger would hang like a cloud for a long time. This made me very nervous and miserable, and when it happened I did not know what to do. So I tried my best to let any such occasion arise.

In this way, when I had completed my study of the second English Reader, I took up Aesop's Fables and also the New Testament, because it was written in simple words and short sentences. When the routine for my household work and my studies was well settled, he said to me, "You should now jot down the daily household expenses."

A brahmin named Vinayak had come to Nasik with us for the first two months. He was in charge of the daily minor expenditure and kept the account. He did it all accurately. I used to keep the whole sum but from time to time, as the need arose, I would ask my hushand and hand over small sums to Vinayak. When I began keeping the account, I used to write it out every day. But there would always be some mistake in my additions or subtractions and I had to spend hours and hours in tallying the balance. Naturally I was not able to do my lessons for the day very thoroughly and this was often exposed. When this happened five or six times, my husband made it a rule to check up the account book every night before retiring. In a few days, he was able to spot where I was going wrong. He explained it to me until I, grasped it fully and exhorted me not to commit such mistakes again. He checked my daily accounts a few times after that and then used to look them up only at the end of the month.

We were eight in our house then. The average monthly expense for food was calculated on the basis of the expenditure for the last two months. On the first of a certain month, he said to me, "You can take hundred rupees for expenditure on food now and make the sum last over the month."

My notions about expenditure were very vague. I thought that the large sum of a hundred rupees could hardly be needed for food alone. To that he said, "So much the better. Even if the amount is not needed, we shall not take it back from you. We shall make a gift of it for your needlework."

I was very happy to hear that. I said again, "This won't include the servants' salaries and subscriptions, will it ?"

He said, "No; this will not include anything beyond expenditure for food actually. For the otner heads you can take more money. But remember, we must get all the savouries and snacks we are used to now. There must be no cutting down. And everything must be paid for in cash. No credit, please."

Even that exhortation failed to warn me. On the contrary I thought, how could such a large sum be spont. All was well till the twentieth of the month. After that I got into the state in which most families with a meagre income are at the end of a month. By the twenty-fifth nearly the whole amount had evaporated. I began to feel thoroughly ashamed and was so worried that I could hardly hide my anxiety. And yet how could worrying help ? The daily expenditure had to continue, but it could not unless I asked my husband for more money. I just could not bring myself to do that. It only added to my worrying.

After a day or two of this, he asked me about it. "Why do you look so depressed these days ? I hope you are not ailing ?"

I was all the more ashamed. I had been taking all possible care so that he might not notice that anything was wrong. I hung my head and said, "Oh no, nothing is the matter."

I those few moments, a hundred times did I think of asking for more money. But my pride would not let me do it.

I got utterly confused and suddenly burst into tears. I could not control myself at all. He had already guessed my state of mind. He did not wait for my explanation any longer and tried hard to comfort me. When at last I muttered that all the allotted amount had been spent, he said, "You can take as much as you need. Where is the need for being so agitated about it ? After all, all the money is with you. You should speak freely about whatever is needed and never brood over things like this. We are not in such want as to be full of anxiety. But habits of thrift and neatness make one alert and inquiring. Household matters can then be managed efficiently and in an orderly way. That is all I wanted to impress upon you. If you had kept this point in mind, you would not have worried like this unnecessarily. You can take what you need, but please be careful about keeping the account." With that he enjoined me to take all the money that was needed.

His salary at this time was eight hundred rupees. I used to keep that whole amount and all the other eash in the house. It was a rule with my husband not to keep even a pie with himself. I do not think he even as much a touched a key of any sort let alone tie it up to his sacred thread. But, though all the money was with me, I never spent more than five rupees more than the sum allotted for household expenses without his permission. He would promptly agree to spending more when I did ask him, never once did he say no. But he did not like it if it was done without asking him. This was our custom, and I never neglected to observe it. So there was never any occasion for anger or displeasure for either of us.

Rao Bahadur Vishnu Moreshwar Bhide was Sub-judge at Nasik when we went there. He owned a garden at Nasik and now wanted to sell it off. We bought the garden. It meant more work for us, and also added a kind of relaxation. Morning and evening we went to the garden, assigned different jobs to the servants and checked up what they had already done. In the mornings, I used to walk to the garden on my own. In the evenings after my husband returned from the courts, both of us and Bhauji would go there for a drive in the tonga. We would walk about in the fresh air for an hour or two and talk happily. He would enquire about the jobs done by the servants. Then we returned home. After that, as I said before, an hour would be spent in my English lesson—an hour all too short. After dinner, he would ask me to read Marathi books for about an hour and a half. Then we would retire for the night. Early in the morning, at about four o'clock, he would ask me to read for an hour and then say, "It is time for you to go to the garden." I used to go with our old orderly as an escort. Mo husband would then call up Bhauji, take his lessons, set him at his copy book at six o'clock and then go on with his own routine.

THE OLD NAIK

Sakharam Naik, who used to escort me to the garden, knew a lot of stories of sadhus and saints of the Warkari Panth. He could also sing a number of *abhangas*. For the first few days, he kept humming these to himself in a low voice as he walked. He would never speak to me unless I spoke to him. He would just answer the questions put to him and continue reciting something softly. It occurred to me that the old man knew a lot of *abhangas*, but recited them softly to himself, out of a sense of courtesy and discipline. So I said to hlm, "Sakharam, if it is your practice to recite *abhangas*, do it aloud. I will not mind it. I like them."

He bowed to me humbly and said, "Very well, madam. Many people would consider it discourteous. They dislike the jabbering of old persons like me. So I was afraid."

So, in the early morning, he would sing an *abhanga* or two and also comment upon it. It was a good diversion for me. I did not contradict or question anything he said. But it often made me laugh the way the words of the *abhangas* were twisted or their meaning distorted. The text these people follow is often very corrupt but they try to wrest a meaning from it.

For instance, instead of "The child Prahlad was born unto Hiranyakashipu", they say "A child in *paral* was born unto a *harina* (deer) and *kasav* (a tortoise)." They even interpret these corrupt readings by saying "We have heard of ten incarnations of God. He had to incarnate himself more than ten times for his *bhaktas*. He had to be born unto a deer and a tortoise and even in *parel*. Just think? This is what God who loves his *bhaktas* so deeply has to undergo for them." All this is expounded with great piety. It never strikes these people that such an interpretation is not plausible. Nor can they bear any one to question it. They cannot be blamed for this. It is all due to their blind traditional faith. They cling to it in simple-hearted piety. They never try to think. That's all.

Our orderly was of sort. Sometimes he would be quite. overwhelmed while narrating the stories about some man of God. But when he would try in interpret these stories, he would distort their meaning as I have just said. Yet, I would listen to him, all attention. I could not think of hurting a pious old man like him. I would narrate all that happened to my husband when we sat down for food, and we would have a good laugh.

This morning walk of mine enabled me to bring home from the garden vegetables and flowers. During winter about four to five hundred roses could be cut and two or three large basketful of brinjals and gourds. My husband loved betelnut scented with rose-petals. So some roses and some vegetables were kept back for our use; the rest of the produce was sent to the market with the servant. The proceeds were credited daily by me in the account for the garden. Once or twice a week, all the produce used to be retained at home, for my husband liked to have it sent to our friends and acquaintances.

WOMEN'S EDUCATION

During that year. the Prarthana Samaj was established at Nasik by my husband with the help of Deshmukh, Ketkar,

Wad and other friends. Rao Bahadur Gopalrao Hari Deshmukh was Joint Judge there, His six daughter-in-law and two daughters were considerably educated according to the standards of those days. His wife was an orthodox lady, but she could read and write well. She was fond of listening to the Puranas and also reading them. She observed all the sacred rites and rituals and on such occasions invited the women of the town for *huldi-kunkit*. That took me to their place pretty often and so we became well acquainted with them. Rao Bahadur Deshmukh and my husband both strongly advocated the cause of women's education. They oncouraged their wives to get the women of the place together at least for *haldi-kunku* and read out to them the lives of women like Sita or Savitri and by such efforts persuaded them to educate themselves. They also exhorted us to pay visits to girl's schools to encourage them by giving prizes and such other means.

Quite soon such an occasion arose. Mr. Caglan, Sessions Judge of Thana, came to Nasik to conduct a session. He stayed there for a little more than a week with his wife and his sister-in-law. They were both young and amiable. They were keen on getting to know Hindu women and so they came to our house of their own accord the morning after they arrived. Naturally, we returned their call the next day. The two Deshmukh daughters, myself, Mrs. Caglan and her sister, all of us were of the same age. So even when we had met only a couple of times, we got to know each other quite well. We used to go out for walks morning and evening, sometimes to our garden or to the river Ghats, to Sundrnarayan temple or Muthe's garden.

During these very days, one Mr. Godbole who was deputy educational inspector came to Nasik to inspect the schools-Dwarkanath Raghoba Tarkhadkar was the headmaster of the high school. His wife, Laxmibai, was a good deal older than I was. But she was very pleasant and cheerful and treated me as a friend of her own age. She taught me knitting and sewing. My cousin-in-law, Sakhubai Thosar had also come from Bombay to spend a few days in her parental home. She was an in-law but was more like a sister to me. So the two of us sisters-in law and Laxmibai became as found of one another as sisters are. We could not spend a day without meeting each other. Either Laxmibai would come to our house or we went to hers. She was a very well-informed person too. Mrs. Caglan also joined us, after she came there.

THE PRIZE DISTRIBUTION

The deputy-inspector completed his inspection of the school and it was decided that since Mrs. Caglan was luckily there, she should be requested to distribute the prizes to the girls. The inspector and Rao Bahadur Deshmukh came to our place to consult my husband and fix up the day. The day was fixed. Feeling that the presence of a large number of women would lend grace to the occasion. they began considering how this could be brought about. They felt that ladies of the old orthodox families and of *jagirdars* would not come in response to a mere invitation card, and that some women must go and invite them personally. The deputy-inspector said that if this task would be taken up by the ladies of our two families, he would arrange to get the wives of pleaders and other officers to attend. Thereafter he went away.

Then it was decided that the two Deshmukh daughters and I should go round to all the families on the list and invite them personally. After this Deshmukh also went away. A day or two later the Deshmukh girls and I went to all the houses and invited the women personally. Accordingly, about fifty to sixty ladies were present on the occasion. We all felt that even that was a considerable number in those days. For, this was the first time that men and women had assembled together for a function in Nasik. The rest of the gentry in Nasik had not been invited. Only about ten or twelve men who approved of women's education and were leaders of opinion had been invited and were present.

The function began with a hymn and a song welcoming the guests. The deputy-inspector read out the report for the previous year and Mrs. Caglan distributed the prizes. Then my husband asked me to read a short speech thanking Mrs. Caglan and giving a word of advice and encouragement to the assembled women. I read the matter and thanking Mrs. Caglan and the audience, sat down. Just then, the deputy brought a try of garlands and bouquets to me. I garlanded Mrs. Caglan, her sister and mother. I left over one garland in the try and passed it back to the deputy. He softly suggested to me that the Sahib was to be garlanded with that one. I refused. I was quite offended. One of the main rites in a Hindu wedding is that the bride and bridegroom garland each other. Orthodox Hindu women, therefore, object to garlanding any other man. Raosahib Deshmukh was watching me. He smiled, got up immediately and taking the tray from the deputy, garlanded Mr. Caglan and gave him the bouquet and scent and the rest. In the meanwhile, the Deshmukh girls had distributed *haldi-kunku*, *pan*, flowers, scent and rosewater to all the assembled women. The function was thus over and we returned to our homes.

As we were retiring at night, my husband asked me teasingly, "Did your meeting go off well? But why should there be such partiality towards women? It was the men who took all the trouble to organise the function. The women just came when all was ready. Why did you garland only the three women and leove out poor Caglan?"

I said, "I would not have minded if I were not a Hindu. I was really surprised and offended to see that a wise old Hindu gentleman like the deputy should suggest that I should garland the Sahib."

"But Deshmukh came to your rescue."

"He is of course incomparable: He is magnanimous. It is not his way to put one on a mean trial".

"You are unnecessarily harsh on the deputy. Probably he too had no mean intentions. He suggested it only casually. Often, one does not think of everything at the first instant. It was rather tactless, no doubt."

The next day Laxmibai visited me. She said, "Our meeting went off well yesterday. But I was so relieved to find that you saw through the deputy's game in a second. I was quite worried."

Our friendly trio was soon broken up. Sakhuvansa went away to her own home. We were suddenly transferred to Dhulia and Laxmibai was left at Nasik. We never met again, for she died a year later.

My husband was not in good health in 1900, and so he was afraid the doctor would not permit him to go to attend the Congress session. He was himself very keen on going. Although he was ailing, he had as usual asked for the voluminous reports of the Social Conference, and continued writing long letters, getting those received read out to him and dictating answers to them, as a matter of daily routine. There was no break in that. The work of preparing summaries of the reports received from various institutions was also being done continually. As the dates for the Conference drew nearer, he had to spend several hours working at a stretch. His article on 'Vasistha and Viswamitra' was to be read in the Conference. He had to work on it unceasingly for four or five days. In the little leisure that he had, the talk always turned to plans and preparations for going to Lahore. He was to leave just about a couple of days later.

I had made up my mind to tell him that I was going to accompany him because he was not keeping well. I thought I would tell him how utterly restless I would be if he went alone and that I simply must go with him. And then I would get my things ready. But, before I could speak, he asked me himself to come with him. It was a great relief to me. I packed up my things with great enthusiasm and also got together, with great care and forethought, his clothes and everything that he would need. My mother-in-law, sister-in-law, Gangabai, Laxmibai, Abasahib and his children were all in Bombay then. So it was decided to leave Sakhu and Nanu with them. But I do not know why my husband changed his mind. This might before leaving he asked me if I had taken everything necessary and also told me to pack Sakhu's things for he had decided to take her along—"When the people from Poona arrive tomorrow, I shall ask them to reserve our seats", he said. "It is very cold in Lahore. Please take a lot of warm clothing, especially for Sakhu."

"How can we take Sakhu alone?" I argued. "If we do take one, the other child must also come. Otherwise neither."

"Please do as I say and don't worry. One should not argue about things which must be done in any case. It is best to do as you are told. We could have taken Nanu too. But it is very cold in that region. We have only two servants with us. Nanu is just a child yet and will need a servant to himself. You will also have to look after him a lot. You will have to manage everything yourself and my ill health will make it difficult. So, it would be best to leave Nanu here. Sakhu is quite grown up now. She will not be a nuisance. She will be quite a help to you and some company. So, I thought, we might take her with us rather than leave her here. Please pack up her things."

I agreed and got together everything in the morning. I did not say anything about the change in the plan to anyone in the family. I had decided not to, till the moment of departure. As everyone knew that only my husband and I were going, many of them kept on teasing Sakhu about it. The poor girl would be in tears and whenever she could, she would go to him, and urge him to take her along. I was also very reluctant not to take her; but only the thought that Nanu would be left alone had compelled me to agree not to take her. Sakhu was very happy when she came to know that she was coming with us. But I was really pained to leave Nanu alone. Nanu was too young to understand all this. When people teased him, he did come to me once or twice and insisted that I take him along. But I gave him five rupees in a tiny little purse and said, "Here's some money to buy pictures for you. Keep this purse, won't you? Don't give it to anyone." He was mightily pleased at that and danced with joy.

In the morning, Nagarkar, Gokhale, Bhide and a few others came from Poona to join us in our journey. My brother-in-law went and reserved our seats in the afternoon. We were to depart the next evening. My husband spent the whole day working and talking to the people from Poona. He did not rest even for a few minutes in the afternoon. So, his daily 'spasm' proved more severe than usual and also lasted longer. He was naturally more exhausted after it. It was an hour and a half since he had gone to bed and yet he could not sleep. He had been writing such a lot the whole of the week. I thought that perhaps he could not sleep on account of a tried brain. So I went downstairs and got some butter. I also asked the night watchman to get some leaves of *erund* from the garden. I rubbed the butter on my husban's scalp and temples and applied the cooling *erund* leaves and then massaged the soles of his feet with butter for a long while. He tried his best to lie quietly and sleep. But nothing would help. It struck one. Instead of sleep, there came on a sharp pain in his chest. Until then, although he could not sleep, he was at least resting in bed. Now even that was denied. The pain in the chest would not let him even lie down. He had to sit up in bed supported with pillows and a bolster. When he managed to sit up like that, I went downstairs, lighted the fire and filled a rubber bottle with hot water. I called up Bajaba and asked him to get another bottle ready and bring it to me upstairs. I went up, applied a mustard poultice on my husband's chest and placed the hot water bottle under his back. Still the pain did not cease. It was six o'clock before it disappeared. Only then could he sleep a little.

As soon as he fell asleep, I sent word to Dr. Bhalchandra asking him to come over. I also told Nagarkar, Gokhale and others about everything. We were all in a quandary about the plan to go to Lahore. My husband woke up at about seventhirty, had a wash and came to the drawing room at about eight. When the others asked him about the pain and sleeplessness he said, "Oh, that happens off and on. There is nothing to worry about. It is an old ailment of mine. It comes up now and then."

Just then Dr. Bhalchandra arrived. He examined him, heard all the details and said, that he could in no case advise my husband to undertake such a long journey. Not only that. He would urge that he should not go at all.

My husband was extremely disappointed. He sat without a word, full of anxiety, for ever such long while, even after the doctor had gone. Then slowly he said to Gokhale, "So let us decide now. What is to be done?"

"How can we say anything about your condition", Gokhale said. "It is best to abide by the doctor's advice. If you give me instructions about everything, I shall go and do exactly as you wish."

"Of course, you will. After all, you will have to look after everything now. But, if all of you feel that I should not go now, I must at least send a telegram."

When they all said that he should not go, he took pen and paper and wrote out a telegram. He read it out to all and said, "After eighteen years, there is a break in my attendance at the Congress." His voice was choked with sorrow and tears streamed down his face.

So the plans to go to Lahore were cancelled. His article, which was to be read out at the session, was handed over to Gokhale. He also sent Abasahib wiih them all.

They left for Lahore in the evening. The next day we went to Lonavala. Friends from Poona came on a visit and urged him to go to Poona for medical treatment. But he refused. He had decided to continue the treatment in Bombay, and would go to Poona only when he felt a little better.

Three or four days later, those who had gone to Lahore for the Congress returned. They gave him an account of the Congress session and the conference and left for Poona the next day. He looked greatly relieved after the account. Reports of the two sessions appeared in the *Times, Advocate, Social Reformer, Punjab* and other papers. He read the speeches of Gokhale and Chandavarkar and wrote to them immediately how happly and relieved he was to find that they had proved equal to the burden. He wrote the letters in his own hand.

We were in Lonavala for only ten days. He did not keep well at all. Rather, his ailment grew worse, little by little. Mentally he was extremely depressed. He would speak to me or to my sister-in-law, again and again, about cutting out such and such expenditure, farming out the orchard on a contract and reducing the number of heads of cattle. He would urge us to tighten up the establishment at Bombay and try to wind up the problems about our agricultural property spread out in so many places. He would say that he was thinking of going on leave for six months and then retiring immediately afterwards. He would point out that he might not return to Bombay for quite some time. He would suggest that the furniture and other household things at Bombay might as well be sent to Poona. He would say all these things very casually, but it was quite obvious that a feeling that the end was drawing near was within him. Such suggestions of his, such an attitude of turning away from life grieved me deeply. It filled me with sorrow. But I had to suppress it all in reselute slience.

SIX MONTHS' LEAVE

When the leave was over, we returned to Bombay from Lonavala and on the eighth, my husband sent an application for six months' leave and proposed to retire after that. "Our income will then be just about seven or eight hundred besides the pension. Will you be able to manage all the expenditure here and at Poona, within that ?" he asked me.

"It will be a little difficult until we buy a honse in Bombay", I said. "Here, the house rent alone means three hundred or more. Could we not wind up the establishment at Poona and stay here together ?"

"Oh, that cannot be", he said. "The establishment at Poona will not be touched, nor will the people there be moved anywhere. All the conveniences they are accustomed to, like *Kathas* and *keertanas*, will be available at Poona alone. They can be comfortable only there. And I must now stay in Bombay. That is why I wanted to ask you whether both the establishments could be run within that amount."

"Oh, yes, they certainly can", I said. "We are not people who cannot do without a particular convenience. All the unnecessary expense could be cut down. You have always urged that one should have only those things whieh one can afford always. You have trained us all to that. So why should it be difficult for me to manage with a little less money ? And after all, it is not such a small sum either. In any case, I think it would be better to buy a house as early as possible. House rent is a great expense here."

"I am thinking of buying a house", he said. "I don't know when it will materialise. We went round five or six houses. They were not bad. You don't like an old house. We need a good, comfortable house in a decent locality and then you must all approve of it. When all these factors combine then alone will there be a possibility of our buying a house." He then despatched the application for leave.

In September, 1900, Mrs. Ranade fell ill, and her doctor declared that she required to undergo an operation. Ranade counselled her to wait a little and try the effect of medicines. She was much perplexed about the matter, as she did not want to bring additional worry upon her husband while his own health was so precarious. However she became much worse, and one day Ranade had to be summoned hurriedly from the Court. Two other doctors who were consulted also advised operation, and Ranade was persuaded to consent, though he pointed out to his wife that even without it she would still be able to go about the house and carriage for drives, and could enjoy reading and writing, and he asked her why she should needlessly take her life in her hands. Ranade had not slept at all on the night of that day when his wife's condition had caused him to be hurriedly called from the Court. She heard him on the other side of the partition, turning from side to side uttering "Ram, Ram" in a dejected voice, and four or five times she was aware of him stealing up to her bed to see if she were asleep—on which occasions she always feigned to be sleeping. Again, on the ntght previous to the operation, he did not sleep at all.

Mrs. Ranade tells us what her own reflections were on the night before the operation, and they afford us some interesting sidelights. She imagined what the effect would be on Ranade if she were to die on the morrow. He was unaccustomed to look after his own more private affeirs, and had come to rely upon her greatly for his personal conveniences. He did not like treatment or attention from any one but herself—e g., in the matter of the service of meals, administration of medicines, massaging of body and head, etc. The other folk in the household were careful and interested, but they did not understand him as she did, and his reserve would prevent him from letting them minister to him as she had done. Moreover, he was himself in such poor health that it seemed a special pity she should be taken away just then. She reflected on the happiness and the glory that had fallen to her, through her marriage. It was true God had denied them the supreme earthly happiness of having children, but both of them accepted that without objection or complaint, filled up the lack in other ways, and rejoiced in the state in which they were. With a becoming modesty she thought how, except for the fact that she was of good family, there was nothing to fit her for marriage with Ranade—on beauty, no talents, no knowledge. It was only through God's gracious favour that there had been given to her the happiness of so blessed a life union, and she had hardly thought of the possibility of its coming to an end.

The operation was successfully performed, and three weeks after it, they decided to go off to Matheran. The doctor, hearing of this intention, said that Mrs. Ranade must on no account be moved for a fortnight more. So Ranade, who was badly needing a holiday, went off alone, at his wife's urgent insistence.

Already in the month of August, the disease, *pseudo dugina pectoris*, which in the end caused his death, had laid firm hold upon him. Its chief symptom was a spasm of the heart, a kind of muscular cramp, that came on regularly about 10-30 every night, and that lasted for 15 or 20 minutes. The spasms ceased on the night before Mrs. Ranade's operation, but ten days or so after he had gone to Matheran, his wife was distressed to get a letter telling her that the old trouble had begun again, and the next day she set out to join her husband. They returned to Bombay at the end of the holiday, and he was able to carry on with his usual work and occupations, though there was constantly present the shadow of these nightly seizures.

Ranade asked the doctors what his disease was called. but he got no satisfactory answer, and he began to think that they were deliberately refraining from telling him. He, therefore, resolved to find out for himself, and in some books obtained from the Medical College he identified his symptoms and made himself familiar with all the details of his disease. At first he showed an anxious interest in his illness and talked much about it. But from the month of October onwards he seems to have attained to an attitude of Stoic indifference. He seems to have resolved that whatever happened he would endure quietly and, as far as possible, let no one see his suffering. When pain was specially severe, he used merely to ask for massage or for foments. Only on his bed would he let himself go a little and would moan as he turned from side to side. Though he knew from the medical books the serious nature of his malady, he did not allow his outward conduct to be affected. But he could not prevent the sympathetic Ramabai from sensing the shadow, and her tender heart was melted with pity and apprehension so that daily she wept over it.

The doctor advised Ranade to rest much, and the home folk pressed this advice on him. But he din not follow it. He would keep reading nnd writing constantly all day. He seemed resolved that not a moment of his remaining time must be lost.

On 24th November, 1900, in the Framji Cowasji Institute, at Bombay Ranade unveiled the portirait of Dadabhai Naoroji. On that occasion he made his last public speech. After describing the virtues of the Grand Old Man of the Indian political movement, he said, "In the modern conditions of life the India that is to be born will have no room for mere distinction of race, creed, colour. We aspire all of us to be Indians first and Indians to the last over every other condition which has separated us so long and made a united India impossible." After saying something of the periods of Conquest and Consolidation under the British Government he continued, "We are in the third condition of Reconciliation or Reconstruction, and for that condition Dadabhai has done his proper duty. The India of the past we can never hope to revive, but the India of the future it is for us to shape and to fashion." While finishing this address, he had one of his seizures, but he leant on a post that was behind him, and as the attack passed off in a few minutes, his audience never knew of it.

In December, 1900, he was eagerly anticipating the Social Conference at Lahore, for which he had written a paper entitled, "Vasishtha and Vishvamitra." But his heart spasms had been getting worse, and it was with very great regret that, on the day before they were to set out, he gave way to the insistence of this friends and decided to obey the doctor's advice not to go to the Conference. Pen and paper were brought and Ranade wrote a telegram to the effect that he would not be able to be present that year. He read to the company what he had written, and told them that for eighteen years there had been no intermission in his attendance—and his voice was thick and his eyes were filled with tears as he spoke. He found comfort, however, in the thought that two such able followers as Gokhale and Chandawarkar, were ready to bear forward the banner that he had so long carried.

Two days afterwards Ranade went off to Lonavla. There he read and wrote, working on a collection of Dharma Sastra Texts useful for Hindu Law, and preparing an essay for C.Y. Chintamani's book on Social Reform. He stayed for ten days, his health getting steadily worse. On returning to Bombay at the beginning of January, he wrote to the High Court asking for six months leave of absence, and he told Ramabai that at the end of it he intended to retire. On the 14th, alarming symptoms developed, but on the morning of the 16th, he felt specially clear-headed, and said that the doctor need not make his usual visit that day. In the evening he had a drive and a walk in company with his wife and his half-brother. On returning home he received a wire intimating the death of a friend, and his comment, after expressing his regret at the loss, was, "What a happy death it is to die while one is working." The time before the evening meal was passed in dictating a number of letters, and in discussing with some visitors the preparations for a forthcoming widow remarriage. After supper his sister sang for him some of his favourite verses from the Prarthana Samaj hymnbook, and then he settled to read a chapter of Justin M' Carthy's *History of Our Own Times*, which together with the Upanishads and Milner's *History of Christiantty* had been his latest studies. Soon however the nightly spasm came on, this time with such extreme severity that Ranade cried, "Better come death than the endurance of this pain." As the seizure did not pass off a doctor who lived nearby was hastily summoned, and he at once saw that this time Ranade was beyond the power of human aid. A quarter of an hour after the seizure began, with his head resting upon his wife's shoulder, he passed away.

When the news of his death spread over the land, a very real sense of loss was felt among high and low, rich and poor. The great concourse of people of different races, castes, and creeds who joined in the funeral procession was cloquent of the high esteem in which he had been widely held. The body with proper ceremony was given to the flames in the burning ghat at Bombay, and the ashes were consigned to the Triveni at Allahabad, where the Ganges, the Jamna, and the Saraswati mingle their waters.

So passed a great patriot and a great social servant. So passed a leader who, if he wrought no sensational deliverance for his Israel, yet by his wise, many sided, and fruitful activities laid broad and deep foundations for the structure of freedom. Sir Pherozeshah Mehta once said that he measured the greatness of England not by her material strength but by her ability to produce men of such intellectual grasp and wide moral sympathies as Lord Ripon and Major Baring. We for our part close this book with the thought that India's greatness may well be measured by the fact that she could produce a Mahadev Govind Ranade.

The idea of holding periodical gatherings in each Presidency for the discussion of Provincial matters of public interest is a legitimate off-shoot of the great National gatherings which have now become an institution of the land. This year these gatherings have been held in all the three Presidencies and it is obvious that this success indicates a healthy growth of public sentiment. In the Madras Presidency the political gatherings in that Province have always been accompanied by the friends of Social Reform utilizing the occasion on the analogy of the great national gatherings of the Congress and the Conference to meet together for the discussion of social subjects, and though hitherto in the political Conferences held in this Presidency, it has rot been found possible to follow this example, it is a matter of great satisfaction to find that our Satara friends have realized the necessity of supplementing the work of the political Conference by inviting the friends of social reform to come together and take stock of our gains and losses in the social sphere of our activities. Owing to the circumstances under which this work had to be undertaken at Satara we have had to content ourselves with a very brief programme, but it is to be hoped that the seed sown to-day will bear a rich fruit hereafter.

I know there are those among us who see no advantage in holding local or national gatherings of this sort for the consideration of social topics. There are others who think that, though such gatherings may have their uses, they should not be joined together in place and time with the political meeting, as they only serve to distract the attention of the workers and lead to no practical results. It may be of use to attempt a brief reply to both these objections.

As regards the first difficulty it seems to me to arise from a confusion of ideas, which is very prejudicial to the right appreciation of our duties both in the political and social sphere. The underlying assumption is that in politics our duties consist chiefly in stating our wants and grievances to strangers who have been placed by Providence in command over us and who are ill-informed about our real condition. Politics in this sense means simply formulating claims for gifts or favours which require no other action on our part. While in the social sphere our duties lie more exclusively with the regulation of our own actions in which outside help is not needed for guidance or control. As I understand it, this distinction between the two spheres of our activities is based on a radical mistake. The integrity of any human being cannot be broken up into separate spheres of activities of the sort contemplated by those raise this objection. For the sake of convenience you may say that the rose has its beauty and its fragrance, but you can no more separate the fragrance from the beauty, and any attempt to do it can only end in the destruction of both. What is true of the individual is true of the collections of individuals whom we may call by any name, tribe, class, or community. These communities are organizations and you can no more separate their activities except provisionally and for the time. Every little village in our land, however poor it may be, has its temple and its chowki, its resting place and watering place, and every town or city must have its township civic life made up of interests which are not wholly political or religious or commercial. The shops and the bazars, the temples and the theatres, the schools and the hospitals, the courts and the barracks, the young and the old, the men and the women, the poor and the rich—it is this variety and concourse which constitute the interest of village, town, and city life. Some may rule, others obey; some may advise, others follow; but the distinction is only provisional and not in the nature of things. You cannot even build a house of your own where you do not keep a place for strangers or the wayfarer. You have to provide for the God's place of worship, a place where the thirsty, hungry, and sick may be cared for, and there is no man so poor and so selfish that he does not share in all these varied interests and recognize their claims. Each concern has to be attended to in its own time and in its own way, but it is the whole collection which makes it a human interest. What is true in our private concerns is equally true of our public life. Politics is not merely petitioning and memorialising for gifts and favours, Gifts and favours are of no value unless we have deserved the concessions by our own elevation and our own struggles. 'You shall live by the sweat of your brow' is not a curse pronounced on man, but the very condition of his existence and growth. Whether in the political, social, religious, commercial, manufacturing, or aesthetical spheres, in literature, science or art, in war or in peace, it is the individual and collective man who has to develop his powers by his own exertions in conquering the difficulties in his way. If he is down for the time, he has to get up with the whole of his strength, physical, moral and intellectual, and you may as well suppose that he can develop one of these elements of strength and neglect the others, as try to separate the light from the heat of the sun or the beauty and fragrance from the rose. You cannot have a good social system when you find yourself low in the scale of political rights, nor can you be fit to exercise political rights and privileges unless your social system is based on reason and justice. You cannot have a good economical system when your social arrangements are imperfect. If your religious ideals are low and grovelling, you cannot succeed in social, economical, or political spheres. This inter-dependence is not an accident but is the law of our nature. Like the members of our body you cannot have strength in the hands and the feet if your internal organs are in disorder. What applies to the human body holds good of the collective humanity we call the society or state. It is a mistaken view which divorces considerations political from social and economical, and no man can be said to realize his duty in one aspect who neglects his duties in the other directions.)

As an example, the present crisis of the famine may well be considered. If our social arrangements were as perfect as they might be made, half the terrors of famine would vanish and the political problem would be much simplified. There is no question which is purely political any more than social or economical, or even religious; and they may make a fatal mistake who suppose that these are separate departments in our composite nature. The same forethought, the same resolution, the same historical spirit, the same comparative scrutiny and the same strenuous endeavours are needed in all the spheres of our activity, and therefore, it will not do for us to say that in politics our duties are clear but not so in other spheres. The whole man has to be developed and perfected for his own advantage and the glory of God, and it is only a conception like this which can strengthen our efforts and crown them with real success. It is on this account that when we take stock of our wants our mind must be open on all sides; the eyes must see, and the ears hear, the hands move and the feet support. This can only be done by our devoting attention to all claims. Owing to our difficulties of everyday life of toil and sorrow we cannot always find time for all things. When we therefore meet for the purpose of taking thought of our political condition, that is just the time when we have the spirit of unselfish devotion stirred up in us to approach our internal man in its most tender moments, and there is an obvious convenience in seeking to utilize the advantages of time, place, company and the enthusiasm which springs from association with equals, and you will thus see why the Congress and Conference gatherings have been joined together. If I had the choice we should long since have added other spheres of work so as to make the national gathering really national in name and aims. The claims of some kind of work might be more absorbing than those of others, but each must have its time and place, and proportional attention devoted to it, and I am glad to see that these considerations have weighed with our friends in inviting us to this gathering at Satara on the present occasion.

But it may be said that our social fabric is not the work of human hands like the political institutions under which we live, and that in regard to these social customs the law has been laid down from time immemorial and we have only to follow it and it is not for us to attempt changes to suit our exigencies. This is another of those misconceptions for which there seems to be no excuse, except a false pride, which makes us cherish dangerous delusions. As a matter of fact the social arrangements at present are admittedly not those for which we can plead the sanction of the great Law-givers whose names we revere in lip worship but whose behests we disobey at every step. Most of the customs which we now profess to follow run counter to the practices observed in the old times, when the Institutes were written. The dependent status of women, the customary limits of the age of marriage, the prohibition of marriage to widows in the higher castes, the exclusive confinement of marriage to one's own division of the sub-castes into which the country has been split up, the ignorance and seclusion of women, the appropriation of particular castes to particular professions, the prohibition of foreign travel, the inequalities made by the license enjoyed by men and the abstentions enforced on women, the jealous isolation in matters of the social intercourse as regards food and even touch, indiscriminate charity to certain castes—for all these and many more alienations from the old standards you cannot hold the Law-givers responsible. They are the work of human hands, concessions made to weakness, abuses substituted for the old healthier regulations. They were advisedly made by men whose names are not known to our ancient history. They are innovations for which no sanction can be pleaded. It may be, they were made with the best intentions. Admittedly they have failed to carry out these good intentions, if any, then entertained; and in seeking to upset them and restore the more healthy ideals they superseded, the reformers of the present day are certainly not open to the charge that they are handling roughly our time-honoured institutions. It is rather for the Reformers to take their stand as defenders of these ancient ordinances and denounce those who have set Cod's law at definance to suit their own purposes.

But, even if this were otherwise and even if it could be shown by a long special pleading that the changes made are to some extent proper deductions from the old texts, it is quite plain that no lapse of time can bar the way of reform, where such is needed by the exigencies of our present difficulties. Above all mere ordinances of Institutes stands the Eternal Law of justice and equality, of pity and compassion, the suggestions of the conscience within and of nature without us. We can no more resist the stream of these influences as working for righteousness than we can roll back the tide. All real prudence would dictate that we should take full measure of these influences and decide how far we must accommodate ourselves to the inevitable. All classes of Society, reformers and anti-reformers alike, unconsciously admit the force of these considerations. The only difference between the two consists in the fact that while the latter yield unconsciously and under pressure, the former seek to use conscious effort to accomplish the same purpose, and between the two victory must be for those who do not wise to drift, but wish to be guided by the admonitions of their inward monitor and the lessons of past history. People will visit England whether their elders like it or not, and the force of circumstances will prevail. The education of women will similarly be encouraged as each year rolls on. The limits of age for marriage will be raised. Inter-marriage restrictions will be dissolved. Caste exclusiveness must relax and the greatest freedom predominate in all transactions between man and man. As prudent men the question for us will be, shall we float with this current or resist it? As these influences are Providential, our duty is clear and this duty becomes more pleasant, when we find that in so acting we are not only obeying God's law, but also returning to the ways of our forefathers, overstepping the obstacles put in by our fathers in the way.

There is one objection still which hampers the way of Reform. Granted that seform is desirable, it is still claimed that only the ecclesiastical heads of the different communities and the caste elders have legitimate authority to act in such matters and that it is not for a miscellaneous crowd of people like ourselves to claim this privilege. To a certain extent the caste elders and even the Acharyas are moving in the right direction. In the great caste conferences held in all parts of India the Kayastha, Vaisya and other organisations that might be named without number, there are visible signs of the dead bones heaving with the life of a new spirit. Even the Acharyas in the South, when moved by Native rulers, and, in some cases when not so moved, spontaneously, have put forth efforts to promote what is right and proper. There is, therefore, no occasion to quarrel with these agencies. They, however, have their vested interest at stake and it will be more than human if they look at these things in the same light as we, who feel the pinch, are disposed to regard them. Their cooperation should be welcomed, but the question does not close here. The duty is cast upon us to see that the commonwealth to which we belong is not endangered by any vested prejudices. We can never forego the right of every human being to act in concert with others of his own way of thinking and make the effort to better our condition with the light that is given to us and with the help that religion and history afford us. Of course, our powers are limited, but the work of education consists in increasing the strength of the powers by propagating both by precept and example what we feel to be right and proper. We may fail or our effort miscarry but the effort will do us incalculable good, and the very failure will serve as a warning. This is the law of all progress and we can claim no exemption from it.

Lastly, it has been said that we are to split up into sects and divisions, castes and sub-castes, that no common concert is possible for the best of us, and that if we mean real work we must being with castes and sub-castes and not indulge in the dream of joint action at least for many centuries to come. This argument is double-edged and has been used by those who do not feel with us, to damp our energies in the political as also the social sphere of action. When we examine it more carefully we find that it is more fallacious than true. Castes and sub-castes have no doubt their particular preferences and dislikes, their own evils and iniquities to accout for, and we see that everywhere from the reports of the Social Conference their best men are manfully struggling to cure these evils. It should, however, not be forgotten that this caste difficulty is the main blot on our social system. The great fight has to be maintained here and not on the outskirts. Quite independently of this circumstance, the differences between the caste merge into minor matters by the side of their great similarities. In the social sphere of our activities all castes and even creeds are alike defective in not recognizing the claims of justice and equality, and according to the respect and freedom due to the female sex, and cherishing the abuse claimed by men as men and by the members of one class of men to the disparagement of other castes. This furnishes the common platform on which all can act, and it is only the education received on this common platform, that can command the elevation and freedom, which alone will help us to be taller, wiser and better, individually and collectively.

I have thus attempted to forestall by anticipation many of the objections which might be and are urged by those who are not disposed to be friendly to the work of our social emancipation. With the work that has been done in the different Provinces by more than a hundred Associations that are in full sympathy with the cause of social progress, it is not my purpose here to deal. The reports of the Conference for the last thirteen years furnish a living record to which all can refer with advantage. It is a record which does not show large achievements in accomplished facts, but to those who can read between the lines the spirit that animates this work, there is a land of promise opening its vistas before them so as to encourage the most despondent. To go no further back than the past five months, I find from the notes of events kept with me that even in this year of distress some seven re-marriages took place: three in the Punjab, one in Bombay, one in the North-West Provinces, one in Madras, and one in the Central Provinces. In Bengal, where the widow marriage movement commenced in Pandit Ishwar Chandra Vidya-Sagar's time. as many as forty-six marriages were celebrated, thirty were celebrated since, and forty-one more celebrated among the Brahmos, making a total of one hundred and seventeen. Including the Central Provinces and the Berars, the Bombay Presidency has, during the last thirty years since the movement began, shown more than a hundred such marriages distributed equally between the Gujarathis and the Deccanis. The Punjab and the North-West Provinces show a total of more than thirty, and Madras presents nearly the same figure. The total of marriages would, therefore, be about three hundred through out India in the several Provinces, in the higher castes.

Miss Manning's "Indian Magazine," in one of its recent numbers, gave the total number of Indians, mostly students studying in England, to be three hundred and fifteen, of whom nearly half, or one hundred and fortyone, were Hindus, seventy-nine Mahomedans, sixty-one Parsees and twenty-two Native Christians. These figures show how the wind is blowing and how the stream of events is steadily on the right side. The Native papers in the Punjab show that during the last five months some seven admissions of converts from Christian and Mahomedan faiths were made by the Arya Samajais, and there is an active controversy going on for the wholesale admission of some hitherto despised castes. The success of Bethune College in Calcutta, and Female Schools and Colleges at Jullunder, Poona, Ahmedabad, and Mysore has been full of promise in this as in previous years. Among legislative events, next after the passing of the Mysore Marriage laws, the most noteworthy event during the past five months has been the enactment of the Hindu Gains of Learning Bill by the Madras Council. The local Sabhas, such as the Deshamukha and Kunbi Sabhas in the Berars, the Rajput in the North-West Provinces, the Saurashtra in the Madras Presidency and the Khatris in the Punjab, have held their meetings and under good auspices passed resolutions in favour of marriage reform. Many instances of late marriages have taken place throughout the country, also of inter-marriages in different parts of India. This is, no doubt, a brief record, but as observed before it is full of promise.

The present crisis through which our part of the country is passing under the stress of plague and famine has intensified the necessity of taking adequate steps for alleviating the distress suffered by all classes. There are particular directions in which all social reform organizations might work with advantage in such a crisis. Many thousands of poor orphans have been rendered homeless and although they are supported through famine by private and Government charity, the time is coming when, with the rains on us, this charity will cease to flow and the unclaimed orphans will have to be provided for when the distress is over. Missionary Societies have pledged themselves not to effect conversion while the distress is at its height, and they are prepared to give over the children to those who will claim them. The rest, who will be unclaimed, will have to be cared for by these societies, and people everywhere must consider the question how to deal with these poor children. Freedom to return to their community is a charity which we all can display, if we have the largeness of heart to understand the issues involved. The economical question here becomes one of religion and social amelioration. Equally affecting is the claim which has been urged on behalf of hundreds of child-widows who have been rendered miserable in consequence of the famine and the plague visitation. In normale times their condition was bad enough, but their misery has been aggravated by the misfortune of these hard times and those who have any heart to feel for their wrongs might well be asked to take thought as to how their misery might well be alleviated. The question of postponing the marriages to the latest limit of marriageable age—to the age of puberty, while the visitations are upon, us, will not fail to attract the attention both of the Reformers and of those who profess to be indifference to this subject. These and other matters will, I doubt not, engage the attention of friends who are assembled to-day. We shall not be able to take any immediate action here, but if these matters allowed claims on our thoughtful consideration, when we go to our places, the work of reform cannot fail to lead to some useful results. For this and work like this, concerted action is needed, and concerted action is only possible under existing circumstances when we think and work together. A committee consisting of all those who sympathise with the progress of Reform is, therefore, sorely needed in this part of the country to co-operate with similar workers elsewhere, and it is with this view that our work to-day will chiefly consist in forming such a committee and laying down the lines on which it is to work. This is a duty in which I trust you will all join, join with a heart that will suffer no disappointment, but will strain every nerve, each within his own sphere, to bring about the practical well-being of our people, in which the well-being of every individual is involved. This is the message that I was commissioned by friends elsewhere to communicate to you here and I now commend this subject to your anxious care, in the full conviction that the work is one in which we can all co-operate with advantage, and in which no progress is possible without such co-operation.

THE MESSAGE OF RANADE

Liberate the Whole Man

Ranade viewed every aspect of life *sub specie aeternitatis*. The last of an untroubled age, he 'combined vision and industry'. Without the ecstasies of the mystic or the contempt of life of the stoic, but possessed of a temperament human and serene, and an imagination that was almost prophetic, he loved life and was conscious of its potentiality and purpose. He disapproved alike of the narrow monkish ideal of single-minded celibacy and the thoughtless surrender to a butter-fly existence of pleasure and comforl. He would have us "realise life in all its fulness and in all its varied relations." Hard of muscle and sinew, humanised in heart and responsive to truth and justic, free of prejudice and superstition, liberated in mind, tranquil in spirit, the men of to-day and to-morrow must be like the rishis of old—'still climbing after knowledge infinite' with infinite courage. "We should learn to be men, stalwart, puritan men, battling for the right, not indifferent not sanguine, trustful but not elated, serious but not dejected." It is a radiant vision of 'liberated manhood' that Ranade continually holds before our wondering gaze. Duty, for him as for Wordsworth, the stern daughter of the voice of God, and her sisters, no less divine, Faith, Hope, and Charity, are the cardinal virpues that should be called into full exercise in the endeavour to regenerate man. For it is a comprehensive task. "The whole existence must be renovated." "The liberation that has to be sought is not in one department of life, or one sort of activity, or in one sphere of thought, but it is an all-round work in which you cannot dissociate one activity from another." The process demands discipline and suffering, "the baptism of fier, and not water." The gallant impatience that cries "Elevate the race at once" for a last and new crusade against life's ills would find little support in Ranade. Step by step, day by day, year by year, in the face of discouragement and defeat, we must build brick by brick. The "helplessness and dependence" caused by a weak fatalism should be replaced by knowledge and effort originating in reverence for the higher self in man. The Law of Karma, widely misconceived but hardest to remove, should be replaced by the Law of Duty. The new idea must come in, that "the Law of Karma can be controlled and set back by a properly trained will, when it is made subservient to a higher will than ours." To hearken to the voice of conscience—"the Divine principle enthroned in the heart of every one of us, high or low"—to respect the God in us, to let nothing come between us and our God, is our duty to both God and Man. "Revera all human authority, pay your respects to all prophets and revelations, but never let this reverence and respect come in the way of the dictates of conscience, the Divine command in us." The way is strewn with difficulties, and "one has to tread upon sharp-edged instruments, carefully balancing the weak limbs and spirits." But "we must bear our cross, not because it is sweet to suffer, but decause that pain and the suffering are nothing compared with the greatness of the issues involved." We may fail, but our cause will succeed. "We may all have to die and become manure for the seeds of life in future generations." The first task is to break the bonds of ignorance and lethargy, to quicken to life a people plunged in intellectual and spiritual decay. The fetters of the mind must be realised as fetters, for then they drop off themselves.

Faith in the Mission of the Indian People

In Ranade sanctity and scholarship, piety and patriotism went together. Deeply read in history, wise with the wisdom of philosophy and experience, he was disposed to see the hand of God in every sublunary transaction. His political and patriotic creed is derived from this implicit faith in God's benevolence. "I profess implicit faith in two articles of my creed. This country of ours is the true land of promise. This race of ours is the chosen race." Ranade's faith in the mission of the Indian people was no mere expedient of popular appeal. It was a real faith, a faith based on reason and fact. "It was not for nothing that God has showered His choicest blessings on this ancient land of Aryavarta. We can see His hand in history. Above all other countries we inherit a civilization and a religious and social policy which have been allowed to work their own free development on the big theatre of time. There has been no revolution, and yet the old condition of things has been tending to reform itself by the slow process of assimilation. The great religions of the world took their birth here, and now they meet again as brothets prepared to welcome a higher dispensation, which will unite all and vivify all. India alone, among all the countries of the world, has been so favoured, and we may derive much strength of inward hope from such a contemplation."

The Religious Experiment in India

The Religious history of India which transcends the record of every other race, justifies the faith in the mission of the Indian people. To us, ths most devoutly religious of peoples, has been assigned the great experiment of evolving an integrated civilization. "All the creeds and civilization are gathered in this land; all the spiritual forms and beliefs are here; all social and political experiments are being tried on a large scale; and this is the only land where you will find all these creeds represented by hundreds and thousands and millions, living peaceably together and partaking of the charities, learning and excellence of each in a spirit of toleration for all, which you will nowhere find on the broad face of the earth." By inheritance, tradition, and discipline the Indian peoples are best fitted to work for "the early dawn, which will before long usher in full blaze, the Sun of Righteousness and Glory which will unite all nations in a common brotherhood." There has been in India a continuity of saints and sadhus who have worked to this end. The nation, spiritual in all its aspirations, gradually ascended to the conception of the purest form of Monotheism the world has yet seen. "One age after another constructed the edifice, laying brick upon brick and layer and storey rose." This highest conception was not only confined to pandits, philosophers and shastris, but it was the common property of every class, including the lowest of the low. But our mission, sad to say, has not been fully accomplished. "Our great ancestors accomplished it in part, their successors failed to accomplish it and suffered the reverses that we are now labouring under." It is the double call of patriotism and religion that we should return to the ways of our forefathers and become "what we were certainly intended to be—fulfillers of the mission which has still not been fully accomplished." But Ranade is opposed to any mock-revival of past glory. Revival is impossible. Reform, based on the old ways and by absorption of the good elements in the new, is the only way of regeneration.

Follow the Lead of Akbar

Ranade's penetrating eye saw the hand of God at every stage in our history. There is a sould of good in things evil, if we would discern it, and Ranade had this ability to read the deep underlying meaning of things. The Mahomedan ascendancy which some would regard as a story of humiliation and sorrow is, for him, a divine dispensation intended to correct and strengthen the character of the Indian peoples. "It cannot be easily assumed that in God's providence such vast multitudes as those who inhabit India were placed centuries together under influences and restraints of alien domination, unless such influences and restraints were calculated to do lasting service in the building up of the strength and character of the people in directions in which the Indian races were most deficient." If the Indian races had not benefited by the contact with the men of stronger muscles and greater powers, they should never have been able to re-assert themselves in the way in which History bears testimony they did. Ranade pays glowing tribute to Akbar and his two immediate successors for realising for the first time in our history the conception of a united, regenerate India. With his broadminded scholarship, he acknowledges in detail the many items of benefit resulting from the contact with Muslim culture. With eloquence and earnestness Ranade insists that the centuries have not rolled in vain, that the lessons of the past have a value not to be put by, and that in this vast country no progress is possible unless Hindus and Mahomedans join together, determined to follow the lead of Akbar and the men of his time. In the struggle for national emancipation, both Hindus and Mahomedans have their work cut out. Our ills are alike, social and political, and together, "we must put our hands to the plough and face the struggle."

A Vision of the Promised Land

Ranade's vision of a united, regenerate India is of the utmost value to our distracted generation, for it is a vision founded on fact and faith, and invested with poetic intensity. It is not invented for a certain kind of propaganda only, but is derived from the facts of history and based on the deepest traditions of the land. It has the memory of antiquity and it dreams of things to come. In a 'timeless' passage, sublime with a sublimity that never sleeps, Ranade dreams the dream and takes us into the deep power of hope and joy.

Here is the miracle of bud and blossom co-existing with the mellowness of autumnal fruit :—

"The end is to renovate, to purify, and also to perfect the whole man by liberating his intellect, elevating his standard of duty, and perfecting all his powers. Till so renovated, purified and perfected, we can never hope to be what our ancestors once were—the chosen people, to whom great tasks were allotted and by whom great deeds were performed. Where this feeling animates the worker, it is a matter of comparative indifference in what particular direction it asserts itself, and in what particular method it proceeds to work. With a liberated manhood, with a buoyant hope, with a faith that never shirks duty, with a sense of justice that deals fairly to all, with unclouded intellect and powers fully cultivated, and lastly, with a love that overleaps all bounds, renovated India will take her proper rank among the nations of the world, and be the master of the situation and of her own destiny. This is the goal to be reached; this is the promised land. Happy are they who see it in distant vision, happier those who are permitted to work and clear the way on to it, happiest they who live to see it with their eyes and tread upon that holy soil once more. Famine and pestilence, oppression and sorrow, will then be myths of the past, and the gods will then again descend to the earth and associate with men as they did in times which we now call mythical."

Glossary

Ahimsa	non-violence
Ashram	home for community living
Bharat	India
Chamar	untouchable caste, a leather worker
Dal	association
Desh	country
Dharma	religion
Ghat	bank of a river
Harijan	a name which Mahatma Gandhi gave to an untouchable
Himsa	violence
Istri	a woman
Jai	victory
Karma	action
Khadi	hand-spun and hand-woven cloth
Khaddar	hand-spun and hand-woven cloth
Kisan	a peasant
Lakh	1,00,000
Nari	woman
Purna	full, complete
Raj	commonly used for British rule in India

Ryot	peasant
Sabha	a meeting or an association
Samaj	an association
Satya	truth
Seva	service
Sawaraj	self-government
Thana	police station
Vakil	lawyer
Zamindar	lawyer
Zamindari	landlordism

Chronology

1842 January 18	Birth of Ranade
1851 to 1856	Education at Kolhapur
1854	First marriage with Sakhubai Dandekar of Wai
1856	Admission to Elphinstone Institute, Bombay
1857	Inauguration of the University of Bombay; Ranade gets a scholarship of Rs. 10 a month
1858	Scholarship increased to Rs. 15 and subsequently to Rs. 20
1859	One of the first Matriculates of the University of Bombay
1860-63	Junior Fellow at Elphinstone College on Rs. 60 a month
1862	Graduates with honours
1863	Double graduate; earns a gold medal
1864	Editor of English Columns of the *Indu Prakash*
1866	Passes LL.B. with honours—eye-sight badly damaged
1866 May to 1867 November	Acting Marathi Translator in Education Department on Rs. 200 a month. During the same period served as Karbhari of Akkalkot and Nyayadhish at Kolhapur

1868	Takes up appointment as Assistant Professor of English and History in Elphinstone College on a salary of Rs. 400 a month
1869	Assistant Reporter in Bombay High Court
1871	Passes examination of Advocate. Becomes known as Prince of Graduates, having stood first in all Arts and Law Examinations; appointed successively as Third Presidency Magistrate, Fourth Judge of Small Causes Court and Acting First Class, First Grade Judge at Poona
1872	Sarvajanik Sabha Report on Material conditions of Maharashtra
1873 February 6	Confirmed as First Grade Sub-Judge on Rs. 800 a month
1876	First wife dies; marries second time Yamuna Chiplunkar (Kurlekar) who became known as Ramabai Ranade
1877	Death of Ranade's father and dismantling of the Kolhapur establishment; Revenue Manual (Editor of Fawcett Committee's Report on Indian Finance)
1878 January 9	Appointed Sadar Amin at Nasik
1878 April	*Sarvajanik Sabha Quarterly* makes its appearance. Paper on Famine Administration in Bombay Presidency
1879 May	Vishrambag and Budhwar Palaces burnt; Revolt of Vasudeo Balwant; Ranade transferred to Dhulia
1881 January 3 to March 22	Appointed Additional Presidency Magistrate, Bombay
1881 March 30	Appointed Sadar Amin at Poona
1881 August 9	Inspection duty in Poona and Satara districts under the Deccan Agriculturists Relief Act

1884 Feb. 27	Appointed Judge of Small Causes Court at Poona on Rs. 1,000 a month
1885	Appointed Law Member in Bombay Legislative Council by Lord Reay
1886-87	Member, Finance Committee on behalf of Bombay Government
1887	Special Judge under the Deccan Ryots Relief Act
1887 February	Made C.I.E.
1890	Industrial Association of Western India started
1890 March	Reappointed Member of Bombay Legislative Council
1893	Lord Harris appoints Ranade as Member of the Council
1893 November 13 to 21	Poona jubilation on selection of Ranade as High Court Judge of Bombay
1893 Nov. 23	Takes seat on the Bench of Bombay High Court
1899	*Essays on Indian Economics* published
1900	Publication of *Rise of the Mahratta Power*
1901 January 16	Death

Bibliography

Primary Sources

Speeches and Writings of Mahadev Govind Ranade.

Writings of Contemporary leaders.

Proceedings of Indian National Congress, relevant volumes.

Secondary Works

Aga Khan, *The India in Transition*, London, 1918.

Andrews, C.F., *The Indian Problem*, Madras, 1921.

Banerjea, S.N., *A Nation in the Making*, London, 1929.

Basu, Aparna, *The Growth of Education and Political Development in India, 1898-1920*, Delhi, 1974.

Bipan Chandra, *Rise and Growth of Economic Nationalism in India*, Delhi, 1966.

Chintamani, C.Y., *Indian Politics Since the Muting*, Allahabad, 1947.

Das, C.R., *India for Indians*, Madras, 1921.

Gandhi, M.K., *Hind Swaraj*, Madras, 1921.

Iyer, C.S. Ranga, *India in the Crucible*, London, 1928.

MacDonald, Ramsay, *The Government of India*, London, n.d.

Mody, H.P., *The Political Future of India*, London, 1908.

Nehru, Jawaharlal, *An Autobiography*, London, 1936.

Pal, B.C., *The Spirit of Indian Nationalism*, London, 1910.

Rai, Lajpat, *The Political Future of India*, New York, 1919.

Setalvad, C.H., *Recollections and Reflections*, Bombay, 1946.

Thompson, Edward, *The Reconstruction of India*, London, 1930.

Woolacott, J.E., *India on Trial*, London, 1929.

Index